W9-COG-257

THE HIGH ROLLERS

Dr. Richard Boggs was a poor boy who made good, first as an honor medical student, then as head of a vast health care organization. Melvin Eugene Hanson was a scuffler who struck it rich with the fabulous "Just Sweats" stores. John Hawkins was a nobody who parlayed his good looks, charm, and sexual skills on New York's Studio 54 disco-drug scene before hitching up with Hanson.

All three had success in common—and failure as well. Boggs' marriage and career were in ruins because of his promiscuous lifestyle and blind arrogance. The "Just Sweats" stores were on the brink of bankruptcy due to Hanson's and Hawkins' aversion to work and addiction to pleasure.

All three men would do anything to get back on top. And all they had to do was get away with murder.

EDWIN CHEN, an award-winning investigative reporter, is a Washington correspondent for the *Los Angeles Times*. During the Gulf War he was the paper's bureau chief in Dhahran, Saudi Arabia. His articles have appeared in *The New York Times Magazine*, *People*, *The Nation*, *Atlantic Monthly*, and *The Los Angeles Times Magazine*. He lives in Washington, D.C.

⊘ SIGNET   ⬡ ONYX

SPELLBINDING DRAMA

☐ **THE DREAMS OF ADA by Robert Mayer.** A true story of murder, obsession and a small town ... "An outstanding book ... The strange twists and turns of the case are more compelling than the finest mystery novel."—*The New Mexican*
(169816—$5.95)

☐ **DEADLY MASQUERADE:** *A True Story of High Living, Depravity, and Murder* **by Richard T. Pienciak.** This true crime chronicle is a deeply human account of a marriage made in hell, and a telling epitaph for the eighties, when everything was not enough.
(170334—$5.99)

☐ **TEXAS VS. DAVIS by Mike Cochran.** Amidst sordid tales of drug dealers, gambling, and orgiastic sex parties at his mansion, Thomas Cullen Davis—heir to a billion-dollar financial empire—was accused of gunning down his step-daughter, his ex-wife, and her lover.
(170547—$5.99)

☐ **FATAL AMBITION:** *Greed and Murder in New England* **by William Sonzski.** The harrowing true-crime story of treachery and greed, forgery, bungled police work ... and of a chilling and complex murder case that tested the boundaries of our criminal justice system.
(402839—$5.50)

☐ **BUTCHER, BAKER by Walter Gilmour and Leland E. Hale.** The true account of the savage sex slayer who bloodied the Alaskan landscape.
(402766—$4.99)

☐ **PRECIOUS VICTIMS:** *A True Story of Mother Love and Murder* **by Don W. Weber and Charles Bosworth, Jr.** Who would believe a mother would kill her two-week-old baby? Here is the terrifying story of the twisted hate that seethed below the surface of a seemingly normal family.
(171845—$5.99)

Prices slightly higher in Canada.

Buy them at your local bookstore or use this convenient coupon for ordering.

NEW AMERICAN LIBRARY
P.O. Box 999, Bergenfield, New Jersey 07621

Please send me the books I have checked above.
I am enclosing $_____ (please add $2.00 to cover postage and handling).
Send check or money order (no cash or C.O.D.'s) or charge by Mastercard or VISA (with a $15.00 minimum). Prices and numbers are subject to change without notice.

Card #_____ Exp. Date _____
Signature_____
Name_____
Address_____
City _____ State _____ Zip Code _____
For faster service when ordering by credit card call **1-800-253-6476**
Allow a minimum of 4-6 weeks for delivery. This offer is subject to change without notice.

W.G. ulm
4/92

CHEATING DEATH

EDWIN CHEN

AN ONYX BOOK

ONYX
Published by the Penguin Group
Penguin Books USA Inc., 375 Hudson Street,
New York, New York 10014, U.S.A.
Penguin Books Ltd, 27 Wrights Lane,
London 8W 5TZ, England
Penguin Books Australia Ltd, Ringwood,
Victoria, Australia
Penguin Books Canada Ltd, 10 Alcorn Avenue,
Toronto, Ontario, Canada M4V 3B2
Penguin Books (N.Z.) Ltd, 182-190 Wairau Road,
Auckland 10, New Zealand

Penguin Books Ltd, Registered Offices:
Harmondsworth, Middlesex, England

First published by Onyx,
an imprint of New American Library,
a division of Penguin Books USA Inc.

First Printing, March, 1992
10 9 8 7 6 5 4 3 2 1

Copyright © Edwin Chen, 1992
All rights reserved

 REGISTERED TRADEMARK—MARCA REGISTRADA

Printed in the United States of America

Without limiting the rights under copyright reserved above, no part of this publication may be reproduced, stored in or introduced into a retrieval system, or transmitted, in any form, or by any means (electronic, mechanical, photocopying, recording, or otherwise), without the prior written permission of both the copyright owner and the above publisher of this book.

BOOKS ARE AVAILABLE AT QUANTITY DISCOUNTS WHEN USED TO PROMOTE PRODUCTS OR SERVICES. FOR INFORMATION PLEASE WRITE TO PREMIUM MARKETING DIVISION, PENGUIN BOOKS USA INC., 375 HUDSON STREET, NEW YORK, NEW YORK 10014.

If you purchased this book without a cover you should be aware that this book is stolen property. It was reported as ''unsold and destroyed'' to the publisher and neither the author nor the publisher has received any payment for this ''stripped book.''

This book is dedicated to Nancy T. Chen,
my mother,
and to the memory of Terry Chen,
my father.

ACKNOWLEDGMENTS

A book like this would be difficult to imagine without the encouragement, support, and help from many people.

Foremost among them was Barbara Lowenstein, my agent. She immediately recognized the potential in the tragic tale of Richard Boggs and his friends from Ohio. I am especially grateful for her advice and insights, always offered with unstinting candor but good cheer.

This book also would not have been possible without the backing of many people at the *Los Angeles Times*. Among them are Shelby Coffey, editor; Mike Miller, national editor; Jack Nelson, Washington bureau chief; and Richard T. Cooper, deputy Washington bureau chief. I am also grateful to Tom McCarthy, Diane Spatz, and Art Pine, assistant national editors in Washington. They were unfailingly gracious in coping with my prolonged absences. In Los Angeles, senior editor Noel Greenwood, nearly alone, understood my desire to rejoin the reporting ranks and to cover the criminal courts—in search of book material.

I began this book while still living in Los Angeles, but in the middle of the project moved to Washington, D.C. That led to eighteen months of extraordinary demands, necessitating numerous trips back and forth across the continent. The endeavor was further interrupted by the Persian Gulf war, forcing me to lug portions of the manuscript to such unlikely places as Baghdad, Amman, Dhahran, London, and Paris. I thank my editor, Michaela Hamilton, for standing by as well as for her superb suggestions as I wrote.

While I alone am responsible for this book, my efforts would have fallen short without the able assistance of my trusty researchers: Judy Shay and Sandi Dawson in Los Angeles, Daphne Eviatar in New York, and Lorna Nones in Miami.

Free-lancer Doug Burrows in Los Angeles undertook many photographic assignments with enthusiasm and good cheer.

In San Diego, photographer Bob Greiser, an old friend, also willingly pitched in when it was most appreciated. Another friend and *Los Angeles Times* colleague, Scott D. Harris, also was generous beyond reason, putting me up in L.A. with easy hospitality. Cousin Robert Peng also provided shelter and warm companionship.

Many other people all across the country generously came forth to offer their assistance and insights. I would like to especially thank Daniel Abraham, Richard Curtin, Edwin Laramee, Dennis Tishkoff, Vincent Volpi, Melvin Weinstein, and Austin Wildman.

I owe a special thanks to Mike Jones for the countless hours he spent patiently answering my questions. Dale Rubin also shared with me information without which this book would not have been complete.

Finally, in the long and lonely hours of assembling this book, two delightful souls provided cheerful company as well as important research when I needed both. One was Meredith Ferguson Chen, a talented writer in her own right. The other is Matthew E. Chen, who may be one of the best ten-year-old map readers anywhere, and self-taught too. It was their patience, support, understanding, and love that sustained me throughout this undertaking. And they have made it all worthwhile.

Author's Note

This is a true story. Most of the dialogue and the dramatic creations of scenes come from court testimony and other statements that were also given under oath, buttressed by subsequent interviews conducted by the author with relevant individuals.

Many innocent people unwittingly got swept up by the events depicted here, and some of them were hurt or badly embarrassed. Thus I have agreed to spare them any further intrusion of their privacy by using pseudonyms. The aliases used in the book are Ed Mulvihill, Jeff Culverson, Alton Prescott, Lucinda Brown, Margaret Kaplan, Georgia Vanderbilt, Stanley Anderson, Jackie Anderson, Gary Johnston, Wilfred Tynan, Margaret Moulson, Tim Browne, Daniel Friedsen, Wanda Livingston and Pamela Johnson. Any similarities between them and living persons, of course, are coincidental.

Prologue

From the instant that he first saw the disheveled doctor in his shabby, unkempt office, Mike Jones had little doubt that the doctor was guilty.

As a fraud investigator for the California Department of Insurance, Jones had seen plenty of down-and-out physicians pulling cheap scams. And even some pretty spectacular ones.

But this, Jones realized, was a cunning, elaborate murder-for-insurance scheme—one that had gone undetected for five months and now threatened to become a perfect crime.

An innocent Los Angeles man was dead, probably killed in the doctor's office, his body passed off as a mild-mannered Ohio businessman with $1.5 million in life insurance.

And now the businessman's gigolo partner—who got all the money—also had disappeared.

Was the doctor a co-conspirator? Was he the actual murderer?

Of that Jones was certain.

"I know, and you know, that you guys pulled a scam," Jones told the doctor. "And this is your only opportunity to tell me."

For a split second, fear flickered across the arrogant neurologist's face. Then he became defiant once more. "You are a stubborn asshole," he told Jones.

The burly investigator didn't bother to reply. Instead, Jones vowed to proceed methodically to nail the doctor and put him on Death Row in San Quentin.

Still, Jones knew it wouldn't be easy pulling together the complex paper trail of circumstantial evidence against the doctor and his now missing accomplices. For one thing, the dead man's body had long ago been cremated—after the coroners ruled that it was a death by natural causes.

But even as he stared coldly at the doctor, little did Jones know on that day that he would play a role in the case that he never had expected.

Mixed Signals

The 911 call came at 7:04 in the morning, just as the sun was rising over the San Gabriel Mountains, basking the foothills with a purple glow.

"Uh, yes, I need some paramedics," said the caller, a physician named Richard P. Boggs.

"What's the problem?" the dispatcher at the Glendale fire department asked calmly.

"Uh, I had a patient call me. He's having chest pains. He came in the office and he's collapsed. I'm trying to give him resuscitation," the doctor said.

"Okay, where are you at?"

"Ah, 540 North Central."

"Are you in Suite 201?"

"Two-oh-one."

At once a team of paramedics from the Glendale Professional Ambulance was dispatched to Boggs's office. As was the routine, local firefighters also responded to the scene, a three-story medical office building on a street corner in downtown Glendale, a well-to-do suburb just north of Los Angeles.

In rushing to the rescue, almost no one had been struck by the oddity of a physician seeing a patient in his office before dawn on this Saturday morning, April 16, 1988. But that was just one of many suspicious circumstances that would emerge in the hours, days, and months ahead.

The first to arrive were four firefighters in a fire engine, led by Captain Stuart Jones, a dark-haired young man with a no-nonsense, almost sullen look about him. Stuart and his men found the front doors of 540 North Central Avenue locked.

As they maneuvered the large vehicle around to the big parking lot in the back, where a lone black Cadillac was parked, a slightly irritated Jones radioed his dispatcher, asking him to contact the doctor inside who had called for help.

By the time they got around to the back, two paramedics and a trainer also arrived, their ambulance lights flashing, sirens blaring. That hardly seemed necessary, since there were no signs of human activity yet anywhere along this stretch of office buildings. At such an ungodly hour on a Saturday morning, the only witness to all the commotion was a well-bundled but unkempt homeless man making his way insouciantly down the sidewalk, pushing an impossibly overloaded grocery cart, lost in his own thoughts.

The arrival of the ambulance was quickly followed by Thomas Brooks, a paramedic supervisor who pulled up in his own car. Having just completed his graveyard shift, Brooks had been on his way home when he heard the call and decided to drop by.

As the growing crowd of rescue workers milled in the back parking lot, pondering how to get into the red brick building, a middle-aged man, perspiring heavily and looking agitated, suddenly appeared at the glass back door.

It was Richard Boggs. He quickly unlocked it.

"Hurry up! What took you guys so long?" Boggs demanded anxiously. Without waiting for an answer, the doctor quickly led them up a flight of stairs to his second-floor office suite.

Brooks was surprised by Boggs's accusatory tone. He knew it hadn't taken his team more than five minutes—at the outside—to arrive on the scene. Brooks himself had been less than a mile away when he heard the emergency call on his car scanner, and since downtown Glendale was virtually devoid of traffic at that hour, he had reached Boggs's office in a matter of minutes. But this was no time to argue. Somebody might be dying upstairs.

As the rescuers raced up the steps, Boggs's urgent manner led paramedic David White, a large man lugging an oxygen tank, to believe that the patient could be saved. "I was mentally preparing myself to go into the resuscitation mode," White would recall.

Inside Suite 201, in a narrow examination room not much larger than a walk-in closet, a bearded man was supine on the linoleum floor, parallel to the examination table, his feet propped up on a pillow.

The room was so small that only White entered, lugging in a first-aid kit and the oxygen tank. The others huddled in the doorway and corridor, exchanging bits of information with Boggs. The doctor, still looking disheveled, had with him the patient's medical file, which contained among other things strips of paper bearing the jagged peaks of electrocardiogram readings.

Inside the examination room, White quickly knelt beside the body to check for vital signs. But there was none. Even more surprising to White, the body was already cold to the touch. "This patient was beyond our help," he recalled.

This was so unexpected that White double- and triple-checked for vital signs. He even ran another EKG on the man. But White got nothing but a flat line.

The paramedic was puzzled. His training and experience in three years as a paramedic and an emergency medical technician told him that the body should have still been warm to the touch—since the man had gone into cardiac arrest less than an hour earlier. Or so the doctor had said.

"I got the impression this person was definitely dead for longer than forty-five minutes," he said later.

And that was hardly the only suspicious sign. When White tried to reposition the man's head, he was unable to do so. Rigor mortis had already set in, especially in the jaw, neck, and fingers.

And since the dead man's blood was no longer circulating, all six pints of it—the average amount of blood in any human adult—had settled along the length of the lower half of the body, drawn there by gravity. The goulishly purple tone is familiar to all paramedics and homicide detectives.

Standing just outside the examination room, White's partner, Brian Reifschneider, also had been immediately struck by the corpse's purplish skin. That meant the patient probably had been dead for a long, long time—much longer than what the doctor had said.

It was time to take a report.

A Telling Tale

Suite 201, with its cheap, rented office furniture and ancient, dog-eared magazines, was small for a physician's office. Only about six hundred square feet in all, it was divided into seven rooms. It also had a slightly tattered look to it; even a fresh coat of paint was unable to conceal the hairline cracks and tiny holes in the walls. The well-worn linoleum floor needed a good scrubbing. This was, in fact, a surprisingly shabby office for a doctor, especially one located in the heart of one of the more upscale communities in all of Los Angeles.

As the Saturday morning sun rose high over the foothills, burning off an early spring chill, Suite 201 was getting stuffier and more crowded by the minute.

Next to arrive were two Glendale police officers, James Lowrey and Timothy Spruill. They had been on routine patrol in the neighborhood. Like most good cops, they were instantly fascinated by a dead body.

The two uniformed officers talked briefly to the fire and paramedic personnel, who were already packing up their gear, preparing to leave.

Before heading out the door, however, Brian Reifschneider pulled Lowrey and Spruill to the side. In a hushed tone he spoke guardedly of his suspicions, telling the officers that he felt the body had been dead "a lot longer" than what Boggs was claiming.

Their curiosity further aroused, Lowrey and Spruill turned to the doctor and led him into a private office for a chat. Boggs repeated what he already had told the others:

He had been home sleeping soundly when the telephone rang, somewhere between three and three-thirty. At the end of each weekday and on weekends, Boggs explained, the telephone at the office was programmed to forward all calls to his home so that patients could reach him in emergencies.

The caller that morning had been Gene Hanson, a heart patient of his for seven years. Speaking initially to the answering machine, a frightened Hanson said he had been drinking and now needed to see Boggs immediately because he was experiencing chest pains. Hanson, according to Boggs, said he felt as if an elephant were sitting on his chest.

At that point, the doctor said, he picked up the telephone cradle and spoke to his forty-six-year-old patient, turning off the answering machine.

Hanson said he could get a ride to Boggs's office if the doctor would meet him there. Boggs said he agreed to meet Hanson there in a half hour to forty-five minutes.

Having arrived early, Boggs was doing paperwork in his office, which overlooks Doran Avenue, the side street, when around five he heard a car out front. It was a light brown Honda. Hanson was in the front passenger seat. Boggs motioned for the car to go around back and then went down and opened the door.

Hanson was reeking of alcohol, Boggs continued. Upstairs, he took Hanson's pulse and blood pressure. An EKG produced an alarming reading, and Boggs, a neurologist, suggested that Hanson immediately see a cardiologist. But Hanson didn't want to, saying he was afraid of hospitals and usually of doctors. Hanson asked to lie down to rest before leaving.

Boggs in the meantime returned to his private office just down the hall to make some notes.

Less than ten minutes later, Boggs said, he heard a thump.

Rushing back into the examination room, Boggs found Hanson on the floor, lying on his right side, face up. Hanson had no chest rhythm and appeared to be unconscious. Quickly, Boggs confirmed with a stethoscope that Hanson's heart had stopped beating.

The doctor said he immediately commenced CPR and tried to summon paramedics. But he said he gave up after twice getting busy signals, followed on a third attempt by a loud squeal. He resumed CPR.

Some forty-five minutes after he initially found Hanson, Boggs said, he finally got through on 911.

There was nothing unusual in seeing Hanson at such a seemingly odd hour, Boggs told Lowrey and Spruill. Hanson, a longtime patient, was a busy merchant from Ohio who often came to Southern California on buying trips for his business. And so Boggs said he always tried to be accommodating. The doctor told the policemen that Hanson was the co-owner of Just Sweats Inc., a chain of sports clothing stores in the Midwest, with headquarters in Columbus.

Hanson had been a patient since 1981, Boggs said, proffering as evidence Hanson's thick medical files, which detailed numerous office visits by Hanson for a heart condition.

Officer Lowrey took the files and began looking through the records with great interest. Lowrey, a handsome young man who looks more like a university professor than a patrolman when he puts on his tweed jacket and wire-rimmed glasses, knew something about heart patients. His dad was a cardiologist right there in Glendale, and as a lad, often talked medicine with his father, accompanying him as he made his rounds. In fact, Jim Lowrey knew who Boggs was.

Hanson's files showed that he had most recently visited Boggs on March 22 and March 29—both times because of chest pains. The files also showed that Hanson had undergone a kidney-stone operation in 1982. Boggs also had treated Hanson for neck and back pains after Hanson was involved in a car accident on June 15, 1985.

One other entry caught Lowrey's sharp eye. Nearly five months earlier, Hanson had been feeling poorly and was experiencing a shortness of breath and a general lack of vigor, and so he had taken a blood test for exposure to the Human Immunodeficiency Virus, the virus that causes AIDS. The test came back negative.

In the examination room, meanwhile, authorities went through the dead man's brown wallet, and its contents certainly seemed to confirm Boggs's account. The two American Express cards and a Citibank credit card all bore the name of Melvin Eugene Hanson. There was even a xeroxed copy of a birth certificate in the man's wallet, and it too said Melvin Eugene Hanson.

None of the authorities on the scene seemed to notice that not a single piece of ID contained a photograph.

And it would be much later that still another curiosity emerged which, in retrospect, also should have sounded the alarm—loud and clear.

Whereas Boggs had told everyone else that Hanson had been driven to Glendale, the doctor had inexplicably told Fire Captain Stuart Jones, amid the commotion, that he himself had driven to Hollywood to fetch Hanson.

At the scene, yet one more clue was overlooked that also could well have tipped off authorities that something was terribly amiss: In the doctor's office was a tray of medicines prepared for just such emergencies. It had been untouched.

Making Sense

Many aspects of Boggs's story deeply troubled Jim Lowrey.

Above all, the cop was struck by the fact that a long-time heart patient who suddenly develops severe chest pains would be stupid enough to go to his doctor's office—rather than rushing straight to a hospital emergency room. And on a Saturday morning before dawn?

"It was an odd time for a doctor's office to be open," Lowrey recalled. And he told Boggs so.

Stuart Jones, the laconic fire captain, also found Boggs's actions curious—bordering, in fact, on malpractice. "It struck me as odd because, in my opinion, anyone with a minimal amount of knowledge would have suggested that the patient call paramedics or called paramedics for him," Jones said.

But since the fireman's role that morning was that of a medic and not an investigator, he kept his thoughts to himself for the time being.

Lowrey, on the other hand, felt no similar compunction. Why, the assertive officer demanded of Boggs, in this day and age would a physician choose to treat a longtime heart patient with sudden and severe chest pains in his office instead of ordering the man to go immediately to a hospital?

"I probably should have done that," Boggs conceded, looking distracted but still affecting arrogance. Under Lowrey's steady gaze, the doctor quickly added, somewhat lamely, that Hanson didn't like or trust the medical profession. As Hanson's personal friend, therefore, Boggs said he felt that it was "my duty" to see Hanson.

Wasn't Boggs worried about the possibility that his actions might be interpreted as malpractice?

Yes, the doctor said wearily, his patience clearly getting short. In retrospect, this might not be something that his insurance company would look kindly upon.

Still, Lowrey persisted. Why did Boggs have to remove Hanson's pants in order to attach electrodes to his legs for an EKG?

Hanson was wearing loose-fitting pants, and the trouser legs could easily have been slipped over his cowboy boots, Lowrey said pointedly.

Peeved, Boggs did not immediately answer the inquisitive officer. But then the doctor noted quickly, as if struck by a fresh thought, that he had helped Hanson remove his pants so Hanson could urinate in the room's sink.

Lowrey, now more suspicious than ever, next picked up the telephone in the same examination room and dialed 911.

As he waited for the phone to ring, Lowrey again studied Boggs. This time Lowrey was struck by how composed the doctor looked for someone who had claimed to have just performed CPR for forty-five minutes. At the same time Lowrey also noticed that the clothes on the dead patient, while somewhat ill-fitting, were not ruffled in the least, as one might expect of a person who had endured forty-five minutes of frantic CPR.

Not surprisingly, Lowrey's 911 call got through immediately.

All told, Lowrey would recall, "none of what he told me made sense."

Lowrey spent close to a half hour talking to the doctor. And throughout, Boggs's demeanor had alternated between frustration and nervousness. By the end of their encounter, Boggs was often pausing to the point of stammering, as if he had to stop and deliberate before answering a question.

When the interview was over, Lowrey had only one thing to say to Boggs:

"Liar!"

Boggs seemed less upset by that than when Lowrey and Spruill summoned the coroner's investigators to the scene to conduct a further inquiry.

But Lowrey's immediate suspicions had to be set aside as still more officials arrived, including a police photographer, criminalists, and Detective James A. Peterson of the Glendale police department, who had come to take charge of the investigation.

At about ten, a young Swedish man arrived at the office. Surprised by the commotion, he worked his way into the medical suite and identified himself as Hans Jonasson, a physical therapist and nurse who worked for Boggs. Jonasson had come to give a patient an injection. But after Lowrey and Boggs exchanged sharp words over whether Jonasson was properly licensed to practice in the United States, Jonasson and the patient wisely decided to postpone their appointment.

Shortly afterward, Lowrey left, but not without conveying his unease to Detective Peterson.

Jim Peterson, forty-eight, was a career Glendale policeman through and through. He had joined the department in 1962 and by 1970 had worked his way up to the rank of detective in the coveted robbery and homicide division. That status meant he usually did not have to work on weekends unless something highly unusual happened.

On this particular Saturday morning, the operations sergeant on duty at the police department had called Peterson at home, requesting his assistance at 540 North Central.

Peterson, a wiry, balding man with a tight-lipped smile, knew of Richard Boggs. The doctor's brother, William, had been a popular detective in the Glendale police department for many years before leaving to join the Drug Enforcement Agency in Europe several years earlier.

Peterson also had met Richard Boggs twenty years earlier, although under decidedly strained circumstances. It had happened one night when Peterson and his partner then, David O'Connor, were doing plainclothes work in the vice squad. They were patrolling a city park that, to the dismay of many Glendale residents, was rapidly becoming a night-time hangout for homosexuals. The officers nabbed Richard Boggs after he grabbed O'Connor in the men's room. Back at the police station, the officers released the doctor to his brother and their colleague, Detective Bill Boggs.

In more recent years, it had also come to Peterson's attention that Dr. Boggs was having financial and possibly professional problems because on more than one occasion, Glendale police had been called to his office to arbitrate disputes between the doctor and those who had come to repossess medical equipment or to evict him from the office altogether—for non-payment.

Peterson, after being briefed by officers Lowrey and Spruill of their suspicions of foul play, thanked the young officers and then condescendingly sent them on their way. He was now in charge.

Then the detective quickly surveyed the medical suite, taking but a cursory look at the corpse. Turning to the dead man's medical files, Peterson almost immediately found what he was looking for: the name and telephone number of the person to contact in emergencies. Gene Hanson was single, and the person he had listed as the emergency contact was one John B. Hawkins, his business partner. Hawkins had a Columbus, Ohio, telephone number.

Picking up the phone in Boggs's office, Peterson reached Hawkins at home right away. Tactfully and gently, the detective informed Hawkins that his business partner had dropped dead.

Much to Peterson's surprise, Hawkins already had heard the tragic and shocking news.

How?

From Dr. Boggs, Hawkins explained. In fact, Hawkins added, he had already made plans to fly out to California later that day.

Did he know if Hanson was gay?

Yes, he was, Hawkins said.

Did he know that Dr. Boggs also had gay tendencies, and did he know if there was anything going on between the dead man and Boggs?

Unlikely, Hawkins replied confidently. "They weren't into the same thing, and they didn't really do anything for each other."

Back at the station, officer Lowrey was stunned when Spruill told him that Peterson had said it would not be necessary for Lowrey to write up a supplemental report on the morning's incident. Lowrey was upset that Peterson so readily accepted Boggs's explanation of the morning's bizarre developments. Lowrey sent a computer message across the room to Spruill, saying he thought Peterson's instructions were bullshit.

As one chagrined Glendale police officer would later point out: "Getting a call from a doctor reporting a death is about as sure a thing as having a mother identify her child." After all, it wasn't just all the IDs on the corpse that had Hanson's name on them. Didn't the corpse match up almost precisely with the Melvin Eugene Hanson described in Boggs's medical files? Both had blue eyes, brown hair, and weighed about 155 pounds.

On that Saturday morning, if Boggs recognized Jim Peterson, the doctor did not let on. And neither did Peterson. The detective never bothered even to talk to the doctor.

Moving Day

By noon, the authorities were nearly done with Richard Boggs, and the doctor was free to go.

But Glendale police sergeant Terry Jones, who had requested the presence of Detective Jim Peterson, had one last request. He asked Boggs if he could follow the physician home. Boggs lived only a dozen blocks away on North Belmont Street, just on the other side of the 134 Freeway, an east–west highway that bisects Glendale. Jones wanted to hear for himself the tape of Hanson's early morning call.

"Sure," Boggs said. "No problem."

Jones, a burglary investigator, initially was sent to the scene because the department's robbery-homicide investigators on duty that morning had been called out to investigate a throat-slashing incident.

As Jones and Boggs departed the office, the doctor casually remarked that it was not at all unusual for him to have seen Hanson at his office during off-hours. In fact, Boggs said, he had met Hanson at his office two or three other times at night, including on Saturdays or Sundays.

Jones and Boggs reached 301 North Belmont in just a few minutes. Inside, Boggs apologized for the disarray throughout the apartment. There were stuffed shopping bags and boxes everywhere, making it difficult to get around the spartan apartment. Boggs and his two roommates were in the process that very weekend of moving to another apartment across town, about two miles away. But beyond the understandable chaos, the doctor's home—like his office—was filled with telltale but unmistakable signs of genteel shabbiness. The few pieces of threadbare furniture gave the tiny apartment the cheap look of a typical off-campus house occupied by college students. It was hardly what one would expect of a physician's home.

The answering machine was on the floor, virtually surrounded by more piles of papers and shopping bags, next to the bed in one of the two bedrooms. Boggs played the tape back for Sergeant Jones.

On it was the panic-stricken voice of a man who identified himself as Gene Hanson, complaining of severe chest pains. Then the tape abruptly ended—apparently at the point when Boggs said he turned off the machine and picked up the phone to talk to Hanson.

Jones took the cassette tape and returned to Boggs's office. There, he turned the tape over to Detective Peterson, who was now just about ready to conclude his "investigation."

Red Flags

By the time investigator Craig Harvey of the Los Angeles County coroner's office showed up at Dr. Boggs's office, most of the other officials were long gone. And a modicum of normalcy had returned to the medical building, which housed more than a dozen other physicians' offices. Several of these were now open for business, and the trickle of patients did not seem aware of the unusual early morning activities in Suite 210.

Nearly five hours had elapsed since paramedics, firefighters, and police had first rushed to the well-scrubbed but unprepossessing brick building, one of many near the freeway that catered to doctors and pharmacists along the city's bustling Central Avenue.

Inside Suite 201, the first thing Harvey did was closely examine the corpse for any signs of physical trauma—bumps, bruises, contusions, abrasions. There was no such evidence of foul play. There also were no needle marks on the dead man's arms. He had not died of a fatal drug overdose, either self-administered or at the hands of another.

Next, Harvey closely scrutinized the corpse for any signs of having been sexually molested, either before or after death. The coroner's investigator performed this examination after Peterson told him that Boggs was probably gay.

Just two weeks earlier, Peterson had said, a gay man from Hollywood had filed a complaint against Boggs, alleging that the doctor had attacked him with a stun gun. But it was clear to Harvey, judging from Peterson's tone, that the gay man's accusations were not to be taken too seriously. It had been, at best, a lover's quarrel. Still, Peterson thought Harvey should know.

But the clothes on the corpse were, if anything, remarkably undisturbed. And there were no other signs of sexual foul play either, a finding that would be confirmed later by a more detailed examination down at the coroner's office.

Harvey then settled in to begin a more thorough examination. He took out a thermometer and set it on the examination table to take the room temperature. Comparing the ambient temperature at a death scene with that of the corpse is a standard way to calculate the time of death, imprecise as that might be.

Next, wielding a scalpel expertly, Harvey made a small, barely detectable incision in the corpse's abdomen, just above the liver. This quickly accomplished, he inserted a thermometer, much like a standard meat thermometer, through the slit into the liver. Its temperature was eighty-seven degrees.

That reading should have been another red flag for authorities because it was inconsistent with Boggs's version of events. Normal body temperature is 98.6 degrees Fahrenheit, fueled by the constant burning of oxygen. But once a person is dead and ceases to burn oxygen, the body temperature begins to drop, eventually reaching the temperature of its immediate surroundings. This rate of decrease varies somewhat, depending on the environment and special circumstances, but it generally occurs at a predictable rate.

Initially, for the first two to four hours, it drops at the rate of one and a half degrees per hour. Thereafter, it falls at a rate of about one degree per hour until it reaches room temperature.

Relying on this widely accepted rule of thumb, then, would have put the time of Hanson's death at two or three in the morning—several hours earlier than in Boggs's account.

That was hardly the only medical clue that investigators overlooked. By the time Harvey conducted his examination, around twelve thirty, the body was at the height of rigor mortis—so much so, in fact, that Harvey found it difficult to bend or move the arms and legs.

That, too, was another unmistakable sign that the body had been dead far longer than authorities had been told by Boggs. Rigor mortis, or the stiffening of the muscles, is a chemical process that occurs after the heart is no longer pumping blood throughout the body to take away waste products. Typically, it takes rigor mortis at least two to three hours before becoming noticeable. The stiffening gets progressively intense, and the body is literally as stiff as a board about ten to twelve hours after death. A body then remains this way for another twelve hours before the rigor mortis gradually dissipates over the next twelve hours.

In his two-page report, Harvey gave the corpse in Boggs's office a 4-plus rigor mortis rating—the maximum. That clearly suggested the dead man had died not around six in the morning but some four hours previously—even earlier, in fact, than the body's liver temperature had suggested.

No one noticed this discrepancy either. But that wasn't Harvey's job. His responsibility was merely to record his findings, write a report, and then transport the body to the coroner's office.

An inventory of the dead man's belongings turned up $53.55 in cash, a ring, a watch, a plastic comb, a pair of sunglasses, and a jacket. The man had no keys. Even more remarkable, not one piece of his personal identification had a photograph on it, not even the driver's license. But this too did not arouse any suspicion.

Finally, with the help of a student worker, Harvey wrapped the corpse in a plastic sheet and drove it to the morgue some ten miles away in downtown L.A. There, Harvey undressed the corpse, weighed and measured it, fingerprinted it, put a tag on each toe, and lifted it onto a gurney. Then he wheeled it down the hall to a large vault chilled to 40 degrees Fahrenheit. There it would remain until an autopsy surgeon became available to do a postmortem.

Harvey put the dead man's personal belongings in a

property safe. His clothing went in a heavy paper sack that also had a toe tag on it. Harvey put the bag in the chilly crypt alongside the corpse.

For Harvey, Case No. 88-03963 seemed no more memorable or remarkable than any of the other five to eight hundred dead bodies he is called on to examine each year. His report said there were no obvious signs of foul play. It looked like a tragic but natural death.

Masquerade

At the Los Angeles County coroner's office early on Sunday morning, Case No. 88-03963 seemed like another routine autopsy to Evancia Sy, one of three hundred she already had performed that year.

The Philippines-born physician had earned her medical degree in 1979 at the Far Eastern University in Manila and then arrived in the United States two years later. After a four-year pathology residency at the University of Oklahoma, Sy landed at the L.A. County coroner's office in July 1987 as a forensic pathology fellow. The office, forever shorthanded and underfunded, was glad to have her. Working under the supervision of Dr. Joan Shipley, Sy by the middle of April 1988 had performed autopsies involving every manner of death imaginable: suicides, natural deaths, accidental deaths, homicides. She had seen them all.

On April 17, barely a full day after Glendale authorities had encountered a dead body on the floor of Dr. Richard Boggs's office, Sy began a routine that had become second nature. After reviewing the report prepared by Craig Harvey, Sy decided there was no need to have a photographer present for the autopsy, a routine practice in cases of apparent or suspected homicide.

In the cramped, antiseptic autopsy room, she identified the body by the toe tag, checking both the name and the case number. The last thing the much maligned coroner's office needed was another case of mistaken identity.

Before opening up the body, Sy performed a cursory external examination, from head to toe. She paused only once, and that was when she studied the man's face a second time. He looked considerably younger than forty-six, the age listed in Harvey's report. At eight-thirty, Sy made the first incision. Working efficiently, with a technician nearby, she deftly removed the tongue and neck organs, followed by the heart, lungs, liver, and all abdominal organs. All the while Sy collected tissue samples from each specimen as well as samples of the dead man's blood, bile, and urine.

She also looked for hemorrhages around the neck, but there was no evidence of strangulation. There were no signs of skull fractures or bruises on the brain either.

All the organs, including the heart and lungs, appeared to be in good condition. Especially the heart. "The vessels that supply the heart were clean." Sy would recall. "There was no evidence of heart attack."

All done, the doctor was stumped. There was no obvious cause of death whatsoever.

Indeed, the only unusual finding was an extremely high blood-alcohol content of .29—nearly three times the legal intoxication level in the state of California. But that was hardly a surprise. The man's greasy fatty liver was convincing evidence of a lifetime of indulgence in alcohol.

Puzzled by the absence of any clues at all as to the cause of the sudden death, Sy prepared numerous tissue slides, ordering a full battery of toxicological tests—for barbiturates, cocaine, codeine, morphine, and other drugs.

Clearly, this was no suicide. But there were no signs of accidental death either. And there were no signs of foul play. Nor, for that matter, was there any sign whatsoever that the man had fallen from an examination table onto a linoleum floor.

Moreover, Sy saw no evidence that anyone had performed CPR, which might well have left subcutaneous hemorrhages in the chest area. Indeed, it is not uncommon to see even fractured ribs as a result of prolonged or vigorous CPR. But here, there were no indications that any form of life-saving measures had been attempted.

By ten-thirty, some two hours after she had begun, Sy was finished. She hoped that the toxicological tests would yield some clue.

A week later, she was still awaiting those lab results when she got a telephone call in her office from a fellow physician.

It was Dr. Richard P. Boggs. He wanted to know what she had found out or concluded about what had killed his former patient.

That, Sy told Boggs, was being deferred, pending additional test results and analytical work. This was in keeping with office policy, but it also suited Sy's indecisive nature just fine.

Speaking in the manner of one physician to another, Sy asked Boggs about his former patient's medical history. Boggs was only too happy to oblige. Mr. Hanson, he said, had been experiencing chest pains off and on for a year, but he refused to see a cardiologist, fearful of most doctors.

Did Mr. Hanson have any viral infections shortly before his unfortunate demise? Why, yes, Boggs replied with expansive intimacy. Only a week earlier.

Grateful for this new clue, Sy went back to the slides containing the dead man's heart muscles. Under the microscope, this time she detected what she took to be an infection in a very small area around the blood vessels that supply blood to the heart.

When the toxicological tests all came back negative, and Sy could find nothing further under the microscope, she completed her autopsy report on June 22, 1988, closing out the case. Sy listed the official cause of death as non-specific focal myocarditis, or inflammation of the heart muscle.

Gene Hanson had died, in other words, of natural causes.

A Hasty Farewell

Kathleen Ann Sealey also worked on that foggy Sunday morning, April 17. Sealey had received a call at the Mountain View Mortuary in Altadena, where she worked part-time as an embalmer.

The caller was John Hawkins. He identified himself as the co-owner, along with the now dead Gene Hanson, of Just Sweats, a chain of sports apparel stores in Ohio and Kentucky.

Hawkins was calling from the Hyatt Regency Hotel near Los Angeles International Airport. He was in town, he told Sealey, to close out the affairs of his late business partner and dear friend. No, Hawkins told her, there was no need to embalm the body. He wanted a quick cremation. And no, he did not wish to view the body. The caller was friendly but businesslike, his voice and demeanor clearly projecting the image of someone used to giving orders.

Hawkins's directions to Sealey were clear and concise: Pick up the body from the coroner's office and have it cremated and the ashes scattered at sea. The sooner the better. He could, Hawkins confided, ill afford any delays, as he was losing money every day that he was in California. But despite the press of business, Hawkins said, he would not leave until the ashes had been disposed of.

Less than two hours later, Hawkins showed up in person at the mortuary, located in a northern Los Angeles suburb high in the foothills of the San Gabriel Mountains, just above Pasadena. He was full of nervous energy, and his youthfulness surprised Sealey, a slender, serious woman who walks with a slight limp.

With his stylishly long hair and casual attire that ac-
centuated his compact but athletic physique, Hawkins
looked more like a student from UCLA than a be-
reaved businessman from the Midwest. Indeed, Hawkins looked for all the world like he could have been
there to sign up for a volleyball tournament at Venice
Beach.

Since Hawkins seemed to be in a big hurry, Sealey
had all the necessary paperwork already prepared by
the time he arrived. There was a release form authorizing her to pick up Hanson's body from the coroner's
office. There was a form authorizing cremation. There
were, in fact, forms galore, and the red tape clearly
irritated Hawkins.

"He was in a hurry," Sealey recalled. "He wanted
everything done as quickly as possible."

Hawkins even had with him Hanson's three-page last
will and testament, plus a notarized power of attorney
signed by Hanson that authorized Hawkins to act on
his behalf.

But there was just one minor hitch, Sealey warily
told Hawkins. She could cremate the body the next
day. But because of a backlog, Mountain View would
not be able to scatter the ashes for perhaps three or
four months.

Not to worry, Hawkins replied. Proceed with the
cremation. He would make other arrangements to dispose of the ashes.

Before leaving, Hawkins counted out $300 in cash
as partial payment, leaving a balance of $370.

Later that afternoon, only hours after Evancia Sy
had sewn up the corpse that everyone assumed to be
that of Melvin Eugene Hanson, Sealey drove down to
the morgue and fetched the body.

Back at Mountain View, she unwrapped the corpse
and put it in the refrigerator. One never quite gets used
to seeing the huge, raw, Y-shaped scars left on a torso
by an autopsy.

The next day, she cremated the body and sent the
ashes to the Abbot and Hast Mortuary in Los Angeles,

which Hawkins had hired to scatter the ashes over the icy Pacific Ocean off the Southern California coast.

After paying Sealey the remaining balance, again in cash, Hawkins had one final request.

He needed three copies of the death certificate as soon as possible. This Sealey did not find unusual or surprising, since as an executor, Hawkins now had a sizable estate to handle. But even so, Hawkins's rush was a bit unseemly.

He wanted the certificates to be rushed by Federal Express to the law firm of Hamilton, Kramer, Myers and Cheek in Columbus, Ohio; to the Farmers New World Life Insurance Company in Mercer Island, Washington; and to the Golden Rule Insurance Company in Lawrenceville, Illinois.

It was time to collect.

Fully Insured

In the fall of 1985, a golden goose had landed on the lap of Ed Mulvihill, an independent insurance agent operating out of the fashionable German Village section of downtown Columbus, Ohio.

Out of the blue, the middle-aged salesman got a call one day from a new businessman in town, saying that he heard about Mulvihill after checking around. The caller said he was starting a chain of sports apparel stores and invited Mulvihill to quote him some prices for life insurance for himself and his partner, plus rates for group health insurance for themselves and their employees. His name was John Hawkins.

Delighted, Mulvihill wasted little time getting back to Hawkins, and the young businessman and his partner, Gene Hanson, liked the rates Mulvihill offered. The first policy was for over $100,000, covering their first store, called Just Sweats, which was located right across the street from the Ohio State University campus.

The store became an instant and phenomenal success, and the two entrepreneurs began opening additional stores all over town. Things were happening at such a dizzying pace that often Mulvihill didn't learn of a new store opening until Hawkins and Hanson came to him for insurance several weeks afterward.

By the following spring, Hanson and Hawkins took out life insurance policies worth $450,000 each with the Golden Rule Life Insurance Company, in Lawrenceville, Illinois.

Less than a year later, as their businesses continued flourishing, Hanson and Hawkins became interested in purchasing additional life insurance coverage. But Golden Rule would not write policies for more than $450,000, which deeply disappointed Mulvihill. He liked doing business with it because he thought it offered better policies for less money. Too, his sales commission was as much as fifty percent of a policy's premium.

And so Mulvihill turned to Farmers New World Life Insurance Company, based in Mercer Island, Washington—the source of ninety percent of his total income even though his commission with Farmers was only ten percent.

Farmers was happy to write $500,000 life insurance policies for Hanson and Hawkins. And that fall, the two businessmen each applied for and received a second, identical life insurance policy with Farmers. Again the monthly premium of $1,580 was paid by a Just Sweats check.

Before issuing each of the term policies, Farmers conducted a routine background check into Hanson's and Hawkins's worth. In addition, both men underwent physical examinations conducted by a Farmers contractor called Porta Medics, which pronounced them both in good health. As an added safeguard, Jeff Dearth, a Farmers underwriting manager whose job it was to review and process life insurance applications, also contacted the men's physician by telephone, speaking directly to the doctor. His name was Richard Boggs. If Dearth had been struck by the oddity that Hawkins and Hanson used a doctor two thousand miles away, he did not say so.

And so by early October 1987, Hanson and Hawkins each had life insurance policies worth $1.45 million. In addition, as a part of Just Sweats' group health insurance coverage provided by Farmers, each man had another $15,000 in life insurance coverage.

And now, in the spring of 1988, with Gene Hanson's sudden death, John Hawkins as the sole heir stood to become a wealthy man.

He wasted little time getting his lawyers in Columbus to begin the insurance paperwork. Hanson sum-

moned Mulvihill to the offices of the company's
attorney, Richard Curtin, where they presented the
pudgy insurance agent with Hanson's death certificates. Mulvihill promised to "take care of everything."

Before the month of April was out, Hawkins sent
Farmers, by Federal Express, a claim on the two Hanson life insurance policies, totalling $1 million. Along
with the claim was Hanson's death certificate, albeit
with a deferred cause of death. Dr. Evancia Sy out in
California still had not made up her mind yet.

In Mercer Island, a Seattle suburb, claims supervisor Shelly Navarre was assigned the case. At that point
there were no questions raised yet about the dead man's
identity. But Farmers was already suspicious about
possible fraud. Several Farmers officials, including
Navarre, wondered if perhaps Hanson had fraudulently withheld vital information about his true medical condition at the time he took out the policies.
Because Hanson's inexplicable death had occurred in
the "contestable" period—that is, within the first two
years of the policies' issuance—Farmers contacted
Equifax Services, a private investigations firm that
works for insurance companies, to look further into
the matter.

Thus Norman MacRae, an Equifax agent in Los Angeles, was dispatched at the end of June to visit Dr.
Richard Boggs. MacRae found the physician disarm-
ing and forthcoming. The solicitous doctor even helped
MacRae make copies of Hanson's medical records.
And when MacRae got back in touch with Boggs in
mid-August for some additional information, the doctor was still pleasant and cooperative. But Boggs had
no information that even suggested that Hanson had
provided Farmers with false information.

"It was all more or less routine at that point in
time," MacRae recalled. His inquiries, he said, were
"typical for any big claim."

At about the same time that Farmers received the
claims statements from Hawkins, the Golden Rule Life

Insurance Company also heard from Hawkins, who was seeking $450,000 from the insurer.

In Lawrenceville, Jennifer Brown was assigned to the claim. She reached Hawkins by telephone at his office in Columbus, and Hawkins readily related to her the circumstances of Hanson's death. He told her his late partner had not been ill until January, when he began experiencing chest pains and shortness of breath.

Why didn't Hanson see a doctor in Ohio instead of this Dr. Boggs in California? Brown asked.

Because Hanson had lived out in L.A. for five years before moving to Columbus, Hawkins said politely.

Brown explained that since Hanson had died within the two-year "contestable" period, Golden Rule too would be conducting a routine investigation into the circumstances of his death. And as a part of that probe, she told Hawkins, Golden Rule needed to know how to contact Hanson's next of kin in order to obtain permission from that person granting Golden Rule access to Hanson's medical history going back ten years.

At that point, Hawkins's courteous demeanor vanished. He balked, "I've been appointed the beneficiary and executor of the will and estate," he said with a dash of indignation. "And I'm not about to grant anybody access to anything without my lawyer's approval. If you want a copy of Gene Hanson's will, call his lawyer."

Sensing Brown's puzzlement at his strong response, and realizing that he had overreacted, Hawkins again softened considerably. He explained that Hanson had disinherited his family six months earlier, and his late partner certainly would not have wanted his blood relatives to learn of his death. Eager to terminate the conversation, Hawkins said he was about to leave town, and they agreed to talk again after he returned in a few days.

Like Shelly Navarre in Mercer Island, Brown now found herself increasingly suspicious about the case of Melvin Eugene Hanson.

Despite Brown's misgivings about the case, Golden

Rule almost immediately sent Hawkins a check for $10,000. "It's standard practice for most insurance companies to do this to help pay for the burial costs that are incurred at the time of death," explained David Grannan, a supervisor in Golden Rule's special investigations unit.

But the rest of the payment would have to await a final ruling by the Los Angeles County coroner's office on Hanson's cause of death.

"You can't pay when you don't know what the cause of death is," Brown said.

But it didn't take long. By the end of June, Dr. Evancia Sy finally ruled that Hanson had died a natural death.

Checks in the Mail

In Seattle, Shelly Navarre was eager to close out the case of Melvin Eugene Hanson. And so throughout the month of May and into early June, the Farmers claims supervisor frequently telephoned Glendale police detective Jim Peterson, hoping for some definitive word on the case. Sensing Peterson's lack of interest, Navarre on June 9 asked him flat out if the Glendale police department had entertained the notion that the dead man was not Melvin Eugene Hanson.

No, it had not, an annoyed Peterson said dismissively. There had been no questions raised about the corpse's identity. Nor was there any reason to suspect foul play in Hanson's death. Leave the police work to us, the tone of Peterson's voice suggested.

But Navarre would not be so easily put off.

Did police compare a picture of the dead man with one taken of Hanson some time before April 16?

"Gee, our technicians did take pictures of the dead man that day," Peterson said. And it certainly would be no problem ordering an earlier picture of Gene Hanson from the California Department of Motor Vehicles in Sacramento. Peterson had to admit that Navarre's suggestion was not unreasonable. Begrudgingly he said he would have no problem with it. Later that day, the veteran detective sent a routine request for a copy of Hanson's driver's license.

Almost a month went by, and nothing happened.

On July 6, Peterson finally made a second request. Yet another week passed before a copy of Hanson's driver's license—with a photograph—arrived for Peterson at the Glendale police station. The license had been issued to Hanson three years earlier. Still, judging from a comparison of the photographs, things seemed to match. "It was fairly close," Peterson recalled. Hanson and the dead man both were five-feet-ten. Both had blue eyes. Both had brown hair and were balding. Both sported a mustache and beard.

And yet . . .

There appeared to be a noticeable age difference. Hanson was listed in all the records as being forty-six-years-old, but the corpse looked decidedly younger. Dr. Sy had made the same mental observation.

Alarmed, Peterson quickly passed the pictures around the police station. Only half thought the dead man was Hanson. And Peterson by now was not one of them.

Still, one couldn't be sure going by grainy snapshots alone. Fingerprints now needed to be compared. With a sense of urgency this time, Peterson once more contacted the California Department of Motor Vehicles, asking for a set of Hanson's fingerprints. When they arrived, even Peterson, no fingerprint expert, readily saw that Hanson's fingerprints did not match the prints taken of the corpse on April 16.

To be doubly sure, authorities also ordered the fingerprints taken of Hanson at the Army Reception Center in Fort Jackson, South Carolina, on April 15, 1965, the day that a twenty-three-year-old Hanson reported for boot camp. Again, the two sets of fingerprints did not match.

On July 13, a chastened Peterson reluctantly called Navarre in Mercer Island. "I don't believe it was the same person," he told her.

But it was too late. Three days earlier, Farmers had sent Hawkins a check for $1 million, and Hawkins had cashed it immediately.

"Everything checked out," Jeff Beyer, a vice president of Farmers' parent organization, Farmers Group Inc., would recall years later. "We had all these reports, and you can't ask for much more." In any insurance claims case, an insurer must strike a balance between caution and expediency, he explained. "And in this case, we did go through some pretty cautious checking. But we had taken about as much time as we could rightfully take.''

The same attitude prevailed at Golden Rule. Like Farmers, it had received by the end of June Hanson's official death certificate, stating that he had died of nonspecific focal myocarditis. And it took Jennifer Brown, her supervisor, and a senior company manager about a week to review Hawkins's claim, going over in some detail the circumstances of Hanson's death. "As far as the information that we had, no misstatements had been made on this application," Brown said.

And so Golden Rule too sent a check to Hawkins, this one for $440,000—plus interest. The company sent the check to Hawkins's apartment in Columbus by certified mail. It did not know, of course, that Hawkins had moved out several weeks earlier—without leaving a forwarding address.

In Columbus, a mail carrier left at Hawkins's old apartment a notice of attempted delivery of the check and then took it back to the post office to await pickup by Hawkins. Luckily for Golden Rule, Hawkins had not yet picked up the check. The insurance company quickly stopped payment on it.

Armed now with irrefutable evidence that a massive insurance fraud, possibly involving murder, had been perpetrated, a red-faced Glendale police department had no choice but to re-open the investigation. Just who was the dead man, if not Gene Hanson? How had he died? Had he been murdered? Where was Gene Hanson? What did John Hawkins do with the insurance money, and where had he disappeared to?

How could Dr. Richard Boggs have mistakenly identified a patient of seven years? Or was the physician also in on the plot? But if he was, why hadn't he fled like the others?

As suspicions of Boggs deepened, it didn't take long for authorities to discover an earlier incident involving the doctor that would prove pivotal in developing the case against all three men.

Close Call

It had been a grueling week at the office, and on this unseasonably warm Friday night in late March 1988, Barry Pomeroy was ready to party.

And the wiry, frail-looking West Hollywood man was hardly alone. Even before he entered The Spike, a bar on Santa Monica Boulevard, not far from his apartment, Pomeroy heard the music emanating from within.

The dark, smoke-filled bar was packed. In the center of the room, people were dancing—some strutting—to the pulsating jukebox tunes. Others clustered around a pool table, idly watching a game being played obviously by amateurs. The Spike had few tables, and so many customers sat on the cartons of beer stacked along the walls, flicking their cigarette ashes onto the cracked cement floor. With numerous pinups of models in leather scattered on the walls, the place looked more like an old warehouse than a bar. In a tiny alcove in the very back, patrons gathered around a few video-game machines, drinks in hand.

Pomeroy, a timid, submissive person, found a seat at the long, crowded bar, under one of the red neon "SERVICE" signs overhead. He ordered a beer from a barrel-chested bartender with well-tattooed biceps and then made small talk with some of the regulars, his cigarette smoke drifting lazily toward the high ceiling.

There was nothing pretentious about The Spike. It was a seedy gay bar in the middle of a rough part of town, along a strip of pawn shops, adult book stores, and a porno movie house. And it catered to devotees of leather and chains. The first thing seen in the bar's entry, upon entering through the black curtains, is the rear half of a large motorcycle, sitting there as if the front had been rammed into the wall and disappeared. And most of the patrons on this Friday night looked as though they owned one.

The night passed quickly, and by the time Pomeroy looked up from a pool game, it was well past one already. He was thinking about leaving, perhaps to get something to eat. At that moment, Pomeroy—and virtually everyone else in the bar—noticed a tall, gray-haired man enter alone through the parted curtains. The man seemed to have an authoritative air about him. But that in itself was not unusual. The Spike was crawling with severe-looking guys who exuded a penchant to dominate. On the contrary, what made the man stand out was his ordinariness.

Soon Pomeroy struck up a conversation with the man, as they absentmindedly watched a fresh pool game, each nursing a Corona beer. The nattily dressed man was a smooth conversationalist and seemed equally comfortable whether talking about motorcycles or architecture or billiards. He introduced himself as Peter Richards, a neurologist who practiced in Glendale.

A half hour later, they decided to go for a bite to eat. By then a gusty chill had descended over the starry Southern California basin, and Pomeroy and Richards walked quickly to the doctor's black Cadillac, parked on a dark side street. They drove down Santa Monica Boulevard to an all-night restaurant called Theodore's, about a mile away. The eatery had just been remodeled, and over hamburgers, the conversation turned naturally to architecture.

Even though it was three, the doctor offered to show Pomeroy some of the new, architecturally innovative high-rises going up along Brand Boulevard in Glendale. Pomeroy readily agreed. As the waiter brought the check, the doctor picked it up with a smooth, practiced motion.

The freeway traffic was still heavy—typical for L.A., especially on weekends—but they still made it to Glendale in under fifteen minutes. By then downtown Glendale was deserted, and Richards slowly drove up and down Brand Boulevard, pointing out the many avant-garde office buildings on either side. Pomeroy was especially struck by one cream-colored high-rise that looked to him like a stack of dominoes.

Breaking the spell, the doctor said he needed to stop by his office to make a few telephone calls. Pomeroy did not mind. The doctor's office was on Central Avenue, just a block west of Brand. They pulled into the back parking lot of the office building and entered through a glass back door, for which Richards had a key.

Inside the doctor's second-floor office suite, Pomeroy sat in the small reception area flipping through some dog-eared magazines while Richards went into his inner office.

When the doctor emerged a few minutes later, he had some color brochures to show Pomeroy. Richards said he was thinking about entering into a food import-export venture, specializing in packaging wines and cheeses in baskets, and he wanted Pomeroy's opinion. Pomeroy, ever eager to please, said he thought it was a fine idea.

The casual conversation then turned to some etchings on the walls in the reception area. They were from England, and Pomeroy remarked that his mother had been born there.

Glancing farther around the doctor's slightly tattered office, Pomeroy became struck by something odd about the many framed certificates mounted on the walls. They all bore the name of Richard Pryde Boggs. Not one certificate in sight had the name of Peter Richards.

Oh, those are my partner's, the doctor remarked offhandedly, and Pomeroy thought no more about it.

After an hour or so, Richards was finally ready to leave. It was close to dawn, and the doctor drove Pomeroy home, dropping him off in front of his apartment. West Hollywood was still teeming with nightlife as they sat in the car and Pomeroy wrote down his telephone number for Richards. The doctor said he would call soon.

Several nights later, Peter Richards telephoned Pomeroy at home, suggesting dinner the following Friday night in a new, popular seafood restaurant in Glendale called The Pelican. Pomeroy was delighted.

"Why don't you meet me at Denny's Restaurant in Hollywood, say around eight o'clock on Friday?" he asked Richards. Denny's was only a block and a half from his apartment.

"Great," said the doctor. "I'll see you there."

Richards was right on time. But at first he didn't see Pomeroy. Denny's was quite crowded, filled with teenage runaways, street people, kids obviously strung out on drugs, and aspiring starlets—all congregating as if they had no place better to go at that early hour. Finally the doctor spotted Pomeroy, sitting at the counter sipping coffee, reading a newspaper, and having a cigarette.

They left almost immediately, again in the doctor's Cadillac. The night was young and, to Pomeroy, full of promise as the twinkling lights of Glendale beckoned.

But once they got off the Ventura Freeway, Richards announced that he had to make another quick stop at his office before dinner; he needed to check on a few patients, and it was much easier to use the telephone in his office rather than in the noisy restaurant. No problem, Pomeroy said.

It was almost nine o'clock and the medical building at 540 Central again was deserted. Upstairs, Pomeroy once more took a seat in the lounge as Richards went into his inner office. A few minutes later, the doctor came back out, leaving the door ajar. Through it Pomeroy could see a large machine in one of the examination rooms. His curiosity was piqued.

"That's an EKG machine," the doctor said. And he invited Pomeroy in for a closer look, launching into an expansive explanation of how the machine works.

Would Pomeroy like an EKG? Richards asked.

Why not? Pomeroy said, somewhat meekly.

"He told me to take my jacket and shirt off, and then he put a lubricant and little suction cups on different parts of my chest, and proceeded with the test," recalled Pomeroy, a rail-thin man who seems even more frail than his five-foot-ten, 140-pound frame.

A few minutes later, a paper printout of the EKG reading emerged.

"Your heart's in good shape," Richards pronounced with a flourish.

Happily, Pomeroy got dressed and exited the small examination room while the doctor lingered inside—apparently to clean up the EKG machine. Or so Pomeroy thought.

Still in the examination room, the doctor turned once more toward Pomeroy.

"Are you ready to go to dinner?" he asked.

"Yes." Pomeroy replied.

The doctor then stepped forward, extending his left arm toward Pomeroy.

Pomeroy walked toward the doctor, re-entering the examination room.

Suddenly Richards pounced on him. Pomeroy felt a sharp jolt in his back as the doctor's right arm shot out, jabbing him with something that he could not make out. It was an electric prod.

At first Pomeroy thought it was a joke. But Richards continued jabbing him furiously, again and again, first in the back, then in his side.

Paralyzed by pain and confusion, Pomeroy nearly blacked out. "I couldn't believe what was happening," he later recalled.

But instead of fainting, Pomeroy took a deep breath and collected himself. Then summoning a burst of energy that surprised even himself, he began fighting back, struggling fiercely against the doctor. That wasn't easy to do, for he was over six feet tall and weighed a good twenty-five pounds more than Pomeroy.

As they fought in the tiny examination room, crashing from wall to wall, Pomeroy began throwing punches at his assailant and kicking wildly. Eventually he knocked Richards's right hand sharply against a corner of the examination table. A little plastic box fell out of the doctor's hand and dropped to the floor. It was a plastic stun gun.

Suddenly unarmed, the doctor immediately backed off, seemingly exhausted.

"I don't know what happened," Richards stammered. "I've been having these problems," he added, gesturing toward his temple with a grimace. Richards apologized to Pomeroy again, adding that he was seeing a therapist for the problem.

Still shaken, Pomeroy didn't press the doctor for a further explanation. He just wanted to get out of there.

During their struggle, Pomeroy had somehow received a cut on the left side of his neck, just under the jawbone. And his blood had stained both his own and Richards's shirts. Pomeroy was still bleeding.

Now the contrite doctor abruptly changed from attacker to healer. Taking a close look at Pomeroy's wound, Richards said he needed stitches. And he offered to sew up the half-inch gash on the spot.

Pomeroy declined. "Just please take me home," he said, almost pleading. The stun gun also had left several burn marks on Pomeroy's back, left arm, and upper chest.

As the doctor continued mumbling apologies, Pomeroy felt somewhat reassured that whatever had come over Richards had now passed. He felt safe again. And when he asked the doctor for something to calm his nerves, Richards obligingly produced two sedative pills.

Finally the doctor offered to drive Pomeroy home. Outside, Pomeroy found the night air refreshing. And he felt much safer still to be out where there were plenty of pedestrians and automobile traffic.

But once they were in Richards's Cadillac, the doctor suggested still another detour. "Let's stop by my apartment," the doctor said. "It's just a couple of miles from here. I may have more sedatives there for you."

Pomeroy did not protest. He could use the sedatives.

When they pulled up to the curb in front of the doctor's Belmont Street apartment, Richards asked Pomeroy to remain in the Cadillac. ''I've got a roommate with a gun. I'd prefer you stay in the car.''

Pomeroy was in no mood to confront another person with a weapon. He just wanted to get home. And so he stayed in the car, grateful that Richards had left the engine running, with the heater on.

About ten minutes later, Richards returned. He couldn't find any more pills, but he now was ready to take Pomeroy home. By then it was ten-thirty, and more than two hours had passed since they met up at Denny's. Pomeroy wasn't even hungry anymore. He went straight to bed.

When Pomeroy's buddies heard about his hair-raising encounter with his new doctor friend, they persuaded him not to let Peter Richards get away with it. But before reporting the doctor to the police, Pomeroy realized he needed to furnish more details about the attack. ''I wanted to make sure that I had the correct name and had the correct office,'' he explained.

And so on the following Wednesday afternoon, five days after the attack, a friend drove Pomeroy to Glendale, cruising up and down Brand Boulevard. Pomeroy recognized the high-rise buildings, but he could not spot Peter Richards's office building. But when they turned onto Central Avenue, Pomeroy right away realized that this was the street. Still, it took several trips up and down Central before Pomeroy thought he recognized the doctor's building; there were so many nondescript structures that catered to doctors and pharmacies along that particular stretch of Central Avenue.

At 540 North Central, Pomeroy and his friend, Steve McGrew, parked in the back lot and entered the building through the glass back door that Pomeroy now clearly remembered. They went straight to the building's directory in the lobby. But there was no Peter Richards listed as a tenant.

Still, Pomeroy believed he could remember the building's layout. Discreetly he and McGrew walked up the stairwell to the second floor.

When they passed Suite 201, Pomeroy thought that was the office. McGrew pushed the door open, and looking in, Pomeroy immediately knew he was right. He recognized the etchings that he had discussed with "Peter Richards" the previous Friday night. Going quickly back down to the lobby, they saw that the directory listed a neurologist by the name of Richard P. Boggs as the sole tenant of Suite 201. Pomeroy at last knew the true identity of his attacker.

Later that same night, when an unsuspecting "Peter Richards" called him at home and solicitously inquired about his injuries, Pomeroy was cool to Richards. Now prepared to file a criminal complaint against the doctor, Pomeroy no longer wanted to have anything to do with him.

On the following Saturday, eight days after he was savagely attacked, Pomeroy walked into the Glendale police department to file a complaint against the man he now knew as Richard Boggs. At the station, a courteous female officer dutifully took down Pomeroy's information. On the following Monday, the complaint reached the desk of a veteran detective. His name was James Peterson.

The detective immediately recognized the name of the alleged attacker. Most of the senior officials in the Glendale PD knew of the doctor's many problems, which often required police intervention. But after analyzing the charges made by Pomeroy, Peterson suspected that this had merely been a lovers' quarrel—a conclusion he reached after talking by telephone separately to both Pomeroy and Boggs.

Peterson asked few questions of Pomeroy and at one point called Boggs "a well-known" and "outstanding citizen" of the community. Pomeroy recalled: "Peterson didn't ask me any questions concerning the assault. He totally discouraged me from actually doing anything."

As for Boggs, Peterson found the doctor's version

of events equally persuasive. "He told me his side of the story, and it was as plausible as Pomeroy's was," Peterson recalled. The only difference between the two accounts was that Boggs said that once at his office that night, Pomeroy "groped" him, and Boggs used the stun gun against Pomeroy only in self-defense.

Peterson nevertheless wrote up his report and, following standard procedure, took the case to a deputy Los Angeles district attorney for review. But prosecutor Phil Heeger agreed with Peterson's assessment, and Pomeroy's charges against Boggs were dropped.

Just four days later, Peterson was called at home on Saturday morning, April 16, and told to go to 540 North Central to direct the investigation of a patient who supposedly had dropped dead while visiting the offices of Dr. Richard Boggs.

That Peterson did so little at the scene that morning—or at anytime afterward—remains inexplicable. Peterson acknowledges that as he drove to Boggs' office that Saturday morning, the Barry Pomeroy incident was still fresh on his mind. "Oh, I was aware of it," Peterson says lamely. "But suspecting and being able to prove something—that's two different things."

Early Yearnings

Dick Boggs was one of the most precocious and resourceful kids in town.

By age ten, the handsome, lanky youth had sweet-talked the circulation manager down at the *Glendale Star-News* into giving him a paper route. And every weekday afternoon Dick Boggs could be seen walking up and down Stanley Avenue, a street lined with eucalyptus and palm trees, enthusiastically tossing the paper onto the porches of the California bungalows and red-tiled, Spanish adobe houses for which the city was famous. On his daily half-hour rounds, Dick Boggs, a spring in his step, seemed like a young man in a hurry. But that was because he had many other jobs to do, for even back then, Dick Boggs was already acquiring an obsession with making money.

"He was always out doing things trying to make money," recalls Beulah "Bea" Boggs, his mother. "He was a real go-getter, and a real hard worker too."

If Dick Boggs was affected by the breakup of his parents' marriage, he did not show it. Instead the child threw his energies into making money to help his mother out.

Pryde W. Boggs had left his wife and three boys in the waning days of World War II. For years afterward, Bea Boggs struggled to make ends meet, taking what jobs came along, including working as a clerk at the neighborhood drugstore. As the eldest boy in the family, Dick Boggs felt a special responsibility to help his mother. And he did so with a vengeance.

Besides the paper route, Dick also got himself jobs mowing lawns, washing cars, sweeping floors at the

Glendale Civic Auditorium, taking care of urns at the Forest Lawn Cemetery, making corsages at the flower shop of a mortuary, waiting on tables and emptying bedpans at the old Glendale sanitarium, and making deliveries for the drugstore where his mother sometimes worked.

The money he brought home was a significant contribution to the family coffers. He even bought his own clothes. In the surprisingly chilly and damp California winter mornings, Dick often would be the first one up—just so he could get a fire going for the family.

"Dick always tried to make things easier for me," Bea Boggs recalled, smiling at the happy memory.

But money wasn't Dick Boggs's only obsession as he was growing up. Even as a toddler, he became captivated by playing doctor. It was an interest that never faded. While other children romped with abandon on the playgrounds, acquiring cuts and bruises along the way, Dick Boggs preferred to play doctor. "As a kid, he used up all my bandages and tapes—wrapping people's arms and legs," said Bea Boggs. "He had always wanted to be a doctor, it seems."

In those early, innocent days, pretending to be doctor was pure kids play. But making money, on the other hand, was a matter of survival. The family, especially after Pryde and Bea divorced, needed every penny.

Richard Pryde Boggs had been born on May 15, 1933, in Hot Springs, South Dakota. At the time, his parents actually lived in eastern Wyoming, not far from Casper, where Pryde W. Boggs worked in the oil fields, supervising the operation of fourteen pumps for a drilling company based in Indiana. Hot Springs was the nearest city with a decent hospital.

A year later, the drilling firm that employed him was bought out by another company, and Pryde Boggs was suddenly out of a job. At a time when steady work was extremely scarce, especially in the oil business, the young couple, with an infant to feed, was terrified.

But Pryde Boggs's reputation as an honest, hardworking man eventually landed him a position as treasurer of the Rocky Mountain Drilling Company in

Colorado. The firm had wells in Southern California and it wanted Pryde Boggs to supervise their operations. "We thought we had become millionaires," Bea Boggs recalled.

In the autumn of 1939, Pryde Boggs was transferred to California. And with six-year-old Richard in tow, the couple looked all over the dry, dusty Los Angeles basin for a house. Bea's aunt said Glendale was a nice place to raise a family, and when Pryde and Beulah saw the town, they readily agreed.

A short time later, Pryde Boggs took his first real desk job, becoming the purchasing agent for another oil company. Every day he commuted to his office in downtown Los Angeles.

As the years passed, in a sturdy frame house on Stanley Avenue in Glendale owned by a devout Seventh-Day Adventist couple, Pryde and Bea Boggs had two more sons. William was born in 1935 and James nine years later—to the day. The two elder brothers, along with their parents, doted on James.

Soon after Jim came along, Pryde left the family, moving to Long Beach, some forty miles away. After that he was rarely ever around, seemingly caring more for the bottle than his three boys.

Life as a working single parent was not easy for Bea. But at least her parents lived across the street and they often helped out with the boys. Still, money was always tight. And the boys did what they could to help out, especially Dick.

Jim also delivered the *Star-News*. In fact, he became the youngest *News-Press* carrier ever. Later, as a young adult, he was more aimless. He worked for a time at an auto dealership and then suddenly quit and joined the Army. After the service, he went on to a successful fifteen-year career with IBM. Today he works in the insurance business in Spokane, Washington.

Bea Boggs was always pretty sure she knew what her middle son would do in life. "Bill was going to be either a policeman or fireman," she recalled. As a teenager, he got a leg banged up while helping local police chase down robbers at a festival in a Glendale park. "He was always doing something like that," said Bea Boggs. "He was a born policeman."

Indeed, Bill Boggs went on to a highly successful career in law enforcement, working for many years as a patrolman and then as a detective in the Glendale police department—the very agency that one day would investigate his older brother for first-degree homicide.

Going Over Big

Back in the placid summer of 1958, the parklike campus of Union College in Lincoln, Nebraska, was a lovely setting in which to fall in love.

A liberal arts college operated by the Seventh-Day Adventists church, the college's fifty-acre campus on the edge of town was home to more than 115 species of trees—more than enough to qualify it as a future site of the Nebraska Statewide Arboretum. The college's four hundred or so students were the sons and daughters of hard-working, God-fearing people of Middle America—and in keeping with the school's clean-cut image.

In that summer of 1958, after four years of study at Union College, Lola Cleveland felt somewhat torn. Having just graduated, the vivacious coed from Forest City, Iowa, was sad to be leaving the school and its comfortable environment. But at the same time she was excited, and more than a little bit nervous, about starting a new chapter in her life. She was heading for California. A devoutly religious young woman, Lola was about to take a teaching job at a secondary school in a high-desert community called Lancaster, some thirty miles north of Los Angeles.

One balmy day, as a gentle breeze wafted across the plains, mutual friends introduced Lola to an attractive, tall young man from out of town. He was in Lincoln to visit friends at Union College.

She was immediately taken by the outgoing young man, whose relaxed demeanor instantly put her at ease. He was from Southern California and was a fount of information about Los Angeles.

Dick Boggs and Lola Cleveland hit it off instantly. Soon they discovered that they had many mutual friends not only at Union College but also at Loma Linda, down in Los Angeles, where he was attending medical school. Much to her delight, he too was a Seventh-Day Adventist.

A faith born and nurtured in nineteenth-century America, the Seventh-Day Adventist Church emphasized winning converts—something that Dick Boggs would become very good at doing. Founded in 1863 in Battle Creek, Michigan, it is based on the belief that the world is in its "last days" and that the end of the world is near. Out of the ensuing chaos and destruction, so the tenet goes, a new earth will emerge in which those redeemed by Christ will live eternally.

Church members emphasize healthful life-styles and many refrain from alcohol, tobacco, and even "unclean" meats, much in the same fashion that Jews observe kosher laws. Dick Boggs eventually bought into the philosophy wholeheartedly, although not for long.

Bea Boggs was a Methodist and her boys were baptized in the North Glendale Methodist Church, which she faithfully attended. But Pryde Boggs had been reared as a Seventh Day Adventist, and over the years his sons gravitated toward that faith.

The Boggs's landlords on Stanley Avenue were active Seventh-Day Adventists and both, in fact, worked at the church—he as its secretary-treasurer and she as the telephone switchboard operator. Young Dick Boggs was further exposed to the church's tenets as a high school senior when he took a part-time job at the Glendale Adventist Hospital. "And so he studied with them and decided to become an Adventist," Bea Boggs recalled.

By the time he was graduated from Glendale High School in 1951, Richard Boggs was a confident young man with a dashing, playful air about him. And everyone, classmates and faculty members alike, thought he had a bright future ahead—an assessment that would be widely shared in later years as well. He had made solid grades and was never a discipline problem, at home or at school.

That fall, he enrolled at the two-year Glendale City College, a small community college just a mile or so up Verdugo Road from home. There, he plunged into student life with infectious fervor.

As a sophomore, Boggs presided over the Associated Students legislature in his capacity as vice president of the student body. He also served as president of the Inter-Club Council, which organized fundraising festivals and sponsored campus blood drives. For the graduation ceremonies, Boggs chaired the committee that was in charge of the program. The 1953 Glendale City College yearbook contains several photographs with Boggs in them, all with him seemingly at the center of attention. There also is a whimsical drawing of Boggs that captured his winning smile.

That autumn, Boggs enrolled across town at the University of California at Los Angeles, where he went on to get a bachelor's degree in zoology. And then, to the surprise of no one who knew him, Boggs went on to medical school. He enrolled at the College of Medical Evangelists, then a little-known Seventh-Day Adventist church institution in Loma Linda, a small community near San Bernardino, some sixty miles east of Los Angeles.

At the Loma Linda University Medical Center, as the school later became known, the austere environment seemed to agree with Boggs. So did the institution's spirit of missionary zeal.

In two successive summers, Boggs joined a twenty-two-member team of students and faculty members in journeying to southern Mexico to provide free medical care in the mountain villages of Chiapas. "Angels on burro back," they were called. "A lot of the villages didn't have anything as elegant as an outdoor john," Boggs would recall. "The ever present pigs were the sanitary crews."

His strong desire to help others was one of his many qualities that immediately appealed to Lola Cleveland. In Southern California, they dated for three years and then got married in April 1961, just before Dick obtained his medical degree.

Like any medical student, Boggs spent a good deal of his time in the library. But unbeknownst to anyone at the time, he was secretly conducting research of a very personal nature. While his classmates pored over medical texts, Boggs read everything he could on the topic of homosexuality. He was by then already feeling the unfamiliar urge, and somewhat frightened, he was determined to learn more about it. Was it abnormal? Could it be controlled?

For the time being, Boggs decided to fight it.

After medical school, he and Lola got a small apartment in Montebello, a community just east of downtown Los Angeles. He began doing an internship at White Memorial Hospital in L.A., and she started her teaching job in Lancaster.

The next few years were happy, but they seemed to pass in a blur. "It was a very hectic time, very busy schedules. So it was certainly not ideal, but we certainly saw each other," Lola recalled. Too preoccupied with their own demanding careers, they decided to begin a family through adoption.

"We had talked for many years about possibly adopting children," Lola said. Initially they went to the Children's Home Society so that they could "check the children as much as possible," she recalled. "But even then it was a little hard finding a match."

In the meantime, Richard let it be known in his medical circles that he and Lola were looking to adopt a baby. "And so one day one said, 'I know of a baby that's available,' " Lola said.

And thus Kevin Scott Boggs entered the couple's life. At the time they had different preferences for names, but he gave in. "The next one," he told her, "is getting Dana Michael."

Bea Boggs hadn't even known that her eldest son and daughter-in-law were contemplating having children. She was working in the drugstore one day when they walked in with the baby. "That's the first I knew of it!" she recalled.

Just four weeks later, Richard and Lola Boggs took in a second baby boy—this time much to Lola's astonishment.

Richard was working at the hospital one Sunday when he called her at home. "Would you like a baby girl?" he asked, saying that one had just become available.

"That would be lovely," Lola said.

But he called back a few minutes later. "I don't know what's wrong with that doctor's eyes," Richard said.

The baby, it turned out, was a boy. But a very cute one, he added quickly.

By then Lola had had more time to reflect.

Much as she loved children, she told him, perhaps one baby was enough. At the time Lola had quit teaching but was working on a graduate degree at California State University–Los Angeles.

"There are a lot of people in the world wanting children," she told him on the phone. "Maybe we shouldn't be selfish and take this one too."

If Richard disagreed, he did not say so. A short while later, Lola went to visit a friend, taking Kevin with her. When she got home that Sunday night, Richard was sitting by the telephone—cuddling an infant.

"Well, here is Dana Michael," he said.

Lola fell in love once more.

Kevin and Dana bore a striking resemblance to each other, and their doting parents took to referring to them as "the twins."

After his internship at White Memorial Hospital, Richard P. Boggs, M.D., did a residency in internal medicine at Los Angeles County General Hospital. There, he won recognition not only for his medical skills but also for his political acumen. It was a time when interns and residents were becoming increasingly assertive, loudly protesting the lack of resources as well as their low wages and long, grueling hours at the hospital. Boggs shared those sentiments, and he was able to articulate those complaints better than

most. They elected him president of the Interns and
Residents Association.

Wasting little time, Boggs organized a ''heal-in'' as
a protest action to get the attention of the Los Angeles
County Board of Supervisors. Lola also got caught up
in the electrifying events, often going down to the hospital to visit her husband and supporters. ''They took
care of the patients in what they deemed was the way
they really ought to be taken care of. Rather than being
just rushed through, they would keep them as long as
they felt was really proper for them to be cared for,''
Lola said, recalling the ''heal-in.''

The protest led to a meeting with the Board of Supervisors. After listening to Boggs's eloquent plea on
behalf of all interns and residents, the board members
voted to grant them higher pay while ordering that they
be required to work fewer consecutive hours. Boggs,
recalled Dr. Ilena Blicker, an intern at the county hospital at the time, ''was pompous, but could be very
charming and personable when he wanted to be.''

After L.A. County General, Richard Boggs received
a scholarship from Harvard, allowing him to pursue
further a specialty in neurology. In addition to his
studies and other duties at the Boston City Hospital,
Richard also took a job working at the Presbyterian
Intercommunity Hospital. Just as he had as a child,
Richard Boggs was working overtime to help feed his
family.

In Boston, they rented a nice duplex, and Lola kept
busy by taking care of the kids. During their two years
in Massachusetts, Lola gave birth to a daughter,
Heather, and then a son, Jonathan.

It was also in Boston, while Lola and the children
were gone back out West to visit friends and relatives,
that Richard Boggs had his first homosexual experience. By then he had reached the conclusion that there
was nothing wrong with being gay. Besides, his curiosity had gotten the best of him. And even though he
was astonished by how gratifying the encounter was,
he never let on to it even after Lola and the children
returned. In any event, he did not view the transgres-

sion as being unfaithful. "I never cheated on Lola," Boggs would insist.

And so, as the 1960s drew to a close, Richard and Lola Boggs and their four children returned to Southern California for good. They were the picture of an All-American family. But unbeknownst to anyone but Richard Boggs, behind all the trappings of a happy young middle-class family clearly on the move, the seeds of disintegration had already taken root.

Seeds of Doubt

During the 1960s, even as much of the country convulsed over political assassinations, urban riots, the civil rights movement, and the war in Vietnam, Glendale, California, remained a tranquil conservative enclave of WASP-ish Republicanism. Largely a bedroom community ten miles north of downtown Los Angeles, with some 100,000 residents, Glendale is nestled in the Verdugo Hills, a stronghold of the status quo tucked into the hillsides between two flat, sprawling valleys—the San Fernando to the west and the San Gabriel to the east.

The tree-lined city was a bastion of Middle American values, a safe haven—or so it seemed—from the offbeat trendiness that engulfed Southern California during the turbulent Sixties.

Through it all, Glendale was able to retain that insular, small-town sense of community. The city services stayed reliable and, above all, its public schools remained strong, their students at every grade level regularly testing well above state and national averages.

But as hordes of new arrivals began pouring into California from all over the United States and from abroad, developers in Glendale were quick to take advantage of the city's many steep hillsides, thanks to a quiescent city government. All over Glendale, powerful developers gouged out tiny lots from the dry, dusty land and threw up houses of all sizes and styles, many of which had a breathtaking view of downtown L.A. or the San Fernando Valley, especially at night, when the entire basin was transformed into a magical ocean of flickering lights. And on the few pristinely clear days of the year, those with strategically located hilltop homes could see clear to the Pacific.

Glendale, in short, was an ideal community for a young, aspiring family like the Bogges. And its medical community was still small enough that a newcomer to the profession, especially a bright up-and-comer like Richard Boggs, commanded notice. "We needed a neurologist at that time, and he seemed to be just what we wanted," said Robert D. Lowrey, a cardiologist and one of the many established physicians who took Boggs under their wing, referring their patients to him for consultation.

"There was a very favorable perception of him," Lowrey recalled. "I valued his opinions. His recommendations seemed to be good ones." Like most who came in contact with him, Lowrey went away with a good first impression. "He was very personable, well groomed, and seemed to be very capable. It seemed like he had a bright future." It was easy to overlook Boggs's arrogance or a tendency to be late for appointments.

Lowrey had hoped that his own son, James, would go into medicine. Instead, Jim became a policeman.

Another older Glendale physician who took a liking to Boggs was Don Fitch, a quiet cardiologist. One night Don and Myra Fitch had Richard and Lola Boggs over for dinner. They were joined that night by Fitch's partner, Bob Lowrey, and his wife.

As Myra Fitch brought out an expensive tenderloin, Lola Boggs, the devout Seventh-Day Adventist, politely but firmly refused to eat it. Richard Boggs, on the other hand, had no such compunctions. He also drank the wine rather freely. Years later, Fitch would chuckle at the memory, saying that he should have become suspicious of the young doctor as of that night.

As it happened, such doubts about Richard Boggs indeed already were surfacing all over Glendale. And beyond.

"A Great Guy"

Dana Boggs was crushed. The high school auditorium was packed with proud parents, and the play in which he had a starring role was about to begin. But Dad was nowhere in sight.

Dana understood firsthand how busy his father could be. Ever since early childhood, Dana had often accompanied his father on rounds at the hospital. Still, it was a blow not to have him present for the big night, Dana thought to himself as he entered the stage. Yet when he looked out, Dana almost right away saw his father's beaming face in the audience. That was just typical of the way Dad came through for him. Dana never forgot that exhilarating moment.

No matter how busy, Richard Boggs almost always made time for each of his children. When he had to work on weekends, he often took one or more of the kids along. "We always knew what he was doing," Dana recalled. "We always knew that he was a doctor and that he was doing something important." The doctor, in short, was as loving a father as any child could hope for, Lola thought.

Yet he could be strict when necessary. "We got spanked, but nothing vicious," Kevin recalled. With Dad the kids could always count on getting a fair hearing. "It worked like this: Just wait till your father gets home," Dana said. "We'd have the whole list ready to go over for the day. So sometimes that meant punishment. But a lot of times that meant working things out that were positive instead of negative."

Richard Boggs also was a wonderful provider. His income of some $200,000 a year enabled them to have a big house, drive fancy cars, and send the kids to exclusive Glendale Academy.

They regularly attended the Seventh-Day Adventist church in town. And when he had the time, he would take the family out to the beach or go eat out. And they went camping up at Yosemite.

On Sunday mornings, he would quietly go into Kevin's room and gently awaken him. Together the two of them would feed the dogs and then drive up to Winchell's to buy donuts for the entire family. "That was our thing," Kevin recalled. It made him, the eldest boy, feel special.

The doctor had a way of doing that with each child. "He's a great guy," Kevin said.

As a child, Kevin especially liked to read and to work with his hands—repairing cars and doing electronics. With every project he got nothing but encouragement and praise from his father.

The doctor was the same way with Heather. "There were times in school when I would struggle and sometimes wonder whether I would make it or not, and he was always really encouraging and positive and showed faith that I could accomplish things," she recalled.

Dana added: "He's always ready to listen. Some people, you come to them and they are ready to give you all this advice. But a lot of times all you really need is to have someone hear it." His dad never turned any of them away. "If it was his kids, everything else stopped. He put it on hold until it was taken care of," Dana added. "He always had time, even though he was busy and on the go quite a bit, doing his work. There was always time."

One Valentine's Day, Heather's father took her out to dinner, just the two of them.

The doctor also made Jonathan, the youngest child, feel special. They seemed able to communicate without using many words. It was as if they could read each other's mind. "He's a brilliant person. He's funny. We think a lot alike," Jonathan said. "It's fun."

As an adult, Dana went on to work for several years

at his father's office. "I actually like working with him and being around him," Dana explained. Today he works with computer hardware and software that have medical applications, taking him often to the familiar milieu of physicians' offices, clinics, and hospitals.

Kevin and Heather too were influenced by their father's work. He became an accountant at the Glendale Adventist Medical Center and she a registered nurse there.

Downward Spiral

From the start, Richard Boggs was able to quickly develop a busy practice. Until he hung out his shingle, there had been only one other neurologist in Glendale, Edison Fisher. And Fisher had more than enough business. Indeed, he looked forward to Boggs's arrival in Glendale, having already heard about him while Boggs was still a star student at Loma Linda.

And so Boggs had no trouble obtaining staff privileges at all three major hospitals in the city, including Glendale Adventist, where he had once emptied bedpans as a teenager. The hospitals were glad to have a young neurologist on board—and a native son at that. He also joined a practice with a group of neurologists and neurosurgeons at White Memorial in downtown L.A.

It seemed like no time before Boggs developed a loyal coterie of admiring patients.

And hardly a year passed before he got a call from Vernon Nickel, the highly respected medical director of Rancho Los Amigos Hospital in Downey, another Los Angeles suburb. The nationally renowned physical rehabilitation facility—with its serene, old Spanish buildings, framed by more than two hundred acres of courtyards, manicured lawns, and tall eucalyptus trees—had an opening for the head of the Department of Neurology, and Nickel wanted Boggs to take the job. Boggs, then only in his mid-thirties, jumped at this, the opportunity of a lifetime.

At Rancho, many people were quickly impressed by Boggs. His energy seemed boundless. Aside from his regular practice, Boggs also taught courses and found time to organize medical conferences, one of which drew top-notch talent from all over the world to Rancho Los Amigos.

As in Boston years earlier, the exposure to a world-class institution like Rancho Los Amigos, and all it implied, proved to be another turning point in the downward spiral of Richard Boggs. It was during this time that he began openly rejecting the austere tenets of the Seventh-Day Adventist church. In Los Angeles, as in few places in America, the unbridled worship of materialism was acquiring the following of a mass cult, one in which old-fashioned values were stood on their heads. If one couldn't afford a house and had to live in a cheap, rented apartment, a shiny BMW—with a sunroof, maybe even a cellular telephone—parked in the carport could go a long way toward making life more tolerable.

Boggs, of course, already had a big house and fancy cars. They owned an imposing Tudor-style house high above Glendale in a community called La Canada-Flintridge, an even tonier suburb than Glendale that was fast becoming home to many leaders of the L.A. establishment. There they threw barbeques for colleagues and even commissioned nearly life-sized portraits of one another, which they proudly hung in the house. And before long Richard and Lola Boggs could be seen driving around town in a Cadillac and a Jaguar.

It seemed as though the new doctor was going to fit in just fine in Glendale. A teacher by training, Lola in the meantime continued with her graduate studies in math and engineering.

Yet behind the facade of success and contentment, all was not well. Richard Boggs was becoming increasingly restless and unfulfilled.

One of the first to sense something askew was Vern Nickel. It was one thing to be late for appointments; traffic, after all, was getting to be impossible in L.A. But it was another when Boggs began to neglect his duties at Rancho Los Amigos in favor of his own private practice. Nickel was severely disappointed, and pretty fed up, too. In time, he developed a nagging feeling that Boggs was consumed by ambition. Or was it naked greed?

"We thought he was very bright. But he was always looking for the easy way out," Nickel recalled. "I was glad when he quit. We didn't have to fire him."

Only three years after he took over the neurology department at Rancho Los Amigos, a prestigious job that for most neurologists would have been the crowning accomplishment of a distinguished career, Richard Boggs severed all ties with the institution. Now with one less distraction, Boggs turned to his private practice with a vengeance. Often he began his days before dawn, making rounds, assisting other doctors in surgery, seeing patients in his office and at various hospitals. Some nights he didn't get home until ten or eleven. Yet few of his patients felt that Boggs had given them his undivided attention. Increasingly he seemed distracted.

By then Boggs also had been affiliated for two years in a group practice with Ed Fisher. But there too it didn't take long before doubts about Boggs emerged. "We discovered that, on call, he wasn't taking care of our patients," Fisher said. Soon Fisher was fielding complaints from patients who said they had called on weekends but were never called back. Boggs often simply did not show up even though he had been given the office schedule of patients he was supposed to see. "I don't know what he was doing," Fisher said.

Neither did Bea Boggs. From the time her son opened his practice, she went to work for him, helping out with all the paperwork, especially the insurance claims. It was better than working in a drugstore. At one time, she recalled, "there were wall-to-wall patients." Yet her son often kept patients waiting endlessly. "Then he would come stormin' in, quite late, huffing and puffing," Bea Boggs said. "I'd get so upset with him."

The young doctor would act contrite, promising to reform, only to lapse into his errant ways a week later.

If Richard Boggs seemed distracted, it wasn't because he was intensely engaged in something he had done, and done well, ever since he was a child: He was dreaming of new ways to make money. The stakes were certainly much bigger now, for Boggs realized that if he could strike it rich once and for all, such financial independence would free him from the constraints of a middle-class existence. Maybe, just maybe, he would no longer have to remain a closet gay while posing as a straight family man. It was, he decided, well worth the risk.

Bitter Medicine

In the 1970s, the business of medicine claimed a prominent place on the nation's domestic agenda. Health-care costs were rising precipitously, pricing many people out of the market altogether. A disenchanted public, its alienation fueled by the likes of Senator Edward M. Kennedy and Big Labor, was growing more and more critical of a distant and seemingly uncaring medical profession. Increasingly there was talk of national health insurance.

This contentious national mood, along with the changing mores of a new generation of young people, prompted many physicians-in-training to contemplate different career paths and life-styles than their predecessors. Instead of setting up private practices, with all the concomitant headaches of escalating malpractice insurance premiums and the mountains of paperwork required by government and private health insurers, many young doctors opted instead for a steady paycheck—by working for somebody else.

And one of the most attractive ways of doing so was hiring on with a relatively new business and health-care concept called Health Maintenance Organizations. In its most fundamental form, an HMO employed a staff of salaried doctors who provided basic services and treatment to members who paid a set fee. Typically, members then would have no deductibles to pay for doctor or hospital services, no charge for lab tests, routine physicals, eye or hearing examinations. For providers of such care, the major incentive was preventive medicine—keeping people healthy and out of the clinics altogether. The concept's one major drawback was that HMO members did not have their choice of physicians since they had to go only to the HMO's facilities.

As a business enterprise, the HMO concept immediately appealed to Richard Boggs. He envisioned heading up an HMO that would serve 100,000 people. But he wasn't motivated solely by the prospect of making big money. He saw the HMO concept as a way to provide relatively low-cost medical services to people who were under-served. By 1970, Boggs incorporated Satellite Health Systems.

Despite being criticized by many of his more conservative colleagues as being a tool for the advocates of socialized medicine, Boggs had little trouble putting together a large group of investors and recruiting more than twenty doctors to participate. But if any of them had crunched the numbers for themselves rather than simply taking Boggs's word at face value, they no doubt would not have parted with their hard-earned money quite so easily.

Boggs, in his infectious enthusiasm for the venture, either forgot or conveniently neglected to work into his projected $1 million-plus monthly income the cost of doing business. He didn't factor in the salaries he would have to pay, the malpractice insurance premiums that insurers would charge, the rent for offices, clinics, and equipment. It was as if everyone just took his word for it. Trust me, he said in his confident, expansive manner.

And so Satellite Health Systems became one of the earliest and most prominent HMOs in Southern California. It was headquartered in a medical building in Hollywood and in Boggs's own office in Glendale. But it had offices from San Luis Obispo to San Diego, covering a stretch of several hundreds of miles along the coast. Before long, as many as 25,000 people had signed up, including the large retail clerks' union.

During those early, heady years, Boggs one day got a call from the president of the United States, encouraging him to push on with the HMO concept. It was, said Richard M. Nixon, a far better way to practice medicine and to provide health care than Ted Kennedy's "giveaway" of national health insurance.

But appearances aside, Satellite Health Systems was ailing. From the beginning, its attempts to get major funding from the Department of Health, Education, and Welfare were mired in disputes over government red tape, caused in part by Boggs's inattention to detail and a proclivity to cut corners. "We just didn't want to deal with the strings," recalled John Pasek, who was the HMO's director of development. "We were whipper-snappers," he went on. "We thought we could do it better and that people would be beating down our doors with funds."

But few did. And soon the first of the oil shocks hit, sending interest rates soaring and plunging the country into a deep recession. Satellite, with a large payroll and far-flung facilities, now was on its death bed. In those early days the prospect of not being able to choose one's own doctors simply did not appeal to the masses, and the initial burst of enrollment quickly reached a plateau. Indeed, Satellite had lost money in every month of its life. The HMO was millions of dollars in debt. At one point, Richard and Lola Boggs even signed for personal loans to try to keep the business afloat.

Finally, the doctor had no choice but to file for business bankruptcy. The list of creditors included the Small Business Administration, countless banks, leasing agencies, and many, many disillusioned fellow physicians and friends.

After that deep embarrassment, Boggs was never the same again.

"That was Richard's downfall," said Bea Boggs. "I don't think he ever got over that." Added a one-time patient: "We just saw him disintegrate. What a waste of genius."

A Mismatch

By the mid-1970s, Lola Boggs could no longer ignore the warning signs that her marriage was in deep trouble. Ostensibly her husband was devoting more and more time to his fast-failing Satellite Health Systems. In fact, however, he had begun spending an increasing amount of time touring the gay bars of West Hollywood. In time he became downright brazen about it, not seeming to care whether other people knew or not. Some days he would show up at his office with disheveled young men in tow, carrying his bags. What they did in the back examination rooms was anyone's guess. The doctor simply seemed unable to keep his private and professional lives separate.

In the privacy of Richard and Lola's bedroom, things also had changed dramatically. Whereas he once had been an attentive, gentle partner, now he had lost all interest in her, though he remained cordial and loving on the surface.

"I was very naive in those things," Lola later confessed. "Even though I found it hard to believe, it became a concern or a puzzle about whether he was gay or not."

She was a woman who kept to herself, and for the longest time she confided her fears to no one. And she put off confronting her husband, hoping against hope that her deepening sense of dread would prove unfounded. Maybe, she thought, he was acting strangely because of the humiliating business bankruptcy, for that indirectly caused them to lose their stately Tudor mansion in La Canada-Flintridge. He was far more disturbed by that than she was. Lola, in fact, never had much desire or use for the big house or fancy cars in the first place.

"At some level, they were incredibly mismatched," said John Pasek, who would emerge as one of the doctor's fiercest defenders. "Lola's sort of salt-of-the-earth. Never been pretentious." Whereas she would have been quite content with a simpler life-style, he had become unabashedly materialistic. "There was something in him that drove him to a lavishness from the point of view of being appreciated," said Pasek.

When she finally confronted him about his sexuality, in 1976, Richard Boggs seemed almost relieved. And he readily admitted to being gay.

But he didn't want a divorce. He wanted to keep up the appearance of a regular family man. Shocked, Lola refused to go along with such a humiliating sham.

And so he moved out of the house, going all the way down to Orange County, where he bought a beach condominium in Laguna Beach, an upscale, artsy community that had a fast-developing gay population. Lola moved to an apartment in the San Gabriel Valley.

Still, Richard kept up his practice in Glendale and often stopped by in the afternoons or after work to see the kids. To that Lola certainly did not object. Hard as it was for them to adjust to the shock of their father being gay, the children continued to love him nonetheless.

But what did concern her, deeply, was that Richard had wasted no time before rushing headlong into his new, liberated life-style down in Orange County. At his beach condominium there was a steady stream of young men—most of them quite unsavory, Lola had heard—coming and going at all hours. She didn't want her children to be exposed to that element, especially since they sometimes wanted to spend the night there, just to be close to the beach.

But Richard told her that whatever else he may be doing, he as a father would continue to put his children's well-being above all else. Even in divorce, Richard and Lola Boggs could agree on most issues pertaining to the children. And never did they denigrate each other in front of the kids. In fact, they rarely even had any conflicts over which parent would spend a special occasion with any of the children. On birthdays, graduations, and other special events, he was always just there. It was almost like old times. When Dana and Kevin graduated from college in June 1987, he joined the rest of the family for a festive lunch celebration in Northern California. And then he took the two boys to Hawaii for a two-week vacation. That was their graduation present.

The couple's divorce became final in 1982. Through it all they remained, as always, civil toward each other. And he was never put off whenever she stopped by his office to collect a child-support check or simply to talk about the kids.

The children too often stopped by his medical office after school, just to chat with their father. Sometimes they stayed for so long that they ended up going out to dinner with him.

It was years before Lola was able to talk about the disintegration of her marriage to even her most trusted friends. For the most part, she found solace instead through counseling.

A Growing Quagmire

Laguna Beach may have been a tiny, safe haven for gay men, but it was still surrounded by Orange County, one of the most righteously conservative, even reactionary, regions in the United States. In time Richard Boggs realized that he still needed to maintain a base of operations in L.A.

And so he bought a luxury penthouse in West Hollywood and lavishly furnished it. Oversized leather couches, marble floors, mirrored walls, a Jacuzzi in the bathtub—no expense was spared.

The co-owner of the penthouse was Jeff B. Culverson, a mild-mannered psychotherapist with a Ph.D. in his mid-thirties. Culverson came from a well-to-do family in the East, and he and Boggs had once briefly shared the same offices at 655 North Central Avenue in Glendale.

Their condominium, like Boggs's place in Laguna Beach, quickly became known for its unending flow of young men coming and going. Many of them appeared young enough to be Boggs's sons, and most looked as if they were runaways from places like Wisconsin and Kansas, fresh off a Greyhound bus. Some of them looked downright bedraggled and even dangerous.

With these pliable young men at his beck and call, life for Boggs was becoming an unending round of drug parties, followed by kinky orgies that involved the use of masks, chains, plenty of leather, and still more drugs.

One night the doctor showed up at the emergency room of the Glendale Adventist Medical Center seek-

ing treatment for multiple lacerations that he refused
to explain. Another night a neighbor thought she heard
gunshots emanating from Boggs's penthouse.

In time Boggs and Culverson had a bitter falling-
out, and they decided to part company. But they were
unable to resolve their dispute over ownership of the
penthouse, and the matter—like just about every other
aspect of the doctor's troubled life—landed in Los Angeles County Superior Court.

Boggs ended up losing the $800,000 penthouse to
Culverson, but the doctor simply blamed his attorney,
Alton Y. Prescott, for the loss. He even went after
Prescott, accusing the attorney in a lawsuit of failing
to file timely responses in the matter against Culverson. As a final insult, Boggs stopped writing Prescott
prescriptions for vast quantities of sedatives, insisting
that he was merely trying to help Prescott break a nasty
cocaine habit. If so, Boggs failed miserably as a drug
rehabilitation therapist. Prescott shot himself in the
head.

Indeed, turmoil was engulfing every aspect of
Boggs's existence, and the bad karma seemed to touch
just about anyone who had anything to do with him.

By 1977, the Glendale Memorial Hospital kicked
Boggs off its staff. Several months later, Verdugo Hills
Hospital followed suit. In both instances his erratic
behavior—not showing up for duty, virtually abandon-
ing his patients, plus a long and growing string of
malpractice complaints—led to the rare disciplinary
actions.

A final indignity came in 1981, when the medical
staff at the Glendale Adventist Medical Center voted
unanimously not to renew his staff privileges. In doing
so, the hospital cited "extensive evidence of patient
harm, patient suffering . . . flagrant disregard for
timely, accurate medical charting . . . an apparent lack
of awareness of wrongdoing . . . patients being subjected to unnecessary and life-threatening diagnostic
procedures . . . inadequate medical management re-
sulting in life-threatening complications and vital or-
gan destruction . . . an admitted practice of

intentionally not visiting hospitalized patients or arranging for another physician to visit hospitalized patients as a matter of practice.''

Despite this unstintingly devastating assessment, Boggs had the audacity to appeal his expulsion to the hospital's board of trustees. He didn't stand a chance. And now he had lost his final hospital connection. The demise of his once promising medical career was now nearly complete.

One of the few people who continued to stand by Boggs was a woman named Lee Reedy, a thin, chain-smoking former patient of his. Reedy and her husband had known Boggs for a decade, and in an odd sort of way they enjoyed his company, finding him to be a refined gentleman with a sophisticated sense of humor. On the spur of the moment, Boggs would call them to offer tickets to the L.A. Philharmonic that night. Or he would drop by, unannounced, at their house high in the hills above Glendale for a late-night visit.

One night Reedy got a call from Boggs that left her shaken. Over the course of a rather rambling monologue, Boggs burst into tears, mourning the loss of his house, his wife, his four children, his friends, and his practice. ''I feel like committing suicide,'' he told her.

But Boggs proved more resilient than Reedy had given him credit for. He quickly regained his spirit even as his travails continued to mount. Increasingly, Boggs was finding himself in the company of lawyers—his lawyers, for he was becoming the target of more and more lawsuits (many of which remain unresolved to this day).

With almost no more legitimate patients left to treat, Boggs also scratched out a living by consulting for personal-injury lawyers, offering expert opinion on hard-to-detect, soft-tissue injuries.

In his spare time he also assisted a La Canada dentist perform surgery because the dentist did not have certain hospital privileges. One of their unsuspecting patients was a woman named Lucinda Browne. The woman, a housekeeper, had initially gone to the dentist seeking treatment for a persistent pain in her jaw, the result of a fall. In all, Boggs and the dentist subjected Browne to eight operations. in which they inserted various jawbone implants. Not one of the procedures produced a satisfactory result. In fact, the devices either slipped out of place or inflicted even greater pain than before. Browne filed suit, but ultimately settled with Boggs's insurance company for $70,000.

Another woman who had an unfortunate—and painful—experience with Boggs was Margaret H. Kaplan. Boggs performed an operation on her that was supposed to relieve her nagging headaches. The operation was to have taken ninety minutes: instead it dragged on for six hours. Afterward, her headaches got no better, her vision worsened, and she became partially paralyzed. Kaplan was awarded $85,000 in damages.

Eventually, such lawsuits against Boggs would take up many shelves in the basement archives deep in the bowels of the Los Angeles County Hall of Records—dusty proof of just how deeply Boggs's life had sunk into a hopeless quagmire of conflict and despair.

Among those who came to regret having befriended Boggs was Edison Fisher, who had welcomed Boggs into his group practice. Fisher ended up kicking Boggs out the door, only to discover that Boggs had stolen his financial records as well as making off with an antique desk. Boggs, a disillusioned Fisher would tell anyone who asked, was nothing more than a sociopath who "had a hard time telling right from wrong."

Another physician who had woefully misjudged Boggs was Georgia Vanderbilt, a practitioner who was getting on in years, though she was not quite ready yet for a retirement home. At the time, Vanderbilt and Boggs shared side-by-side medical suites at 655 North Central Avenue in Glendale.

In April 1973, Satellite Health Systems was going under, and Boggs was on the prowl for a fresh infusion of funds. Persuasive and charming as always, Boggs managed to entice Vanderbilt into joining the HMO as a salaried physician, telling her that he had $1 million in liquid assets. Vanderbilt also was immediately intrigued by the prospect of regular, set hours—and fringe benefits to boot. After hearing his pitch, Vanderbilt readily turned over her office, her equipment, and her patients—all in return for a promised monthly salary of $3,000 a month, plus health insurance and a leased car.

The BMW never appeared, and Vanderbilt's paychecks stopped just a few months later. One day she showed up for work to find the office locks had been changed. Soon the HMO collapsed altogether. And when Vanderbilt's patients asked Boggs where she was, he refused to tell them. Eventually, after much grief and legal expenses, Vanderbilt won a $57,000 judgment against Boggs and had it exempted from the protection of bankruptcy on the basis that the damage had been inflicted as a result of fraud.

But the line of people and businesses with hard-won judgments against Boggs was a long one, to say the least, and it seemed to get longer by the day. But no one could be sure whether he or she would ever see a penny of the money that Boggs had stolen from them.

Yet, despite his ever growing legal problems and rising attorney fees, Boggs nevertheless continued to have money to spend, allowing him inexplicably to go on living in the lavish manner to which he had grown accustomed. In fact, Boggs now was cruising around town—Glendale by day, West Hollywood by night—in a silver Rolls Royce.

Even though he earned $155,000 in 1981—doing what nobody could quite figure out at the time—Boggs fell woefully behind in his child-support payments. And so Lola Boggs too was forced to join the long line of plaintiffs against him, suing to collect $33,000.

By then Boggs's private existence had become so rife with ugliness—and violence—that he began carrying a pistol. And on several occasions he even threatened to kill Lola, telling her menacingly: "I could hire someone to do that."

Lousy Tenant

Stanley Anderson never saw the speeding car come up on his right. The retired accountant was driving his wife, Jackie, to Beverly Hills for an eye-doctor appointment. From Glendale there was no easy way to get there. It was a tedious, circuitous route and it required getting on the busy Ventura Freeway.

The accident happened right where the freeway forks, continuing westward in one direction and splitting off in another, joining the northbound Hollywood Freeway. The Andersons were in the slow lane, westbound, when the car zoomed past them on the right and then, realizing it was headed for the Hollywood, suddenly jerked to the left. Anderson slammed on the brakes but not quite fast enough. When both vehicles finally came to a stop on the shoulder, leaving a quarter-mile trail of twisted chrome and metal, Anderson was still shaking with fear.

Soon afterward, the couple put their Belmont Street condominium in Glendale up for rent. They wanted to live in West Los Angeles, much closer to Jackie's doctor in Beverly Hills. Jackie Anderson, a retired show business publicist, was experiencing severe medical problems with her eyes and eyelids. And that required frequent visits to a specialist in eyelid reconstruction.

Having found a nice apartment in the upscale Park La Brea Towers in West L.A., the Andersons were anxious to find a tenant for their Glendale condominium. And they were thrilled when their real estate agent one afternoon called to say that a nice, well-mannered doctor was very interested in renting the apartment, with an option to buy.

Almost from the start, however, Richard Boggs was late with his $1,300-a-month rent. Within months the doctor also was being cited repeatedly for violating various condominium regulations, including being too noisy and having at times up to four persons living with him—mostly bedraggled young men who had little means for support.

In November 1987, with about two months to go before the two-year lease was up, the Andersons were ready to return to Glendale. Jackie's condition had improved sufficiently so that they no longer needed to make frequent trips to Beverly Hills. The couple wanted to be closer to their friends.

Still, the couple solicitously offered to let Boggs extend his lease by another year if he wished. They only asked that Boggs let them know his intentions without delay, since they would need to give sufficient notice one way or the other at the Park La Brea Towers.

Boggs obligingly replied that he very much would like to buy the condominium, noting ostentatiously that his financial adviser had told him he needed additional tax shelters.

This statement the trusting Andersons now greeted with some skepticism. Boggs twice before had offered to buy the condominium, only to fail to follow through. Still, they became persuaded by the doctor's sincerity.

True to form, however, Boggs failed to open escrow on December 1, as promised. The doctor said indignantly that he had been told by a realtor friend that the agreed-upon sales price of $168,000 was at least $14,000 over its market value.

Now thoroughly disgusted, the Andersons three days later officially cancelled the sale, demanding that Boggs vacate the premises by January 31, 1988, the expiration date of his lease. In the meantime, the Andersons gave notice at Park La Brea Towers and began making final plans to move back to their Belmont Street home.

In the ensuing weeks, the couple continued to remind Boggs at every turn that their Park La Brea Towers apartment had been rented to another tenant and therefore they must be able to get back into their own condominium by February 1 and not a day later. In addition, the Andersons told him, Jackie had to undergo yet another operation at the end of January, and the last thing they wanted was more hassle with the condominium. Boggs said he understood.

But six days before his lease was up, the doctor informed the Andersons that he had no intention of moving out by January 31. The combative Boggs said he was prepared to stay on indefinitely.

It took the Andersons and their lawyers until mid-April to get Boggs evicted. By then the couple's condominium was in shambles. The floors, walls, fixtures—had all been severely damaged, requiring thousands of dollars' worth of repairs.

"He destroyed the apartment," said Jackie Anderson.

All in the Family

Dr. Gary Johnston, a dentist, sat in his lawyer's posh office in West Los Angeles and warily eyed an obsequious Richard Boggs. Though the two physicians had more or less fallen out of touch with each other, they had known each other for more than three years, ever since Johnston had taken an adjoining office suite in Glendale.

Of the two, Johnston had clearly done better in life. He had expanded his practice and moved to the more affluent West Side. His financial standing was such that he could clearly afford the services of Wilfred Tynan, a leading Beverly Hills divorce lawyer and financial adviser.

Even on that side of town, Boggs's string of business failures and the collapse of his marriage became pretty widely known. And so when Boggs out of the blue called him one day, asking for a face-to-face meeting, Johnston became at once curious and leery. Suspecting that Boggs wanted money, Johnston invited him to meet at his lawyer's office on Santa Monica Boulevard.

When Boggs was ushered into the well-appointed conference room at Tynan's law firm, Johnston could hardly contain his shock. Boggs was a shadow of himself, wearing a wrinkled work shirt and baggy trousers whose cuffs were frayed. Boggs's eyes also seemed bleary, as if he had been up all night. Even Tynan, who had never met Boggs before, was dumbfounded by his appearance. This is a Harvard-trained physician? wondered Tynan, himself an Ivy Leaguer.

There was only a modicum of pleasantries, for

clearly Johnston and Boggs now had nothing in common but a few distant, shared memories.

"Gary, I need about $13,000," Boggs said. "The IRS is after me again."

But instead of asking Johnston for a flat-out loan, Boggs had a proposition. He asked Johnston to co-sign a bank loan.

Johnston shifted uneasily in his chair and turned knowingly to Tynan. They had clearly scripted out the scenario before Boggs arrived. This, after all, was not going to be a casual understanding between old friends but a cold business deal.

Johnston's friends had advised him against even meeting with Boggs. No good could come of it, they said. They reminded him of Boggs's now well-known pattern of reneging on his word. They reminded him that Boggs had lost his staff privileges at all three Glendale hospitals. They reminded him that Boggs had failed again in yet another attempt to set up a Health Maintenance Organization; this was in California's agricultural San Joaquin Valley. And now, they noted, the venture was mired in litigation, and Boggs once more was playing hide-and-seek with a growing list of creditors that included the IRS. When, for instance, Los Angeles County sheriff's deputies had shown up recently at Boggs's office at 655 North Central to repossess his $40,000 Rolls Royce, they discovered that his office had been closed by the IRS for default on back taxes.

After the HMO in Salinas failed, a defeated Boggs returned to Glendale, determined to somehow resurrect his once thriving medical practice. Faced with abysmal credit ratings, Boggs began hitting up old friends and acquaintances for loans to get started. But to little avail. Most wanted nothing to do with him.

Still, Johnston could not turn down Boggs's request for a meeting. And now Boggs was pleading with Johnston, acknowledging that he was unable to obtain a loan in his own name because of a "tarnished credit reputation."

Then to both Johnston's and Tynan's surprise, Boggs

offered to "provide whatever security was necessary" as collateral if Johnston would only co-sign the bank loan. They had not expected Boggs to be able to come up with any such collateral.

While trying to resurrect his medical practice, Boggs said, he was beginning to find steady work as a medical consultant and expert witness in personal-injury cases. The work, he admitted, was for the most part pretty routine. All he had to do was review the facts leading up to some accident, give his opinion as to how an injury or purported injury came to occur, and then testify if necessary as to its debilitating consequences for the victims.

Persuaded, Johnston nodded to Tynan, signaling his intention to help Boggs. In a series of subsequent meetings at both Tynan's office and his Pacific Palisades home, the three hammered out an agreement. The collateral would be a $59,483 promissory note that belonged to Beulah Boggs, the doctor's mother, which originated from the sale of a piece of her property in Sunset Beach.

Repeatedly, Johnston and Tynan emphasized to Boggs that the $13,600 bank loan must be paid on, or before, the due day of January 12, 1979. Otherwise, Johnston would have no alternative but to seize the collateral immediately upon default, as he too had financial obligations that made for a tight cash flow, especially every January. Boggs said he understood and signed the papers.

As a part of the arrangement, Johnston's bank, Crocker National, required the dentist to take out a $11,000 loan and place the proceeds in a Crocker branch in Glendale. This would serve as additional security and collateral for the $13,600 obtained from the bank by Boggs and Johnston, the co-signatories. Beulah Boggs also signed the necessary papers stating that Johnston would become the full and sole owner of the collateral $59,483 note upon default of the loan. The package of agreements further stated that in the event of a default, Boggs would also pay for all of Johnston's attorney fees and foreclosure costs. Not that any of this was going to happen, of course, everyone agreed.

The deal was completed in the middle of October. Throughout the next three months Boggs regularly assured Johnston that he would have the loan paid off in full before January.

But with just four days remaining, Boggs called Johnston to say that he needed two to three weeks more before he would be able to pay back the loan. Johnston was shocked and angered—as much by Boggs's nonchalant attitude as by his failure to keep his word. Johnston was barely assuaged when Boggs disclosed with expansive intimacy that he already had secured an extension from Crocker National.

Fine, an annoyed Johnston said, "clear it up as soon as possible."

But of course things would not be so simple. On January 17, Boggs told Johnston that he needed until the end of the month. The dentist repeated his exhortation, adding that he would not exercise his right to the collateral until January 23.

But that date too came and went. Still, Crocker had not received a penny from Boggs. The next day, Johnston had to sell various stock holdings at a loss in order to meet his own financial obligations, including a sizable payroll.

Boggs finally paid off the loan on February 8, issuing Crocker National Bank a check for $14,157.89. But that did not deter Johnston from filing suit against Boggs to recover his losses—and to take legal possession of the collateral note.

In a legal reply filed in court, Boggs argued that Johnston's lawsuit should be summarily dismissed because the issue was now moot, since he had repaid the loan in full. Never mind that it had been nearly a month overdue and that Johnston was legally entitled to the collateral. Boggs went so far as to ask the court to award him $3,500 in attorney fees and court costs.

But in the event that the court disagreed with his reasoning, Boggs continued, he would be willing to pay Johnston "$1 and nothing more." Boggs asserted:

"I had absolutely no way of knowing that a delay of up to thirty days in the payment of the $13,600 loan to the bank would in any way cause a cash-flow problem for Dr. Johnston that would in turn require him to sell stock at a loss." He claimed that he had been unaware of the full contents of the collateral agreements at the time he signed them and therefore the documents were "illegal and unenforceable."

As the lawsuit dragged on month after month, Boggs attacked on another front. He filed a complaint against Tynan, Johnston's attorney, with the State Bar of California, the body that licenses and disciplines lawyers in the state. Boggs accused Tynan of having acted fraudulently in the handling of the loan agreement between Johnston and himself. The state bar dismissed Boggs's complaint as being without merit. And eventually the two physicians settled their dispute out of court, with Johnston forfeiting his claim on the elderly woman's note.

Still, the mere threat that Beulah Boggs might lose a note worth nearly $60,000 created a huge flap in the Boggs family. Bill Boggs had angrily demanded that his older brother pay off the loan and remove the cloud over their mother's nest egg. "He felt we were butting in," said James Boggs of his eldest brother.

The family's relations were never the same again. From then on, Beulah too took a different view of her eldest son. "I just quit having business deals with Dick after that," she said.

Poisoned Medicine

One radiant Southern California afternoon in the autumn of 1985, Hans Jonasson was walking along Santa Monica Boulevard, on his way to visit a friend after work, when a middle-aged man with gray hair cruised by in a black Cadillac and struck up a conversation. The driver ended up giving Jonasson a ride. It was a short drive, but just long enough for Jonasson to learn that the man behind the wheel was Richard Boggs, a Glendale physician who, as luck would have it, was in the market for an employee with just his talents.

The doctor's unorthodox recruiting practices notwithstanding, his job offer held immediate allure for Jonasson. The twenty-two-year-old Swede was, like both of his parents, a nurse by training. But in the year he had been in the United States, Jonasson was quickly getting emotionally burned out in his job taking care of dying AIDS patients in Torrance, a South Bay suburb that was a long bus ride away from home.

A month later, Jonasson began working for Boggs at 540 North Central Avenue in Glendale. His duties included showing patients to the proper examination rooms, taking blood pressure and pulse, drawing blood, giving injections, supervising physical therapy, and keeping supplies in stock. Shortly after that Jonasson moved in with Boggs. They had become lovers.

Jonasson had been only nineteen the first time he came to the United States. He did some traveling but spent most of those six months with friends in Las Vegas, instantly enamored by the fast and loose living in that gambling mecca. After returning home, he realized that the U.S. was where he wanted to live, especially with its liberal attitudes toward gays. Jonasson also had no stomach for socialism and, more important, he despised his abusive stepfather. Three years later, in 1984, he landed in California for good.

A rangy, slightly angular man with a spiky flat-top haircut that looks more porcupine than punk, Jonasson speaks slowly and with a Swedish accent. His eyes have a cold, unfeeling look about them, and they are accented by full lips that seem permanently set in a cruel sneer. His light-colored skin is set off by the dark shirts and pants that he favors, along with ridiculously skinny ties. If Hollywood's central casting were looking for someone to play the role of a steely Russian soldier, Jonasson would certainly be a strong contender.

At Boggs's office, Jonasson fit in easily, affecting a jocular manner. There was just one other full-time employee. That was Jean Walker, a quiet, easygoing middle-aged black woman who ran the office from her perch at the receptionist's desk, separated from the waiting lounge by a sliding window. Through thick and thin, Walker had stayed with the doctor for a decade. She did a little of everything, from keeping patients' records to scheduling appointments to billing insurance companies. She even made the coffee. In any other doctor's office that might have been too much for one person to handle. But with as few patients as Boggs had, the job was a snap. Walker often had nothing at all to do. And Boggs was rarely there.

"You couldn't find a better employer and friend," she recalled. "He never breathed down your neck. And when he asked you to do something, it was always with a please."

About two or three months after Jonasson had joined the cozy office, a patient burst in one day with severe chest pains that required urgent medical attention. He was already blue in the lips and hands. But Boggs was nowhere to be found.

Quickly, Jonasson asked Jean Walker to show him the emergency medical equipment. Walker told him there was none.

The incident deeply shook Jonasson, and afterward he told Boggs that it would be a good idea to have handy in the office a tray of emergency medicines for just such occasions. Boggs said that was a fine idea: it was as if the thought had never occurred to him. And he casually told Jonasson to go ahead and prepare such a tray.

Left to his own devices, Jonasson looked up a medical journal that contained a list of recommended medications for such an emergency tray. After assembling the supplies, he stored it under the sink in the lab room, where all the medications were kept. From time to time he would check the tray to make sure that it was clean and updated.

A little more than a year after Jonasson began working for Boggs, one of the doctor's sons, Dana, came on board and was put in charge of doing billings and keeping track of accounts receivable. As a boy Dana had often accompanied his father on his rounds. And now, fresh out of college, it seemed natural for him to go to work for his father until he had decided for sure what he wanted to do with his life. In the office Dana scrupulously referred to his father as ''the doctor'' or ''Dr. Boggs.'' He didn't want anyone to think he got the job just because he was the doctor's son.

Being of the same generation, Hans Jonasson and Dana Boggs shared many common interests. One was playing computer video games in the back room. And there was plenty of time for that because as time went on, patients were rapidly becoming an endangered species at the medical offices of Dr. Richard P. Boggs.

Three times his office had been shut down by the Internal Revenue Service, dating back to when it had been located at 655 North Central, across the street. Then the doctor would mysteriously come into some money, settle up with the government, and then re-open the office. Then he would have Jean Walker call up all the patients to let them know that he was back in business, urging them to return.

But despite Walker's phone calls, Boggs's patients increasingly took their business elsewhere, fed up with appearing for an appointment only to find the doctor not there—or, worse, to find the front doors padlocked by the government. "We just never saw them again," Walker said.

After one such closure, Boggs carted some three hundred boxes of patients files over to Lee Reedy's house high in the hills for Glendale. She let him store the boxes in her garage. Another time he brought over about twenty potted plants, most of them already dead. The woman eventually managed to nurse a few back to life.

"After Salinas blew up," recalled Reedy, a one-time patient, "he had very little down here in the way of a practice."

One afternoon Reedy went down to Boggs's office to help Jean Walker, her friend, do some paperwork. What she found in the billing ledger was page after blank page. He had almost no patients at all.

"It wasn't very busy," Walker agreed. "The patient load wasn't that heavy at all." Some days there were only two or three patients. On a good day, maybe five. Eventually most of the older patients either died or found a new doctor. And Boggs was getting few referrals.

Besides playing video games, Jonasson also spent a lot of time in the back "lab" playing chemist. With Boggs's encouragement, Jonasson began going in on weekends to try to make methamphetamines. A major source of Boggs's income now was coming from peddling prescription drugs, and now he was interested in converting a portion of his office into an illegal drug lab. In addition to selling steroids and other difficult-to-get prescription drugs, like methaqualone, Percodan, tranquilizers, and assorted sedatives, Boggs also sold a fair amount of cocaine, although he did not like using it personally. Instead he got hooked on methamphetamines, also known as speed or crystals, and soon he was injecting the crystals almost every day.

Often he got so spaced out that he would write prescriptions for patients with dosages that were wildly inaccurate, prompting concerned calls from Riley's Pharmacy downstairs in the same office building.

Alarmed, Walker and Jonasson quickly realized that they had to double-check every patient's prescription before he or she left the doctor's office. In late 1988, one of Boggs's female patients died of a multiple drug overdose, and a family member filed a complaint with the state medical licensing board, alleging that Boggs had irresponsibly provided the drugs. On another occasion, a deputy Los Angeles district attorney got so hooked on cocaine supplied by Boggs that she had to be taken to a detox center and then spent weeks afterward in rehabilitation.

Hans Jonasson had been a good chemistry student in high school, and had even started a chemistry club. But try as he did, Jonasson was unable to come up with the right ingredients or the recipe with which to manufacture methamphetamines. After a year of trying, Jonasson quit after he came down with a severe bout of hepatitis. Instead, Boggs had to go out and buy the methamphetamine crystals.

About that time a third person, Paul Simmermacher, shared the Belmont Street condominium that Boggs was renting from the Andersons, occupying the second bedroom. Almost every day Simmermacher and Boggs were injecting methamphetamines and finally Jonasson succumbed to curiosity. He allowed Boggs to inject him with the substance. Jonasson became an instant convert, and soon he too was shooting up methamphetamines everyday as well as abusing "basically everything I could get my hands on." At one point Jonasson was availing himself of so much Demoral, which Boggs kept in the top drawer of his desk at the office, that the alarmed doctor took the stuff home and put it in a small safe that he kept in a bedroom closet.

Because he had so few legitimate patients, Boggs's presence in the office was becoming increasingly rare. Some weeks his staff was lucky if they saw him three days out of five.

The only real action in the office were the phone

calls and visits from creditors, and it was all Walker could do to keep them at bay. Among the steadiest visitors were agents for June H. Causey and Frank A. Rhodes, Jr., owners of the office building. Boggs was behind on rent at 540 North Central by more than $44,000.

Boggs also was late on several occasions in meeting his biweekly payroll. But he was never late by more than three days, and Walker was now used to this indignity.

Jonasson, on the other hand, was becoming increasingly disgusted with his boss and roommate. Three times, with Dana Boggs's help, he wrote out his resignation. And even more often than that, he yelled at Boggs, saying he was sick and tired of the way Boggs was behaving. "I was trying to make him to be more in the office than he was and to take care of his patients," Jonasson later explained. Mostly, though, the three of them—Hans, Jean, and Dana—just commiserated with one another. And played video games in the long dry spells in between patients.

One day in late 1987, shortly after Boggs had missed another payroll, an angry Jonasson stormed into Boggs's office, demanding to be paid on the spot—and clearly prepared to quit. But Boggs took him by surprise, disclosing that he had just come into nearly $50,000. This, he said with a broad smile, meant that they could all get paid—and with plenty left over to pay the Internal Revenue Service $35,000 toward settling the back taxes. Boggs didn't explain the source of the large sum, but he did pull out a receipt to show Jonasson that he indeed had applied most of the funds toward the whopping debt to Uncle Sam.

The turn of events typified the unpredictable love-hate relationship between Boggs and his petulant young lover.

Once Boggs actually threatened to kill the Swede. This occurred after the doctor had learned from Paul Simmermacher that Jonasson had had an afternoon tryst with two men out in the San Fernando Valley. And when Boggs got home that evening, he was in a rage. He threw Jonasson down on their bed, jumped on him, and started pummeling him. Then Boggs shoved a .38-caliber pistol in Jonasson's face, threatening to kill him. But after they had made up, Boggs showed Jonasson that the gun was not loaded.

The pistol, which Boggs kept under the bed, wasn't the only weapon he possessed. The doctor also had purchased a small collection of stun guns, those battery-powered, pocket-sized devices that emit high-voltage charges and were popular as personal security weapons.

Boggs bought the stun guns after a young, emotionally distraught patient wearing Army combat fatigues one day stormed into the office, demanding to see Boggs. When told that the doctor would not see him just then, the man climbed through the sliding window at the receptionist's desk and confronted Boggs, who was meeting with a lawyer. The intruder began screaming obscenities at the doctor, adding, "I've killed before. I'll kill again. I'm a Green Beret!" It took awhile but Boggs finally managed to calm the man down, who then apologized and left.

Brent Salmon, a friend and patient of Boggs's for twenty years, was in the waiting lounge at the time, and he witnessed the entire commotion. Afterward, when Boggs entered the examination room to see Salmon, the doctor was still somewhat shaken.

"If this continues," Boggs said, "I'll have to get a gun or something to keep these people at bay."

Salmon knew something about self-defense. He was the holder of a sixth-degree black belt in karate and had trained numerous policemen, FBI agents, and even the Royal Canadian Mounted Police. In the mid-1970s, Salmon also served for three years as the security director for members of the royal family of Saudi Arabia.

"Guns," he told Boggs, "cause more problems than they are worth. These walls," he said, rapping his knuckles against the dry-walls, "are so thin that a stray bullet can easily penetrate them and strike a bystander."

Better to get a stun gun, he advised Boggs. With these devices, Salmon explained, lapsing into quasi-military gobbledygook, "momentary contact results in momentary scrambling of the neuronic signals across the nervous system. The patient or person collapses in a heap, and they go down in a very confused state."

Boggs was immediately intrigued.

"It just so happens," Salmon said, "that my son-in-law has a security store up in Ventura called Code Three that sells stun guns."

Boggs bought four of them, keeping one for himself and passing out the others to Dana, Hans Jonasson, and Jean Walker. He charged her $60 for it.

By now, it seemed, the art of healing was the far-thest thing from the minds of those who wiled away the hours in the medical suite of Richard P. Boggs, M.D. It was during one of these many lulls that the subject of poison first came up.

"I was talking about my bad relationship with my stepfather and how I had wanted, when I was living with him, to kill him," Jonasson said, recalling a con-versation with Boggs.

And when Jonasson began fantasizing out loud about poisons that he might use to kill his stepfather without leaving a trace, the doctor looked up with interest.

What, Boggs asked, would you use as the agent?

Brucine, replied the one-time high school star chemistry student. It comes, Jonasson said, from a rare breed of South American tree frog.

"You lick that frog, you die."

Nervous Energy

April 15, 1988, proved to be a grueling and somewhat depressing day for Hans Jonasson. After a nasty, protracted dispute with the lawyers for Stanley and Jackie Anderson, he and Dr. Boggs were being evicted from the Belmont Street condominium.

Jonasson spent much of the day packing and moving boxes from there to a smaller, less expensive apartment on South Street, just a few miles away. It was as if their lives were inexorably shrinking, going from bad to worse—a fact that further hit home in the late afternoon as Jonasson filled out his tax returns.

It was well past eight by the time he finally got home, looking forward to spending his first night in the new apartment. But no sooner had Jonasson settled down in front of the television before a nervous Richard Boggs walked in.

The doctor was full of nervous energy, and almost immediately he began pacing back and forth, stepping around the piles of boxes and bags strewn throughout the apartment.

After doing some methamphetamine with Paul Simmermacher, their apartment mate, Boggs announced suddenly that he was going back to the Belmont Street apartment to finish packing. They were to clear out of the Andersons' condominium by Sunday.

Boggs also said that he would not be returning that night. He was going to sleep at the Belmont Street apartment, for he still had his telephone answering machine there—just in case a patient in distress should call.

On his way out, almost as an afterthought, Boggs

told Jonasson, "If anybody ever asks, you don't remember anything that happened tonight."

Puzzled, Hans simply nodded and went to sleep. He had a patient appointment early the next morning.

Big Dreamers

Emerson Cheek III was one busy lawyer in 1985. After fifteen years of practicing law, the Ohio man had reached the pinnacle of the legal profession in his hometown of Columbus. Barely in his mid-thirties, Cheek had become managing partner of one of the city's oldest law firms: Hamilton, Kramer, Myers & Cheek.

And as chairman of the twenty-member firm's management committee, Cheek practically ran the firm singlehandedly. Still, he found time to practice law, specializing in commercial litigation as well as representing commercial landlords and tenants. One of his clients was an older woman who owned a vacant storefront on High Street, right across from Ohio State University.

That summer, a pair of unlikely businessmen from Kentucky showed up at Cheek's law firm, asking about renting the property. Cheek would never forget his first impression of the two.

The suave, older businessman was resplendent in a smartly cut Armani suit, smoking one cigarette after another. His handsome young partner was a picture of good health, clad in shorts, a T-shirt, and sneakers.

But they had big plans for Ohio.

Gene Hanson, forty-three, and John Hawkins, twenty-two, wanted to open a chain of stores in Ohio to sell sweat clothes and other leisure-time apparel. Only months earlier, they had opened a store called Just Sweats in Lexington, Kentucky, and it had been an instant success. In Columbus, they told Cheek, the vacant storefront across from the bustling Ohio State campus, with its 71,000-plus students, faculty, and staff, seemed the ideal location for selling their wares.

On behalf of his client, Cheek successfully negotiated a six-month lease with Hanson and Hawkins, and the first Just Sweats outlet in Ohio opened for business just in time for the Christmas season. And just as Hanson and Hawkins had brashly predicted, the Columbus store—with its youthful and attractive sales staff, which projected a squeaky-clean image—was an immense success. The shop was overrun by students and townfolk alike.

Faced almost overnight with the need to expand, Hanson and Hawkins again called on Cheek. So impressed were they with Cheek's professional demeanor and negotiating skills that the two now wanted Cheek to represent them.

The selection of Hamilton, Kramer, Myers & Cheek made a lot of sense. As newcomers to a booming city full of opportunities, it would be a decided asset to be represented by one of the city's most respected law firms, one with roots going back to nearly the turn of the century. The firm's clients included a broad cross-section of Columbus's fast-growing business community, including scores of closely held corporations, partnerships, and sole proprietors, many of whom were rapidly acquiring a national, even international, flavor. It seemed an ideal time and place to start a new business.

But Cheek, with his time-consuming administrative responsibilities, could not personally take on the Just Sweats account. Instead the work went to Richard A. Curtin, another young partner in the firm.

To Curtin, a quiet, low-key attorney with a passion for golf, Hanson and Hawkins were not very different from the droves of ambitious newcomers drawn to the bustling capital of Ohio, a rare oasis in the heart of the nation's Rust Belt. They dreamed of striking gold, and many talked of doing it quickly. "We had people coming in all the time with big ideas," Curtin recalled.

And yet in other, important ways, Hanson and Hawkins were distinctly unlike all the rest. They made no bones about making it big, and doing it quickly, and then cashing in—retiring to the good life. They made no effort to conceal their get-rich mentality. Indeed, they boasted about it.

"We don't want to sell sweat clothes for the rest of our lives," they told Curtin.

"John said he wanted to do a lot of living because he felt he was not going to be long for this world," the attorney recalled.

And so Curtin dutifully sat down with Hanson and Hawkins that autumn in his law firm's well-appointed conference room and began helping them think through their professional relationships to each other and to their company. Right from the start, one of their paramount concerns was insurance. "They seemed very interested in getting life insurance," Curtin recalled.

Even more oddly, the two partners seemed more interested in the legal niceties involved in cashing out the business than in establishing a sound legal framework to sustain a thriving business over the long haul.

Changing Times

When Gene Hanson and John Hawkins decided in the mid-1980s to establish their business headquarters in Columbus, they became part of a much larger movement that was rapidly transforming Ohio's capital into a crown jewel of America's heartlands. Whereas so many cities in the Midwest, like Cleveland, Buffalo, and Detroit, had plunged into seemingly irreversible declines, Columbus was a striking exception—thanks largely to the city's two biggest employers, the state government and Ohio State University. Together they cushioned Columbus from the economic shocks that devastated cities and towns throughout the Rust and Farm belts, starting in the late 1970s.

Columbus also had always been blessed by its central location. In the early nineteenth century it was a frontier trading post at the end of the old National Road, which led west from the Atlantic Seaboard. In today's jet age, Columbus is no more than ninety minutes away from eighty percent of the U.S. population, and the city has become one of the nation's leading distribution centers for corporations such as Kroger, J.C. Penney, Nestle, and Borden. Among the businesses that, like Just Sweats, chose Columbus as their headquarters were Wendy's International, the hamburger giant, and The Limited, one of the country's largest specialty retailers.

As the city's economic base became increasingly diversified during the 1980s, more than 100,000 new jobs were created, and they were pretty much evenly distributed among finance, service, insurance, technology, and manufacturing—thus ensuring a large base of well-heeled, upwardly mobile young urban professionals with plenty of disposable income. Today, the Columbus metropolitan area is home to more than 1.3 million people, whose average age is less than thirty-two. Despite the sharp growth, the demographics of the population have remained remarkably Middle America—so much so, in fact, that dozens of national manufacturers continue to use Columbus as their test market for new products.

By the mid-1980s, with an increasingly young, well-educated, white-collar, cosmopolitan work force, Columbus was hardly the bland town of cornfields, steak houses, and roller-skating rinks that it once was. True, one could still see cows grazing within sight of downtown. But that's only because an Ohio State University farm is located there.

Newcomers like Hanson and Hawkins were quickly helping change the face, if not the soul, of Columbus. The novelty of going to fancy restaurants that served raw salmon or foie gras was quickly overtaken by the offerings of newer, even more imaginative entrepreneurs, all vying to capture a piece of the action. A spanking new mall in the heart of downtown, the City Center, became home to exclusive stores like Gucci and Henri Bendel's, where a slender mannequin in an $8,800 black-beaded dress sat on a velvet piano seat, a red rose eloquently poised at her side.

And by the droves, artists, actors, musicians, and other free-thinkers from near and far were drawn to Columbus. At a local church, people spent one evening dancing to Stravinsky beneath a stained-glass image of Jesus Christ. All over town, a new tolerance was in the air. Soon Columbus had a bowling league for homosexuals that its four hundred members claimed was the largest in the country. Even lesbian Republicans were coming out of the closet.

One of the most distinct faces of this new, exciting Columbus was found along High Street, across from the Ohio State University campus just north of downtown. At one time a combat zone rife with condemned buildings used by drunks, addicts, and prostitutes, the area was rapidly becoming home to funky art galleries, interesting restaurants, and specialty shops.

Perhaps the most successful of them all was a glitzy, new sports apparel shop with colorful, inexpensive T-shirts and tasteful sweat clothes, staffed by cheerful, clean-cut young men and women from Ohio State.

And when Just Sweats overnight became a raging success, it hardly seemed possible that just a few years later, it would become an embarrassing blot on the city's well-cultivated image.

California Dreaming

Among the hundreds of raw recruits who reported for Army boot camp at Fort Jackson, South Carolina, on that glorious morning in 1965 was a wiry young man with a slight southern accent. Like packs of unkempt sheep, Gene Hanson and all the other "trainees" were herded from one station to another, getting their heads shaved, filling out a baffling array of government forms, and receiving their baggy fatigues and rock-hard leather combat boots. It was already well into the afternoon when the recruits were told to line up to be fingerprinted—a seemingly innocuous act at the time, but one that would prove more than two decades later to have enormous consequences for Private Hanson.

After eight weeks of arduous basic training and another eight of on-the-job training—all based on the supposition that most of the recruits would then be shipped out to South Vietnam—Gene Hanson found himself ordered to West Germany, much to his delight. There, during an uneventful three-year hitch, while war raged in Southeast Asia, Hanson acquired a special liking for Europe. And he vowed to go back there one day as a civilian, preferably a very rich one.

An obsession with money was one that Hanson had developed early in life.

Born in 1941 in Ocala, Florida, he grew up as Melvin Eugene Snowden, Jr., in rural north-central Florida, where attitudes and accents quickly told an outsider that that part of the Sunshine State was decidedly more Deep South than Disney World. Like Richard Boggs, Gene Hanson grew up in a family of boys, reared by a lone, financially strapped mother.

Katherine Snowden was a pious woman who hailed from a long line of southern Baptist preachers. After a brief marriage to Melvin Eugene Snowden, the tall, wiry woman left her philandering husband in 1943, taking with her their two sons, Gene, who was then two, and Donald, who was just six months old. The three of them ended up in Leesburg, not far from Orlando, where Katherine worked two menial jobs in order to pay her mother for room, board, and baby-sitting.

Three years later, Katherine married Cecil Hanson, a truck driver and a deacon in the local Baptist church. He adopted Gene and Donald, and the boys and their mother took the Hanson name. Together they moved to Jacksonville, and Katherine and Cecil went on to have two children of their own. Years later, Katherine would recall that her second husband was a good Christian but never became entirely comfortable with his adopted sons.

Young Gene, a bit of a loner, was no scholar, but he did well enough to get accepted at Florida State University. He spent two desultory years in Tallahassee, but short on money, he decided to join the Army and thus become eligible for GI benefits afterward.

But when he returned from West Germany, Hanson was no longer interested in continuing with his education. Instead, in the spirit of that era, he spent a couple years doing odd jobs while traveling around the country, as if waiting for some epiphany that would help him figure out what to do with the rest of his life.

In time, Hanson was drawn to Atlanta, which was rapidly emerging from the cataclysmic civil rights struggles as the enlightened mecca of the Deep South. There, Hanson landed a job as a trainee at Rich's department store. A diligent worker who pushed himself to learn the trade, Hanson quickly worked his way up to assistant buyer and then to a shoe-line builder. He also became fast friends with the store manager, Cecil Tanner, a man thirteen years his senior, to whom Hanson would develop a strong attraction.

In Atlanta, Hanson found himself in more ways than

one. He not only became a star merchandiser but also gradually came to terms with himself as a gay person. Until then he had been deeply torn, and he even consulted a psychiatrist to try to sort things out. But in Atlanta, Hanson was struck by Tanner's candor about his own homosexuality, and with Tanner's gentle encouragement, Hanson slowly embraced a similar attitude as well.

Being a loner, few of Hanson's colleagues knew much at all about his private life. They only knew him as an ambitious, indefatigable worker with a penchant for tailor-made Italian suits and strong black coffee.

After a few years in Atlanta, Hanson moved to Richmond, Virginia, where he got a much better-paying job as a buyer for Thalhimers. "He showed promise right away. He was good and we expanded his responsibilities after a short time. He was energetic, and everybody liked him," recalled Ben Berkowitz, who was Hanson's boss in Richmond. "He was bright, with exceptional taste—very well thought of."

But Hanson found the stodgy capital of the Old Confederacy too conservative for his liking. And so, like the legions of young people in the late 1960s and early 1970s, Hanson went west. "We were sorry to see him go," Berkowitz recalled.

Hanson worked for a few years as a contemporary salon buyer for Goldwaters in Scottsdale, Arizona, and then he took a similar position at Meier & Frank in Portland, Oregon.

In 1979, Hanson, by then thirty-eight, at last landed in California—and his life changed forever.

In Los Angeles, he took a $50,000-a-year job as a shoe buyer for Robinson's, a ritzy chain of upscale department stores with outlets all over Southern California. For the first time in his life, Hanson felt truly well-off. He drove a fancy car and was able to afford a nice apartment in the right part of town. He attended private, catered parties in secluded, landscaped backyards with immense swimming pools around which entertainment tycoons and beautiful movie stars mixed easily with politicians and the elite of California. At the same time Hanson was captivated by the stunning wealth that seemed so easily attainable in Los Angeles—and so easy to flaunt.

It was at one such lovely summer party in 1981 that Hanson's pal from Atlanta, Cecil Tanner, introduced him to an engaging young man, the sort that always seemed to be around whenever glamorous people gathered—ready and willing to provide, whether it was sex or drugs. His name was John Hawkins.

The young man seemed the quintessential ladies' man. He was good-looking, well built, and had a magnetic personality. And yet . . .

Something about Hawkins strongly attracted Hanson, and they both knew it.

A Double Life

From across John Hawkins's bedroom, Margaret Moulson could almost feel his admiring gaze caressing her as she approached, tingling with anticipation, her long strawberry blond hair falling across her bare, damp shoulders. As she climbed into his bed, she deftly let her fluffy towel unravel and fall to the floor.

Moulson, a slender but bosomy woman in her early twenties, with large green eyes, was used to that look of lust that men often exhibited when they saw her, especially when she was nude.

And Hawkins, a handsome, athletically built young man with a raging testosterone level, was certainly no exception. But as he reached out for her, it was what he said that surprised her.

"You remind me of my mother," Hawkins told her.

As they locked in frantic embrace, Moulson had little time or inclination to contemplate that comment. Only later—much later, when things turned terribly sour—would that chance remark come back to haunt her.

Moulson was a senior at Ohio State University and worked as a waitress at Max and Erma's, one of many singles bars and restaurants near the campus. She and Hawkins met at one such bar in the spring of 1987. And when he spoke with a burning passion of leaving Ohio and moving to Hawaii to start a cruise business, Moulson knew she was hooked.

To a woman who had hardly traveled outside of Ohio in her twenty-three years, Hawkins came across as a dashing adventurer. He was also an accomplished businessman, drove around town in a variety of ex-

pensive sports cars, worked out at the gym everyday—
and unfailingly summoned enough energy each night
to party hard. She was even charmed by the six straws
that he habitually put into each drink—for good luck,
he said with a smile.

But above all, what made Johnny Hawkins happy
was his mother. He spoke of her in almost reverential
tones, and she spoke of him the same way. "Johnny,"
Jackie Cerian would tell friends and strangers alike,
"was a charmer, a real ladies man." During a 1987
Christmas vacation in Hawaii, with a group of close
friends, she seemed just as proud as he was with every
conquest—especially that one day when Johnny slept
with four different women.

In time, Moulson came to suspect that the love between mother and son "exceeded the bounds of ordi-
nary familial love." During long-distance telephone
conversations that were often conducted in hush-hush
tones, Hawkins would tell his mother over and over
again, "I love you." By mail, Cerian sent him small,
naked statues that were, in his words, "in her image."
And once, when Moulson complimented Hawkins on
his sexual prowess, he boasted that his mother had
taught him how to please a woman.

Yet it wasn't so much the relationship between
mother and son that troubled Moulson as Hawkins's
roving eyes and short attention span. And in time he
came to view her friends as spies. For, whenever she
heard that he had been with another woman, Moulson
would break off the relationship, only to relent after a
few days or weeks because she craved his attention.

Like most young, impressionable women, Moulson
found Hawkins extremely charming and charismatic.
"When he talked to you, it was as if nothing else
existed or mattered," she would recall. "He treated
me like a million dollars."

Indeed he did. Hawkins bought her clothes. He
bought her a diamond necklace. He even paid for her
to have her breasts enlarged.

But John Barrett Hawkins, Jr., hadn't always had
money to burn. Like Richard Boggs in California and

Gene Hanson in Florida, he also was raised by a young, single mother struggling to make ends meet.

Hawkins was born in St. Louis in 1963, and before he was two, his parents divorced.

John Barrett Hawkins, Sr., a welder, then moved to Florida. Jackie moved West, ending up in Las Vegas with her cherubic son, whom she adored and pampered. In Nevada the stunning woman became a dealer in the casinos, captivating many a gambler with her beautiful eyes. It was certainly a much better-paying job, and a far more glamorous line of work, than being a hairdresser.

Early on, young Johnny acquired a knack for sweet-talking and displayed a capacity for hard work. He went door to door all over Las Vegas, peddling an odd assortment of goods, earning enough spending money to buy things for himself, such as sports equipment. For, in his spare time Hawkins was developing into a well-tuned athlete. And by the time he was a teenager, Johnny Hawkins had already begun developing a strong interest in girls. He spent hours on end working out, honing a manly physique that became widely admired—and not just by the giggly girls at the local high school still wearing padded bras.

By the time Hawkins dropped out of high school in the eleventh grade, he had become a tall, muscular young man with a cascade of dark curls and a winning smile. And with his ocean blue eyes and a charming demeanor, Hawkins had his choice of girls—and women.

But the bleak, landlocked desert never suited him. Hawkins was drawn to the sea. And so he went down to Florida to learn welding with his father. But that didn't last long. He liked the work less than the desolate Nevada landscape. It was disgustingly pedestrian, he thought. "He just knew that he didn't want to be a welder with burns on his hands," Gene Hanson would recall.

Back in Nevada, Hawkins worked on a pipeline project, but again he found the work distasteful. And so at age seventeen he bought his mother's silver Ford Econoline van and headed for California.

For a time Hawkins made an honest living in Los Angeles, including doing construction work. He even found time to get his GED equivalency. But like so many aimless young people drawn to L.A., Hawkins ended up on the seedy fringes of show business. He found a one-room apartment in a Hollywood building where pornography was produced.

Hawkins also tried his hand doing stand-up comedy at the many bars that offered amateur nights. But this too Hawkins found demeaning—having to stand on a tiny stage in the hot spotlight in some smoke-filled bar filled with drunks who paid him little attention. Still, that experience made him realize that in the big city of L.A., he could live by his wits.

So Hawkins went back to doing what he knew best—hustling. And the only thing he had to sell was his considerable good looks. But in a city where appearances are far more important than reality, that was quite an asset. And it wasn't unusual to see women—and a surprising number of men—turn their heads unabashedly for a second look after Hawkins had walked by.

At first Hawkins escorted wealthy older women around town. But as word of this glamorous newcomer circulated, men came clamoring—many of them high-powered executives in the world of entertainment who had money to burn.

"He was a gigolo, a male prostitute," Jackie Cerian said. "I'm not ashamed of what my son did. For Johnny, it was only a stepping-stone."

By the time Hawkins was eighteen, he was making quite a name for himself in Hollywood—and beyond.

Party Boys

The exclusive "back bar" at Studio 54 was rocking as usual. Reserved for only the crème de la crème of the world's superstars, the intimate party room on any given night held more recognizable faces than probably any other room in the world. Celebrities from virtually every walk of life vied with one another to gain entry into the hottest nightspot on the face of the earth.

The Manhattan club's clientele was a who's who in American entertainment and arts and letters. Among its regulars were Bianca Jagger, Andy Warhol, Christie Brinkley, Cher, Calvin Klein, Halston, Liza Minelli, and Barry Diller, the brilliant Paramount studio chief.

Nightly, as such beautiful people convened for the ritualistic celebration of themselves, camera-laden gawkers would fill the sidewalks outside the club, ogling the rich and famous. The more audacious would actually line up to get in. They would be content merely to get past the front doors, perhaps to rub elbows with the many lesser-known writers and aspiring socialites who were banished to the club's main, outer room.

The true measure of one's status, however, was the ability to gain admission into the back bar, where anything, it seemed, was available—for a price. And in the early 1980s one of the main providers—indeed, a major attraction—was John Hawkins.

From California, through his growing contacts in the upper echelons of Hollywood, Hawkins had easily made the transition from one coast to the other. And shortly after he arrived in New York, while escorting an attractive, wealthy Middle Eastern woman in her forties, Hawkins was driven by a sleek white limousine to Studio 54. There, the club's co-owner, Steve Rubell, immediately developed a crush on Hawkins, and he hired him on the spot.

As a bartender, Hawkins in no time began dispensing a lot more than a well-tossed Manhattan. Word quickly circulated that the handsome gigolo bartender had an inexhaustible supply of every imaginable type of drug. And Hawkins was far from coy about it, often showing up for work brandishing like trophies large glass bottles filled with hundreds of pills. These he obtained from a down-and-out physician out in Southern California by the name of Richard Boggs.

Hawkins had met the Glendale doctor through one of Studio 54's regulars, a dapper merchandiser named Gene Hanson, who had a $75,000-a-year job as a shoe-line builder for the Palizzio division of Michael G. Abrams & Co. Like so many men and women on both coasts, Hanson fell madly in love with Hawkins. Hoping to curry favor with the handsome young bartender, and sensing the scammer in him, Hanson one night proposed the drug-selling scheme, and Hawkins jumped at the idea.

As Hanson had predicted, Hawkins began raking in thousands of dollars every week. And he was being invited to several private parties a night. Sometimes he made as much as $5,000 in one night. And once a Middle Eastern potentate, flush with petro-dollars, flew Hawkins to London, where he starred at an all-night orgy that featured spiced lamb, curried chicken, and scantily clad young men and women flown in from as far away as Bahrain.

For Hawkins, scamming was becoming a way of life.

During a short trip to L.A., virtually on impulse, Hawkins pulled off an insurance caper that netted him a quick $25,000. Using a rental car, he and a friend staged a hit-and-run accident in West Hollywood. Hawkins acted as a pedestrian who was struck by a car while crossing a busy intersection. After being "hit," Hawkins collapsed to the pavement, writhing in pain until he was rescued by paramedics. Hawkins's insurance company promptly paid his claim after his physician vouched for Hawkins's injuries, saying that he would be unable to work for three months. The good doctor was Richard Boggs.

"There's no risk," Hawkins boasted. "I've got Boggs in my back pocket. And when you have a doctor who can verify everything, there's no way the insurance company can nail you."

But by the mid-1980s, Studio 54 had lost its allure, and the fast-spreading AIDS epidemic was putting a screeching halt to rampantly promiscuous gay life. An alarming number of Studio 54 employees and patrons were succumbing to the deadly infectious disease, and a worried Hawkins began having his blood tested every few months.

Hanson and Hawkins weren't exactly burned out just yet, but they too began to slow down somewhat and to take stock of their lives. Hanson's career in particular seemed to be stalling.

It was in the waning days of Studio 54 that another gorgeous woman entered Hawkins's life. She was Missy Hughes, a soap opera star and aspiring model and actress. They quickly became inseparable and at one point even talked of marriage. As Gene Hanson's sales career appeared to be taking a dive, Hughes began encouraging Hawkins to strike out on his own, perhaps in some business, given his ability to sell himself and whatever he seemed to believe in. Hughes even offered to buy in with seed money if Hawkins could come up with the right ideas.

Hawkins was intrigued, but eventually he got spooked by her increasing talk of marriage and children. He had seen his mother go through three unhappy marriages. He just wasn't interested.

And so Hawkins again began thinking about heading for California—this time in the company of his bosom buddy, Gene Hanson.

A Disappearing Act

He was alternately outraged and inconsolable. Even as the police car finally arrived on the scene, the young man was still hysterical.

Several roughnecks—obviously gay bashers—had beaten him up, kicked the hell out of his shiny Porsche, and then set it on fire, the sobbing, screaming young man told the police officers. Dutifully they took a report and then went on their way.

Several weeks later, an insurance check for $9,000 arrived in the mail for the Porsche's owner, John B. Hawkins.

Again it had been a snap, although this time the scheme was dictated by urgent necessity.

A frantic Gene Hanson had called from Europe, where he was staying at a fancy hotel, running up a large tab that they both knew he could not pay.

Sit tight, Hawkins confidently told Hanson, promising, "I'll take care of it."

Hawkins went out and bought a nice-looking but barely functioning Porsche that badly needed a new engine—writing a $5,000 check that he knew would bounce. Then he drove it down to lower Manhattan and parked it on a deserted street just around the corner from a gay bar. After dark, he bashed it in and then set it on fire.

Hawkins had carefully chosen this remote gay bar so that he could act effeminately and hysterically in a convincing manner after emerging from the bar to find his car destroyed.

The $9,000 more than covered Hanson's bills in Europe. Hawkins had netted a profit of $4,000. Insurance scams, he now realized, was a pretty easy way to make a living.

It certainly was easier than trying to sell shoes in Europe, an endeavor that had taken Hanson overseas in the first place. After only five months, Hanson had been laid off by Abrams & Co., for the retail industry was sliding fast into a recession and sales executives were being let go by the droves. Still, in a matter of weeks Hanson managed to land another sales job, this one with Arpiedi Shoes. Almost right away the firm put him in charge of its California division, delighted to have in Hanson someone with a long experience and firsthand knowledge of the California life-style and consumer tastes.

The company gave him expensive shoe samples worth tens of thousands of dollars and a considerable cash advance, and then sent him on his way. Or so it thought.

For the next few weeks Hanson over the telephone repeatedly gave Norma Sztaimberg, his supervisor, one excuse after another why the shoes were not selling. Then one day she called him only to discover that his telephone in California had been disconnected. "I lost my money and the shoes, and I never heard from him again," said Sztaimberg.

Unbeknownst to her, at about that same time a small import-export business quietly started up some 2,500 miles away, in Beverly Hills, California. It went by the name of Hawkins-Hanson Enterprises. On paper the company was to be an Italian shoe-import concern. The idea was to make counterfeits of the Italian shoes Hanson had in his possession, and then market them, relying on Hanson's extensive contacts in shoe-retailing business, especially in Europe.

But even though Hawkins had had no trouble raising the funds to get Hanson off the hook in Europe, they soon realized that the shoe-selling scheme was not going to prove lucrative. At least not quickly enough to satisfy them.

And so even as Hawkins-Hanson Enterprises in Cal-

ifornia died a quiet death in February 1985, that very
month, back in New York, the two were setting in
motion their most audacious insurance-fraud scheme
yet, one that held the promise of a huge payoff.

No Sweat

Gene Hanson and John Hawkins picked a frigid February afternoon to move out of their high-priced Manhattan apartment.

The two of them spent much of the day loading furniture and paintings into a rented U-Haul truck. But the work proved too strenuous for Hanson, who spent as much time sitting down gasping for air and smoking cigarettes as he did loading the truck. And so he and Hawkins hired a young, strapping Latino man to help out, paying him $20 an hour for four hours of labor.

Even so, the three men were unable to complete the task before dark on that winter day. Their Latino helper agreed to return the next morning at 11:30.

The following day, at 11:20 Hanson was sitting alone in the truck, behind the steering wheel, when another Latino man jumped into the cab from the passenger side and shoved a gun in his face.

He ordered Hanson to drive across town to the west side, where they were joined by two other Latino men. There, they locked Hanson in the back of the truck and then drove off. After about twenty-five minutes, they stopped and yanked open the back of the truck. Blinded by the sudden burst of sunlight, all Hanson could see was a huge metal door, which he took to be that of a warehouse.

The men quickly unloaded the truck's contents—valuable paintings and expensive antiques—and then locked Hanson back inside the vehicle. Then they drove off again. After what seemed like another long ride, they stopped and apparently abandoned the vehicle, but not before menacingly ordering Hanson to wait inside a good half hour before seeking help.

Hanson waited a few minutes and then, certain that the robbers were gone, he began banging frantically on the door, yelling for help. After someone finally came to his rescue, Hanson stepped out and saw that he was in Harlem.

The only problem with this account, given police by Hanson, was that it didn't happen.

What did transpire was even more improbable.

In February 1985, Hanson and Hawkins were ready to leave New York for greener pastures, but first they needed to pull another scam to buy into their next venture, whatever that was going to be. Increasingly pressed for money, they could no longer maintain their lavish life-style—especially the elegant $5,000-a-month brownstone they were renting on Lexington Avenue at 26th Street, a few blocks north of Gramercy Park. Their two-bedroom duplex looked all the more stunning because of its top-quality decorator contents. The high-ceilinged apartment was filled with original lithographs and oil paintings, one of which was worth $10,000. The entire apartment was furnished with expensive Victorian antiques.

All of it was rented.

And all of it was covered by a homeowner's insurance policy.

And on February 5, Hanson and Hawkins, using the pretext of a move, arranged to have it all appear to have been stolen—and then calmly collected $109,000 on their homeowner's insurance policy.

They fooled not only the cops and the insurance company but even the professional movers they had hired for the job.

With the help of Tim Browne, a childhood friend of Hawkins's from St. Louis, they rented two moving trucks, from different locations and using different names. On moving day, the hired hands showed up promptly at eight and methodically began loading one of the U-Haul trucks, which clearly had more than sufficient capacity to hold all the men's belongings. The second truck was nowhere in sight.

The brawny movers worked quickly and by lunch time their job was almost done. Before going off to eat, the men secured the contents by ropes and then covered them with heavy tarpaulins supplied by Hawkins and Hanson.

As soon as the three movers left the apartment, Browne pulled up in the second, identical U-Haul truck, which he had parked around the corner out of sight. Then Hawkins drove away in the first truck as Browne quickly pulled into the vacant spot at curbside.

Inside the second truck was a similar-looking pile of furnishings—also covered by identical tarpaulins. When the well-fed, unsuspecting movers returned, they quickly finished loading up the truck and then, once paid, went on their way, never the wiser to the truck switch.

The rented artworks and furnishings Hanson and Hawkins returned to their rightful owners. Then they drove the second truck, containing the junk furniture, to a landfill in New Jersey—returning with an empty vehicle, but now with Hanson inside the cargo compartment. Hawkins drove back into Manhattan and abandoned the truck in Harlem—with Hanson still inside, ostensibly as a robbery victim.

New York police detective John Miles, a gruff but friendly man with a weather-beaten face in his late fifties, didn't know quite what to make of Hanson's bizarre account. Somehow it didn't ring true. "It was his manner of telling it," the veteran cop recalled. "He remembered some things too well, some things not at all." But Miles attributed Hanson's inconsistent account to the strain of having been hijacked, with a gun in his face.

Hanson, of course, didn't tell Miles that the supposedly hijacked goods were all rented—and well insured, important facts that clearly would have made the detective far more suspicious from the start.

After giving the initial report, Hanson proved extremely difficult to reach, and he and Miles ended up speaking only twice more on the telephone, each time only briefly. Further following up on the incident, Miles one afternoon drove up to the Harlem neighborhood where Hanson said he had been driven. Nobody there could recall anything resembling the incident that Hanson had described.

"It never happened. He made it impossible for us to trace it," Miles eventually concluded.

As for Judy Schiff, Hanson and Hawkins's landlady at 83 Lexington Avenue, she was relieved in early 1985 to bid them farewell. As soon as they moved in, they had had the living room painted a shiny brown, which Schiff detested. More to her liking, though, they installed louvered shutters and filled the apartment with expensive art and elegant antiques. They told Schiff that Hanson was Hawkins's stepfather, which sounded plausible to her, given their age difference.

Hanson was away a good deal of the time—because his shoe business required almost constant travel, especially to Italy, he told Schiff. In Hanson's absence, Hawkins begrudgingly looked after Lady, a yappy little dog that Hanson seemed to cherish. But what really kept Hawkins company, to Schiff's increasing annoyance, was a steady stream of visitors to the apartment at all hours, including the actress Missy Hughes and lots of handsome young men. Hawkins told Schiff that he was a model and an aspiring actor.

For years, Schiff, a stocky woman in her forties, knew nothing about the insurance fraud that her former tenants had perpetrated. Police never bothered to question her about Hanson and Hawkins.

In any case, Miles's report on the alleged robbery was good enough for the Chubb Insurance Company. Without further ado it sent Hanson and Hawkins a check for $109,000.

At last the schemers had enough money to start a legitimate business. It had been no sweat.

Untapped Markets

The first Just Sweats store opened in June 1985 with great fanfare, complete with a ribbon-cutting ceremony and plenty of picture taking of the many civic leaders who turned out for the happy event.

The store was in Lexington, Kentucky, the hometown of a key investor, Missy Hughes. Even though she and Hawkins had begun going their separate ways romantically, she nevertheless retained a soft spot for him. And in those dark, waning days of Studio 54, when Hawkins had spoken so poignantly about finding his way into some legitimate business, Hughes could not have been more encouraging.

And so in March, when Hawkins came back from California, bursting with enthusiasm over his newest get-rich project, Hughes was all ears. He got his idea while in Los Angeles, where there was a wildly successful chain of sports clothing stores called Pure Sweats. While out on the coast, Hawkins even paid a high-level Pure Sweats employee to tell him everything he knew about the company and the industry, from merchandising to profit margins. Hawkins, who had an uncanny ability to absorb a great amount of complex information, returned to New York convinced that this was the way for Hanson and himself to invest their ill-gotten insurance proceeds.

Hughes agreed that he had hit on an idea that couldn't miss—selling T-shirts, socks, and sweat clothes to an exercise-crazy America. By then doing even better in her acting and modeling careers, she kicked in a large sum of her own money to help Hawkins and Hanson get started. Her brother became the Lexington store's manager.

Almost overnight the brisk sales confirmed what Hanson and Hawkins had known instinctively: the Kentucky capital, in the heart of the nation's storied bluegrass country, was a largely untapped market for the stylish yet inexpensive sweat clothes that were becoming extremely popular as everyday casual wear and not just for exercise.

And so the prospects of becoming millionaires were no longer just a pipe dream. And when the time came to think expansion, Hanson and Hawkins simply looked north across the Ohio River.

Just as Atlanta earlier had become a magnet of the Deep South, drawing young, ambitious people, Columbus, Ohio, now enjoyed a well-deserved reputation as one of the most desirable cities in the Midwest. More important, for the second year in a row, the Ohio capital was ranked by the Louis Harris Poll as having the ninth most favorable climate for business.

Columbus, in short, had become a modern-day boomtown. And Just Sweats was only one of more than a thousand new businesses that started up in the Columbus metropolitan area in the mid-1980s.

But none was more successful than Just Sweats, thanks in no small measure to the bright, clean-cut, and enthusiastic young people that Hanson and Hawkins hired.

Typical among them was Melissa Mantz, a pretty Ohio State University coed who confidently walked into the first Just Sweats store in Columbus shortly after it opened, seeking a job. Hawkins liked the way Mantz looked, especially her gorgeous figure and bright, infectious smile. But he had no job openings.

Mantz was undaunted. ''I'll show you,'' she said.

In the course of that afternoon, an amazed and bemused Hawkins watched Mantz outsell all the other salesclerks. He hired her on the spot to be the store manager.

Mantz was a fast study, and she quickly learned the merchandising trade from inside out, even playing a role in decorating the store to appeal to youthful tastes, from rock music to the bright, colorful decor.

The demand for Just Sweats goods seemed insatiable. Within months of opening that first Columbus store and establishing the company's headquarters out on East Broad Street, Hanson and Hawkins quickly opened ten more outlets in Ohio. Back across the river in Kentucky, it was the same fantastic story.

After only a year, Just Sweats had twenty-two outlets, generating more than $8 million in sales. In the frenzied chaos the two elated businessmen worked punishingly long hours. Hanson supervised the firm's day-to-day operations. Hawkins took care of the merchandising and advertising end of things. He even cast himself and some friends in Just Sweats commercials that aired on local TV, turning them into celebrities around town.

To Dick Curtin, the company's attorney at Hamilton, Kramer, Myers & Cheek, the two entrepreneurs no longer seemed like run-of-the-mill dreamers with just another cheap get-rich scheme. Sure, they still came across as flim-flam artists. But what businessman doesn't have a touch of the con artist in him? Persuading people to part with their hard-earned money, after all, comes with the territory. And sure, Hanson and Hawkins were hardly the most organized businessmen in Columbus; indeed, some of the Just Sweats outlets were opened simply because Hawkins had vastly over-ordered.

But who had time to find fault when the company was expanding with such breathtaking speed, raking in money almost faster than could be counted? Certainly not *Entrepreneur* magazine. It named Just Sweats as an "Opportunity of the Month."

For months on end, it seemed, Hanson and Hawkins worked at a feverish pitch, finding fresh outlets, signing up new vendors, arranging for deliveries, buying advertising, fielding an unending barrage of queries from would-be investors. All over town, owners of commercial buildings were clamoring to have Just Sweats as tenants, so eager were they that many provided interior decorating for free, providing virtually everything but the cash register.

For a time Hanson and Hawkins seemed truly caught up in the business frenzy, taking little personal compensation, instead plowing their earnings right back into the business. To the good people of Columbus, this unlikely pair of newcomers seemed like modern-day Horatio Algers who were rapidly realizing the American Dream.

But of course it was too good to last.

Out of Control

John Hawkins was working late at the High Street store just across from the Ohio State campus, supervising an inventory in preparation for an audit the next morning. It was an enchanting spring evening, the end of the first truly balmy day after a long Midwest winter, and every pretty coed who walked by the store, it seemed, was wearing a tight T-shirt and hip-hugging shorts.

"The chicks are really out tonight," Hawkins said somewhat ruefully, staring out the store's picture windows.

Finally, it was too much. Hawkins just couldn't concentrate anymore. "You finish up," he told Dan Norris, a store employee. "I gotta get out of here."

With that, Hawkins walked over to the cash register and removed a fistful of $20 bills that he didn't even bother to count. Stuffing the cash into the back pocket of his green gym shorts, Hawkins disappeared into the Ohio night.

Flush with sudden wealth, such diversions increasingly became a way of life for Hawkins and Hanson as they succumbed once more to the simple pleasures of life. "His life-style was: wake up, go to work, go home, go to the health club and work out, and then hit the bars," one Hawkins buddy would recall.

If Hanson and Hawkins had hired a professional business manager to run Just Sweats early on, that person surely would have sounded the alarm that the firm was perhaps growing a little too fast for its own good. What little controls that were in place would have been inadequate even for an established retail store, much less one that was growing by leaps and bounds. But for Just Sweats, the absence of an adequate accounting system amid the breakneck pace of expansion nearly proved to be its downfall. Merchandise? Nobody seemed to know for sure what was being sold where, when, or for how much. The company's financial books were worse than nonexistent. Except for some daily sales figures, they were in utter chaos. At the same time, many of the hundreds of callers seeking a Just Sweats franchise never had their calls returned.

Before long, suppliers and most anyone who had any business dealings with Just Sweats were calling the company to ask about unpaid bills. Among this rapidly growing line of unhappy creditors was the law firm of Hamilton, Kramer, Myers & Cheek. Things soon deteriorated to the point that whenever Hanson and Hawkins called with a new business problem, Dick Curtin politely informed them that there could be no more legal advice until they had first paid his firm for services already rendered.

"They basically abused everyone. They would get the goods or services, and then not pay and not pay," Curtin recalled.

But pay Hamilton, Kramer, Myers & Cheek they did, for Just Sweats was finding itself increasingly mired in legal squabbles of one sort or another, just about all of them its own making.

UCLA sued Just Sweats in federal court in Columbus for trademark infringement. The university had fifty domestic licensees, including five right in the Ohio capital. Just Sweats was not one of them, yet it was blatantly selling sportswear with UCLA's trademark logo. The suit eventually was settled out of court, with Just Sweats agreeing to stop selling such unauthorized products after paying UCLA a nominal fee.

Closer to home, Ohio State University also got dragged into a prolonged dispute with Just Sweats over a licensing agreement. In this case at least, Just Sweats was a legitimate licensee. The dispute arose after the university set out to determine how much in royalties the company owed it. For what seemed like the longest

time, university officials got little cooperation from
Just Sweats. And when the university's accountants finally gained access to Just Sweats' financial data, they
found its books riddled with inconsistencies, containing information that made little sense.

"We talked. We had meetings. And we conducted
audits. But they didn't follow through," recalled Les-
lie A. Winters, director of contracts administration.
"They did not keep accurate records or controls."

With their business now firmly established as an immensely successful cash cow, Hanson and Hawkins inevitably grew arrogant as businessmen. From the
beginning they had paid their employees the bare minimum wage. And now, thinking they could do no
wrong, they began cutting other corners—ordering, for
instance, the sale of damaged merchandise at full price
and instituting an in-your-face, no-refund policy.

In the meantime, the business partners quickly became bored with the mundane chores required in running a successful business. And so once more they
channeled their considerable energies into enjoying the
good life. Hanson bought a posh condominium at the
exclusive Park Towers, just east of downtown. And if
he seemed to have lost a step or two as a party animal,
Hawkins clearly was just hitting stride.

While playing basketball one afternoon at the trendy
Continental Athletic Club uptown, he met a kindred
soul named Erik De Sando, a good-looking bachelor
in his twenties, with a head of thick, curly dark hair.
On and off the court, De Sando had no trouble keeping
up with Hawkins. He also was in sales, specializing
in the construction of outdoor decks and patios.

Hawkins at the time also was in the market for a
new roommate, since his lifelong pal, Tim Browne,
had returned to St. Louis to resume his studies after
ostensibly working for Hawkins at Just Sweats but in
reality simply partying with his buddy. Hawkins
thought De Sando was the ideal person with whom to
share his two-bedroom apartment on the city's lively
North Side. And De Sando agreed. Soon the two became virtually inseparable.

Before long, De Sando was helping Hawkins write Just Sweats commercials, and then he too began appearing in the company ads. But mostly they just partied. "We just wanted to have fun and we did," De Sando said.

Still, Columbus was not L.A. or New York. More and more, Hanson and Hawkins began speaking wistfully of selling their company and retiring to some exotic, faraway place in the sun. Hawkins talked specifically of starting a cruise company in Hawaii dedicated to having fun. "The Booze Cruise," he would call it.

Such talk hardly surprised their friends, acquaintances, and employees. Who, after all, didn't dream about an early retirement blessed with a golden nest egg? But what they couldn't know at the time, of course, was that for Hanson and Hawkins, this was not idle chatter.

The two partners had become scam artists through and through. And unbeknownst to anyone else in Ohio, they were about to spring their final scam.

Well Covered

Erik De Sando was nearly panic-stricken. Like Tim Browne before him, De Sando did occasional business errands for his roommate, John Hawkins. And while driving down to Kentucky to make some deliveries at the Just Sweats outlet in Lexington, De Sando had gotten into a nasty accident, demolishing the company's leased truck.

Now, as he walked through the front doors of Just Sweats' headquarters back in Columbus, De Sando was dreading having to face his temperamental roommate. Luckily, Hawkins was out to lunch. In fact, everyone but Gene Hanson was gone.

And when De Sando told the co-owner what had happened, Hanson seemed unfazed. "Don't worry," he said, looking up with a smile at an immensely relieved De Sando. "That's what insurance is all about."

On another occasion, when a young salesclerk casually mentioned that her car had been involved in a minor accident, sustaining about $1,000 in damages, Hanson offhandedly offered to help her file an insurance claim that he said would net her thousands of dollars. "You can lie about stuff like the amount of damages," Hanson told her.

As time went on, insurance seemed increasingly on Hanson's mind even as he became more and more disengaged from the affairs of Just Sweats. Out of the blue one day in late 1987, he remarked to Dan Norris, another Just Sweats worker: "I don't know why people buy life insurance. Why would you buy life insurance when you wouldn't be around to get any of the money?"

But as owners of a thriving business, Hanson and Hawkins of course were well-insured. Through two different companies each man had nearly $1.5 million in life insurance, with each other being the beneficiary. In addition, through their company's group health plan, each man had another $15,000 in life insurance. And when Hanson treated himself to a $68,000 Porsche, he took out another $50,000 in life insurance to cover the outstanding loan on the car—just in case he died.

And as 1987 was drawing to a close, Hanson began talking openly as if he would not be long for this world. He was ready to cash in.

Selling out

On a slate-gray afternoon in late December 1987, a solemn Gene Hanson invited Erik De Sando into his office for a chat. For weeks now, rumors had been circulating throughout the company that Hanson was seriously ill. Indeed, De Sando had to admit, the man looked like death warmed over. Hanson smoked three packs of cigarettes a day, sometimes more. And he gulped down coffee by the urns. His pale face was deeply lined and he looked downright unwell.

As De Sando entered Hanson's large office, he braced himself for the worst. And Hanson didn't let him down.

He had a serious, and quite likely terminal, heart condition, Hanson somberly told De Sando. "I've only got a few months to live," he said. Before De Sando could gather himself and reply, Hanson went on, saying he was about to move to Los Angeles, where he knew a doctor who could provide him the best medical care possible.

He then invited De Sando out to his condo, and as a grand farewell gesture he bestowed upon the befuddled young man his television set, video cassette recorder, and some potted plants. But Hanson still wasn't done.

Noting that De Sando was about to start a new job in February, as an insurance agent, Hanson with a flourish flung open the doors to his huge walk-in closet and insisted that De Sando take some of his expensive Armani suits as well.

De Sando's private meeting with Hanson was just one of many tête-à-têtes that the co-owner of Just

Sweats held in the waning days of 1987. Another who had such a meeting with Hanson was Paul Colgan, the company's accountant. With Hawkins also sitting in, Hanson told Colgan that he was doing such a superb job that the firm was awarding him a two-week, all-expenses paid vacation to Europe. Immediately.

Colgan was stunned—but also dubious. Just days earlier, Hawkins and Hanson had taken away his check-writing duties, causing him to fret that his career at Just Sweats was on thin ice. But Hawkins later had taken Colgan aside, assuring him that, with a new year approaching, the co-owners had merely resolved to assume tighter control of the company in general and its finances in particular—especially the flow of company funds.

Only somewhat reassured, Colgan suspected that Hanson and Hawkins might be negotiating to sell Just Sweats and that they didn't want a key officer like Colgan to be around who might somehow muddy the waters.

Colgan was less than thrilled to be traveling alone on a winter holiday to Europe, and on such short notice too. But he resolved to enjoy himself nevertheless. "I was paranoid. I didn't think I'd have a job when I got back," Colgan recalled later. He certainly didn't relish the idea of being out of a job after serving just two years as the company accountant. Yet, he had to admit, the job was becoming less and less challenging. All he seemed to do anymore was field telephone calls from angry creditors demanding payment.

Just before taking off for Europe, Colgan left with Hanson several company checks made out to Just Sweats' vendors that required Hanson's signature.

Shortly after that Hawkins also left town, taking his mother, sister, De Sando, and several other buddies from Columbus for an all-expenses-paid vacation in Hawaii. It was his treat. Caught up in the Christmas spirit of giving, Hawkins and Hanson had given each other a $20,000 bonus. Hanson used the money as a down payment for a Porsche, but Hawkins was determined to spread the good cheer.

In Hawaii, Hawkins bedded down young women left and right. But he also found time to go out on a party cruise—two nights in a row—to better prepare himself for starting his own "booze cruise" one day, he told De Sando.

Left behind in Columbus, Hanson now was in place to set in motion their final get-rich scheme.

An Aborted Scheme

It was every merchant's dream. The store was absolutely mobbed. Even a good quarter hour before opening, shoppers had begun congregating outside despite the below-zero wind-chill factor.

It was the day after Christmas—the single busiest day of the year in the cutthroat world of retailing. That the store was busy was not in itself a surprise. But what caught Gene Hanson and Melissa Mantz, now Just Sweats' corporate merchandiser, off guard was the crushing throng that jostled one another, many elbowing their way to get at the bargains galore. It was all the more unexpected since Ohio State students—normally the store's steadiest customers—were home for the holidays.

But then, this was a sale to end all sales. Everything in the store, even the top-of-the-line brands, was marked down by fifty percent.

Hanson had ordered the steep discount at every one of Just Sweats' outlets, and the overwhelming turnout instantly netted the firm hundreds of thousands of dollars.

It was to be a one-day blowout. Thus Mantz was stunned when, near the end of the day, Hanson put out the word to extend the sale by three weeks.

A bright, ambitious young woman in her twenties, Mantz had been one of the few corporate Just Sweats officials, along with Hanson, who worked through the holidays. Fearing that a prolonged half-price sale would deplete the company's inventory, Mantz argued fiercely with her boss. But Hanson could not be dissuaded. The company, he said rather cryptically, needed cash—lots of it, and fast.

Unbeknownst to Mantz, Hanson also was secretly accumulating cash by sitting on the company's bills, refusing, for instance, to sign and mail the checks to vendors that Paul Colgan had left with him before going to Europe.

When the sale ended in mid-January, just as Mantz had feared, Just Sweats' shelves were virtually bare, its warehouses nearly empty. Mantz eagerly awaited the imminent return of John Hawkins, intending to plead with him to assume more responsibility in the company's day-to-day affairs since, in her view, Hanson had clearly lost his touch.

But just before Hawkins was due to return, Mantz's grandfather died and she left town to attend his funeral. When she got back, the well-tanned Hawkins was livid.

Hanson was nowhere to be found, and neither were $1.8 million from the company coffers. Together with Colgan, who had just returned from Europe, they pulled out the financial books for a closer look.

Because of the company's shoddy bookkeeping practices, aggravated by the fact that it had numerous accounts in different banks around town, it took several days before they figured out roughly how much Hanson had taken. When Colgan opened Hanson's desk drawer, he saw the checks he had left still sitting there, untouched and now long overdue.

There was no choice, Hawkins, Mantz, and Colgan agreed, but to call in Dick Curtin, the company's attorney. And when they showed up at the offices of Hamilton, Kramer, Myers & Cheek, Curtin was joined by another of the firm's partners, Austin P. Wildman. The two men were longtime friends and had been partners in their own law firm before merging it with Hamilton, Kramer almost three years earlier.

At once Hawkins flew into a rage, ranting about the many creditors hounding Just Sweats for payment and denouncing Hanson for absconding with the money.

Where could Hanson have gone? the attorneys wondered. Hawkins had no idea.

Then Mantz spoke up. Just before Hanson disappeared, she now remembered, he had sent several large boxes by United Parcel Service to California. The destination should be on the copy of the invoice. Hawkins said he would look for the papers.

At the mention of California, Curtin surmised that Hanson might have developed AIDS and had gone out West in search of exotic, untested treatments for the disease.

Turning to Hawkins, Curtin added gravely that if there was even a hint that another jurisdiction was involved in the embezzlement, he had no choice but to immediately "march yourself across the street"—to the Federal Bureau of Investigation.

With that, Hawkins's demeanor abruptly changed. For the first time he seemed to be genuinely focused on the problem. "I'm not quite ready yet to go to the FBI," he said. "Let me see if I can find him out there."

Reluctantly, Curtin and Wildman agreed. But they told him there was little time. The life of the company hung in balance.

Within days, a smiling Hawkins was back in Columbus—with a big duffel bag stuffed with cash and interest-earning bearer bonds that totaled about $1.6 million. And he regaled everyone with a colorful account of how he had managed to track down Hanson in L.A., using a variety of ruses, disguises, and other ploys that fooled even hotel dicks.

When he at last caught up with Hanson, Hawkins said, a contrite Hanson said he simply wanted out of the business and had taken the $1.8 million because he felt that amount represented his rightful share of Just Sweats stocks—based on some closed-door discussions with prospective buyers in 1987. But Hawkins said he had managed to convince Hanson that his shares were worth far less than that. In the end, they agreed to let Hanson keep $243,583.06, and Hawkins—now as sole owner of Just Sweats—brought the rest home.

At the time it seemed like a plausible account. Hanson was capable of such erratic behavior. "I, for one, believed Hawkins," admitted a sheepish Austin Wildman. Even the bearer bonds that Hawkins brought back from California had the same serial numbers as those taken out by Hanson, the lawyer noted. But in hindsight, there is little doubt that Hawkins and Hanson had worked hand in glove in plotting the embezzlement scheme.

Their plan first called for Hanson to abscond with the $1.8 million—his share of the proceeds. The scheme's second act would be trickier to execute. It required them to find someone who bore a strong physical resemblance to Hanson. And with the help of Dr. Richard Boggs they would kill this person and then mis-identify the body as that of Gene Hanson. That accomplished, Hawkins would receive $1.5 million as the sole beneficiary of Hanson's various life insurance policies. Boggs was to get $100,000 for his role in the dual embezzlement and murder-for-insurance plot.

The scheme collapsed, however, when a likely murder victim could not be readily found in early 1988, after Hanson had set the complicated plot in motion by disappearing with the $1.8 million. With their attorneys insisting that the FBI be called in to investigate the embezzlement, Hawkins and Hanson had no choice but to abandon their scheme and return the money—after improvising the Hanson buy-out.

But of course the two businessmen regarded the setback as only temporary, for they knew that out in Los Angeles, their doctor friend was on the prowl nightly for somebody who looked like Gene Hanson.

Crisis Management

By late January, the contrast between Just Sweats' besieged headquarters and its depleted stores could not have been more stark. At the corporate offices, the phones were ringing nonstop. Nearly every call was from an outraged vendor or some other Just Sweats creditor, screaming like never before about not being paid. From Seattle, Roger Larsen, a sweat suit supplier, called to demand payment of $27,000. In Pittsburgh, Max Joel, owner of LBJ Sales, another supplier, had nearly $120,000 coming. In Atlanta, Jeff Adair, the owner of Riada Mills, was staring at a pile of bills that Just Sweats had not paid for four months. Even right in Columbus, Jeff Scheiman, president of SOS Productions, had been waiting for almost two months for his $30,000 payment for producing Just Sweats TV commercials.

The company's stores, in the meantime, were virtually devoid of customers, its shelves depleted by the prolonged after-Christmas half-price sale. And because Hanson had marked down every last piece of merchandise across the board instead of discounting only the lower-quality goods, all the top-of-the-line stuff now was gone, leaving just the dregs, the mismatched outfits that nobody wanted. All this meant, of course, the firm was generating almost no sales revenues.

Morale, not surprisingly, hit rock bottom at both headquarters and the outlets. Clearly it was going to take every last ounce of charm and talent that Hawkins could muster to calm the mob and to stabilize the ship. But Hawkins seemed determined to do both as he threw himself into the task. And for the most part, he succeeded, as few vendors quit Just Sweats. The company still held an allure.

"People would go into his office mad as hell and then, ten minutes later, come out with a smiling Hawkins, his arm around their shoulders," recalled one Just Sweats employee.

Hawkins also sent letters to the company's vendors, suppliers, and creditors, candidly telling them what had happened, though he spared them the colorful details. And he pleaded for their patience, promising to straighten matters out.

Still, the task before him was daunting. No one seemed to know for sure how much money, if any, Hanson had left behind in the firm's many different accounts. Nobody could say what new merchandise had been ordered, if at all. Nobody knew just what the company's debts and financial obligations were.

Somehow Hawkins managed to obtain some new loans from sympathetic bank officers, allowing long-overdue bills to be paid and Mantz to at last begin buying fresh merchandise again. Just Sweats also hired a public relations and advertising firm that launched a local campaign to bolster the Just Sweats image.

In due course the firm began getting back on its feet. With the able assistance of loyal and indefatigable people like Paul Colgan, Melissa Mantz, the company's legal advisers, Hawkins had succeeded in cleaning up the mess left by Hanson. Above all, Hawkins seemed convinced now that the company needed an experienced professional manager to come in and take charge of Just Sweats' day-to-day operations.

And so as winter loosened its grip on the heartlands, there were many people in Columbus who believed that Just Sweats soon would be poised once more to attain new heights.

A Full Accounting

On a blustery March afternoon, Edwin A. Laramee was reading the Sunday paper in his ranch-style house in a fashionably semi-rural Columbus suburb when a "blind" want ad in the *Dispatch* caught his eye. It said a locally headquartered company was looking for an experienced comptroller. It didn't give much detail, but invited interested persons to submit a resumé and write for more details.

Laramee, forty-six, was immediately interested. A native of Boston, he had moved to Columbus right after graduating from the Bentley College of Accounting and Finance in Waltham, Massachusetts. For the next two decades, Laramee had worked as an accountant for a succession of clothing stores and shoe retailers throughout Ohio.

But if his resumé seemed checkered, it was because of the proliferation of corporate mergers and acquisitions during the laissez-faire era of the Reagan Administration. No sooner had he settled comfortably into one job, it seemed, before the company was either bought out by another or had taken over somebody else. This may have been great for the junk-bond kings, but it meant uncertainty and chaos for tens of thousands of salaried employees.

In the 1980s alone, Laramee faced the prospect of moving his family to Cincinnati, Florida, Texas, and New York. But he and his wife had developed strong roots in Columbus and they had no desire to leave. Also, they had a son at Ohio State and a daughter still in high school. When one job took Laramee to Cleveland, he simply bought himself a sports car and began commuting on weekends. But that job had ended in the fall, and since then Laramee had been on the lookout for work closer to home.

Hence when he saw a local firm's ad for a comptroller that Sunday afternoon, Laramee wasted little time in responding. A few days later, he got a call from John Hawkins. It was the first time Laramee had ever heard of Just Sweats. At Hawkins's invitation, Laramee went to the company's downtown headquarters several evenings later to meet the businessman after office hours.

Walking across the virtually empty company parking lot, Laramee was impressed to see by the front door a shiny Mercedes-Benz and a brand-new Porsche parked side by side. He knocked on the door and waited, checking the knot of his tie one last time.

Then a handsome, well-built young man with an engaging smile opened the door to let him in. He was wearing sneakers, shorts, and a sweatshirt, and his long, dark curls tumbled out from under a Chicago Cubs baseball cap. Laramee wasn't sure who the man was until he introduced himself. "Hi, I'm John Hawkins," he said with a smile, extending his hand. "I'll be right with you."

Laramee could barely conceal his surprise. "I was a little taken aback because he was so young," he recalled.

Soon Hawkins emerged from his back office, and the two of them walked across East Broad Street to a stylish restaurant called Vasso's and, over lamb chops and prime rib, began getting to know one another. Hawkins was his usual animated self and did much of the talking. "He was very charismatic and enthusiastic about the business," Laramee recalled. Initially, Laramee thought to himself that the niche that Just Sweats had staked out was too narrow. But the more Hawkins elaborated on the concept, the more he became convinced of its genius. "Everyone from toddlers to grandmothers are wearing sweats," he thought.

But the thing that Laramee would remember the most about the entire evening was Hawkins's candor.

As other diners came and went, Hawkins spared no detail, from Missy Hughes's early financial backing to Gene Hanson's embezzlement just two months earlier. Hawkins's recitation left Laramee somewhat dumbfounded. And so he just sat there listening as Hawkins rambled on.

Because the embezzlement had painfully underscored the company's need for sounder financial controls, Hawkins confided, the Fifth Third Bank of Columbus had strongly urged him to hire an experienced comptroller. If he did that, Hawkins said, the bank stood ready to loan him another $250,000 for expansion.

Nearly three hours later, Laramee and Hawkins emerged from Vasso's into the chilly Columbus night. When they got back across the street to Just Sweats, the office's front doors were locked and Hawkins didn't have his keys with him. The president of the company had been locked out.

Laramee offered Hawkins a ride anywhere he needed to go. But Hawkins declined, sure that someone would be coming along any minute with a key.

A few nights later, the two had a second dinner at Vasso's. This time the conversation was more like a conventional job interview, with plenty of give-and-take before Hawkins and Laramee finally got down to the specific responsibilities of the job. Hawkins said he needed someone to take over the duties of Paul Colgan, whose performance he had found wanting. Laramee said that with some sound advice from smart lawyers and reliable CPAs—along with a crack in-house comptroller—he saw no reason why Just Sweats could not quickly and fully recover and then go forward from there. John Hawkins's charm had worked its magic once more; Laramee became a true believer.

Several days later, Hawkins called to offer him the job. Laramee was elated. They picked March 22 as his starting date. It is a day now etched in his memory, for this was one career move that Laramee soon would live to regret.

Good-bye, Gene

Ed Laramee hit the ground running and never looked back. Like a whirlwind, he toured Just Sweats stores in Kentucky as well as in Ohio, stopping to chat with employees and store managers alike, taking inventory and watching with a broad smile as trucks bearing new shipments of merchandise finally began arriving again.

Back at headquarters, rather than taking a corner office, Laramee shrewdly opted for a desk in the general, open area—a more strategic vantage point from which to monitor the flow of information and people. From that perch Laramee quickly saw that nearly every aspect of Just Sweats' operations, like its financial data management, was in a state of disarray. "They had had phenomenal success and they were just overwhelmed," he said.

With Gene Hanson long gone from Just Sweats, Ed Laramee now was the "granddaddy" at the Just Sweats headquarters. Most everybody else there was still in their twenties. Laramee, a wiry man with a wry sense of humor, good-naturedly went along with his new role, and eventually he too got swept up by the infectious enthusiasm of the bright, eager kids at the office. In time he stopped wearing neckties to work, although he still didn't feel entirely comfortable showing up in sneakers, as everyone else did.

With Laramee's arrival, Colgan was given the title of treasurer but few of the duties traditionally invested in such an office. It became Colgan's responsibility to clean up the company books and help the outside accountants prepare the firm's year-end financial statements. Just Sweats operated on a fiscal year that ended May 31.

Laramee, meanwhile, was to focus on the coming fiscal year, with a mandate to implement sound fiscal controls, thus starting more or less with a clean slate. Even so, he couldn't help noticing that the books were in a total mess—months behind. Laramee was further appalled by the lack of data on inventories—the lifeline of such a fast-moving retail business. "They didn't know what inventory was where," he said.

Aside from the continuing calls and visits from bankers, vendors, suppliers, and other creditors, prospective investors also were still calling Just Sweats almost daily, looking for franchise opportunities—despite its recent troubles. "Everyone wanted to make a deal. It was incredible," Laramee recalled.

As things gradually moved toward an even keel, Hawkins once more, following a now familiar pattern, began losing interest in the company's day-to-day affairs. His presence at the office again could no longer be counted on. Often he would disappear for days at a time, and nobody knew how to reach him. "I was never sure if John was going to be in," Laramee said. "And if he was around, I wasn't sure what he was going to be working on."

Increasingly, Hawkins seemed to be detaching himself from Just Sweats. He didn't seem interested even when Laramee brought up serious company matters to discuss. "He just didn't seem to pay a whole lot of attention to them," Laramee recalled.

About the only thing that Hawkins did focus on was the company's need for more cash. On numerous occasions he talked openly about the $1.5 million in life insurance that he would collect after Gene Hanson, supposedly gravely ill out in California, had departed from this life. The company sure could use such an infusion of capital, Hawkins would say.

The first time Laramee heard Hawkins talk this way, he reacted viscerally, snapping: "You can't spend what you don't have."

"I know Gene isn't dead yet," Hawkins replied, unfazed. "It's just a book-making arrangement."

Still, Hawkins was obsessed with the idea that Hanson would soon die, and he continued to openly anticipate receiving $1.5 million in death benefits. The final time Laramee heard Hawkins speak this way was early on Monday morning, April 18. Hawkins was standing in the door to Colgan's office, talking to the company's treasurer when Laramee happened by and overheard Hawkins.

Laramee interrupted him and said with unconcealed exasperation: "John, you can't base business decisions on those kinds of assumptions!"

Hawkins turned to Laramee and said innocently, "Oh, didn't you hear? Gene died. That's where I was over the weekend. I was out there making the arrangements."

A New Beginning

In the days and weeks following Gene Hanson's death, John Hawkins was not a pleasant fellow to be around. But it had nothing to do with being morose over the death of his friend and former business partner. Rather, Hawkins was growing more irritatingly impatient by the day about getting the $1.5 million payoff from the insurance companies.

And no one found it harder to be around Hawkins than his roommate and fellow party animal, Erik De Sando. Whether at the gym over a workout or at home across the breakfast table, Hawkins badgered De Sando with questions about insurance. To Hawkins there was no better person than De Sando to furnish the answers, since his roommate now was working full-time as an insurance salesman.

De Sando, on the other hand, was peeved by the constant barrage of questions. Only weeks earlier, he had gently tried to engage Hawkins in a discussion about insurance, hoping to entice Hawkins and Hanson to change their insurance carrier, bringing their business to De Sando's new employer. But Hawkins could not be bothered. Eventually, De Sando let the matter drop. "It was really kind of a strain on our relationship," he recalled.

But now, suddenly, with Hanson's death, Hawkins couldn't get enough talk about insurance.

"What," he asked De Sando, "if a man fell off a boat and the body was never found? Could the beneficiary collect his life insurance?"

"What if the coroner in L.A. found the presence of drugs in Gene? Could they rule his death a suicide?"

There seemed no end to the what-if scenarios that Hawkins posed.

"John started asking me a lot of questions about the policies. He was worried about not getting paid," De Sando said. "A lot of what happened in the doctor's office was kind of unclear, and they weren't sure if maybe Gene hadn't committed suicide, which at that point might void the policy itself, so John wouldn't be paid. So he had a lot of questions that he asked me."

At the office, Hawkins's comportment also puzzled many people. Despite its phenomenal growth Just Sweats remained a relaxed place to work. Many of its two hundred or so employees were youthful part-timers who were students at Ohio State. At company headquarters, Hawkins set the tone with his casual personal dress code. Hanson, the old man of the bunch, also had contributed to the low-key corporate culture even though he continued wearing his $800 Armani suits with their distinctive sloping lapels, slouchy fit, and casual elan.

Only about a half-dozen people worked at the cozy, laid-back Just Sweats headquarters out on East Broad Street, and everyone on that Monday morning in mid-April quickly learned of Hanson's sudden death. But, to Ed Laramee's astonishment, the mood of the office hardly changed at all. "It was strange in the sense that nothing unusual happened," he said. "It was business as usual. It was kind of like: Gene's dead. So what?"

Sure, Hanson had hardly been a beloved figure, given his brazen and clumsy attempt at embezzlement, which nearly killed the company. But still, Laramee thought, the co-founder deserved some kind of gesture.

Hawkins set the tone. He went right back to work. Among the first calls he made was to the company's lawyer, Dick Curtin. It had all happened so suddenly that something about the fast-breaking chain of events struck both Laramee and Curtin as odd—Hanson's sudden death, Hawkins's overnight trip to L.A., the autopsy, the cremation . . . and here was Hawkins, on

Monday morning, already back in town, ready to go forward—and so eager to collect the insurance money.

What the company really needed now, Hawkins told Curtin unabashedly, was the life insurance payoff. That could really help Just Sweats get off and running again. Curtin had to admit that he couldn't agree more, and he vowed to get on the telephone right away with the insurance companies.

With his lawyers quietly at work behind the scenes, Hawkins's mood lightened considerably. And he spoke openly about plowing the $1.5 million that he had coming back into the company coffers. In the meantime, the Fifth Third Bank gave Just Sweats another $200,000 loan.

As spring turned into summer, Laramee recalled, "the bills were being paid, and everybody was happy and enthused again."

After not hearing from the insurance companies for nearly eight weeks, Dick Curtin, like his client, was chafing. He realized that one issue he would need to take up with them was the question of interest on the money, which was accumulating at a rate of several hundred dollars a day. And so Curtin began calling the insurers nearly every day, trying valiantly but without much success to break through the first level of claims adjusters.

"I knew the insurance companies certainly had a right to investigate," he said. And so he and Austin Wildman offered to help the insurers in any way they could to expedite the process, never failing to remind the insurers that Hawkins desperately needed the proceeds for his business.

And when Farmers New World Life asked for Gene Hanson's dental records, Curtin was only too happy to oblige. But when he got in touch with Hanson's former dentist, he found an angry voice at the other end of the line. Never mind that his former patient was dead. The dentist said Hanson still owed him hundreds of dollars. Not only that, the dentist fumed, Hanson had repeatedly broken appointments without bothering to call ahead. Taken aback by the depth of the dentist's anger, Curtin politely endured the dentist's wrath. In the end he managed to persuade the dentist to part with Hanson's dental records.

Austin Wildman, in the meantime, tried to work with the authorities out in California, hoping to help them close out the case expeditiously. "We really wanted to help," Wildman said.

"What can we do?" he asked Detective Jim Peterson of the Glendale police department.

Nothing. Nothing at all, the cop replied icily, resentful of the distant pressure.

But all the frustrations evaporated on Friday, July 8. Amid the stack of mail that arrived at the law offices was a Farmers New World Life Insurance Company check for $1 million. Quickly a jubilant John Hawkins swung by Wildman's office to pick it up.

"I got my money!" he screamed when he tore open the envelope and saw the check.

From there Hawkins bounded down the street, heading for the Fifth Third Bank to deposit his money. He was a sight to behold, Wildman thought, chuckling to himself as he looked out his window at Hawkins. His client was wearing cutoff jeans, a loud Hawaiian shirt, and a Cleveland Indians baseball cap. The check was in Hawkins's leather briefcase.

"I'll never forget the day that he got his money," Wildman said. "Hell, we were proud of the job we had done in getting him that money."

Questions

On a muggy afternoon in early July, a perspiration-soaked mailman walked gratefully into the elegantly appointed, air-conditioned lobby of 6195 Bush Boulevard, a swanky high-rise apartment building on the North Side of Columbus. Among the mail he hoped to deliver on that day was a registered letter to John B. Hawkins. It was from the Golden Rule Insurance Company. But to the best that the mailman could determine, Hawkins was not home, and so he left a notice of attempted delivery, which further informed Hawkins that he could personally pick up the letter at the post office.

The Golden Rule letter held a check for nearly $450,000—the death benefits from one of Hanson's life insurance policies. But Hawkins never got the notice or the check, for several weeks earlier, he and De Sando had moved out hurriedly, and they had neglected to leave a forwarding address.

Hawkins and De Sando had been evicted from their apartment after getting into a nasty, name-calling dispute with the building manager. After some scrambling around, they found a nice two-bedroom condo on Ellerdale Drive, about four miles away. But after completing the move, they simply didn't get around to leaving a forwarding address—until, that is, well after the mailman tried to deliver the Golden Rule check.

And so as far as Hawkins and Dick Curtin were concerned, they still had not heard from Golden Rule. In mid-July, Curtin once more placed a call to the insurance company's headquarters in Indiana. When he politely suggested that the company's check to

Hawkins must have been lost and that perhaps Golden Rule should consider stopping payment on it, Curtin was surprised by the response of the claims supervisors at the other end of the line.

She laughed. "Oh, we'll be happy to stop payment on that check, Mr. Curtin," she finally said, "but not for the reason you might think."

Puzzled, Curtin asked to be let in on the little joke. But the woman continued to play coy, suggesting that Curtin ought to call Farmers New World Life for the real low-down.

"She acted like she didn't want to tell me," Curtin would recall.

After some further coaxing, though, the woman finally relented. She told Curtin that questions had arisen in California over the identity of the dead man. She understood, she told him, that authorities out there now believed that the dead man was somebody other than Gene Hanson.

Bewildered, Curtin called Farmers immediately. Its officials confirmed everything that the Golden Rule claims supervisor had told him—and provided even more details about the stunning development. Furthermore, they demanded to know where Hawkins was and what he had done with the $1 million.

Reeling, Curtin said he believed that his client had deposited the check right away. He said he would try to locate Hawkins immediately for a full explanation, for he too had lots of questions for Hawkins. Surely there was some mistake.

It might take a day or two to track Hawkins down, Curtin added, for he had heard that Hawkins may have left town, possibly to visit his father in Florida.

The lawyer didn't know it at the time, of course, but John Hawkins had already decided to become a fugitive.

Few Answers

With a sinking feeling, attorneys Dick Curtin and Austin Wildman silently walked the few blocks to the law offices of Emens, Hurd, Kegler & Ritter, where they had an appointment with Mel Weinstein. He had invited them over, promising to show them convincing evidence that the man who had died in California and been identified as Gene Hanson was in fact clearly not Gene Hanson at all.

Weinstein was one of about sixty lawyers in the law firm that for years had represented Farmers New World Life in Ohio. And when an alarmed John Patton, one of the insurer's senior claims managers, called in mid-July, it was Weinstein with whom he spoke.

"Mel, we've got a problem that we need you to look into," Patton said.

Initially the focus of Farmers' concern was on how Gene Hanson had died and whether he had withheld any vital medical information when he purchased the life insurance policies. But now, Patton told Weinstein, it appeared that the dead man may have been somebody other than Hanson. The insurance company might have been swindled out of $1 million.

"All there was," Weinstein recalled, "was a question of whether the corpse indeed was Hanson, based on the photographs."

Quickly getting himself up to speed on the case, Weinstein asked not only for the photographs of the corpse taken in the doctor's office and at the morgue but also other, known photographs of Hanson. In addition, Weinstein, forty, also wanted to be able to make a fingerprint comparison—a much more reliable means of identification than grainy snapshots taken by some criminalist.

Weinstein was deeply disturbed when he compared the photographs of the dead man and those of Hanson. He became even more alarmed when the very first person to whom he showed the pictures—a longtime friend of Hanson's—was not willing to say that the dead man was Hanson.

Weinstein next placed a number of calls to California and ended up speaking to a Los Angeles County coroner's investigator named Kurt Stoutsenberger. "We don't think it's the same guy either," Stoutsenberger said.

But the pictures of Hanson that authorities in L.A. possessed were either Xeroxed or faxed copies that were of poor quality, Stoutsenberger said. Weinstein advised them to get their hands on the originals, and fast.

Between the L.A. County coroner's office, the Glendale police department, the California Department of Insurance, the California Department of Motor Vehicles, and the Federal Bureau of Investigation, it took a full month before the fingerprints of the corpse and those known to be that of Hanson—taken at his 1965 Army induction in Fort Jackson—were finally compared by experts. Their unanimous verdict: The dead man was most certainly not Gene Hanson, despite what Dr. Boggs had said and despite all the IDs on the body that bore Hanson's name.

Only after Weinstein had in hand an affidavit from California authorities attesting to this fact did he telephone Curtin and Wildman one steamy afternoon, inviting them over to see for themselves.

Curtin and Wildman wasted little time getting themselves to Weinstein's office. Arriving a few minutes earlier than expected, they were ushered into a well-appointed conference room with a sweeping view of the Columbus skyline, including the oddly shaped state capitol building across the street.

They didn't wait long before Weinstein entered, carrying a folder that he put down on the mahogany con-

Richard Boggs as a child.
(Courtesy of Beulah B. Boggs)

Right: Dr. Richard P. Boggs, the young neurologist. (Courtesy of Beulah B. Boggs)

Below: Dr. Richard Boggs at his trial in the summer of 1990. (Doug Burrows)

Melvin "Gene" Hanson.

John Hawkins in Hawaii.

Melissa Mantz, the young coed who rose to the top of the
Columbus-based Just Sweats chain of clothing stores,
cofounded by Melvin Hanson and John Hawkins.

Dr. Richard Boggs's office building in downtown Glendale, California, where, he claimed, Melvin Hanson suffered a fatal heart attack in April, 1988. (Doug Burrows)

The Boggs family. From left to right: Dana, John, Heather, Lola, and Kevin. (Courtesy of Beulah B. Boggs)

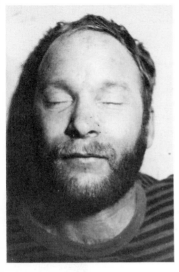

Ellis H. Greene, who only much later was identified as the corpse found in Dr. Richard Boggs's office.

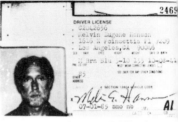

Melvin Hanson's California driver's license became an important piece of evidence for the Glendale police department.

The Bullet, the Hollywood bar where Ellis Greene had his fateful meeting with Dr. Richard Boggs. (Doug Burrows)

Vincent Volpi, the Columbus, Ohio, private detective hired to investigate Melvin Hanson's mysterious death.

Vincent Volpi's team of investigators. From left to right: Lucy Ciferno, Gus Tripodis, and Leisa Tremper.

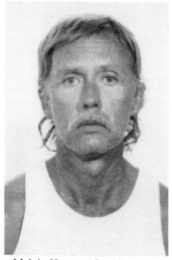

Melvin Hanson after his arrest at the Dallas-Fort Worth airport. At Tarrant County Jail, Texas, January 30, 1989.

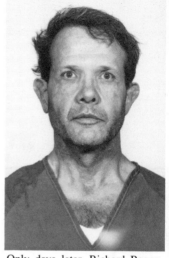

Only days later, Richard Boggs was apprehended in California. At Los Angeles County Sheriff's Department, February 6, 1989.

John Hawkins in early 1988 before fleeing the United States.

Jon Perkins (left), the Glendale homicide detective who worked on the case, and Al MacKenzie, the Los Angeles County Deputy District Attorney who prosecuted Dr. Richard Boggs. (Doug Burrows)

Dale Rubin, the chief defense counsel for Dr. Richard Boggs. (Doug Burrows)

Charles Lindner, the second of Dr. Richard Boggs's attorneys. (Doug Burrows)

John Hawkins, with a drastically new appearance, about one year before his arrest in Sardinia on August 2, 1991.

John Hawkins, the fugitive.

ference table. Inside were a number of photographs, among them a full-face shot of the dead man previously identified as Gene Hanson. With Weinstein looking on, perhaps a bit too smugly, Curtin and Wildman realized instantly that their worst fears had been confirmed. There was no way the dead man was Gene Hanson.

"It was clear," Curtin recalled later. "It wasn't even close. It was the final nail in the coffin."

The two lawyers left Weinstein's office in a state of shock, knowing full well now that, in Wildman's words, "a giant scam had taken place." The two certainly had nothing to hide, but they both realized that at that very moment they themselves probably were being regarded as possible accomplices.

After they left, Weinstein rushed to the Franklin County Common Pleas Court and obtained from Judge Dale A. Crawford a temporary restraining order barring John Hawkins from spending the $1 million that he had received from Farmers'.

Hawkins, of course, was not present during that August 24 court session. By then he had been gone for nearly six weeks. Like Hanson, he had vanished.

And out in California, red-faced officials still couldn't say who the dead man was.

A Second Look

One muggy day in late June 1988, Kurt Stoutsenberger was summoned by his boss, the head of a special operations unit at the Los Angeles County coroner's office. Carl Harris had received a hot tip that he wanted Stoutsenberger to check out immediately—and as discreetly as possible.

Earlier in the day, Harris had gotten a call from a friend who was a retired Los Angeles police department homicide detective. The friend, now a private investigator, suggested that the coroner's new special operations unit really ought to take a closer look at a case up in Glendale involving a man named Gene Hanson, especially at the mysterious circumstances under which the corpse had been identified. The rumor going around was that the body was not Gene Hanson at all, that it had been deliberately mis-identified as a part of an elaborate insurance-fraud scheme. Harris was grateful for the tip, for he had not heard that rumor yet.

Right away Harris decided that twenty-nine-year-old Stoutsenberger was the right investigator for the sensitive assignment. The thoughtful young man was diligent, smart, and, above all, tactful—a quality that would surely come in handy if the investigation should prove that someone else within the coroner's office had botched the initial, routine probe.

The unit that Harris headed had been created only a few months earlier—as a response to the rash of insurance scams in the 1980s involving fraudulent death certificates, although rarely involving murder. Even though Stoutsenberger had been with the coroner's office only two years, he had been among the first to be chosen for the elite unit, having proven himself as a sharp-eyed investigator of the first order.

After conferring with Harris, Stoutsenberger went straight to work on the case. And when he pulled out the case file and began studying the facts surrounding the verification of the dead man's identity, Stoutsenberger was immediately intrigued. The doctor had acted suspiciously, having seemed overly eager to sign a death certificate and dispatch the corpse to the mortuary. Luckily, two local patrol officers had summoned the coroner's office, whose personnel not only examined the body but also took fingerprints. After further studying the various after-action reports, compiled by Glendale police officers Jim Lowrey and Tim Spruill, by the firefighters, and by the paramedics, the inconsistencies in the statements given by Dr. Richard Boggs leaped out at Stoutsenberger. The case was rife with all the hallmarks of an insurance scam. Perhaps it involved only a case of deliberate mis-identification. But maybe it also involved murder. Stoutsenberger quickly realized that there were ample grounds for deep suspicion.

Eager as he was to proceed, he was also stumped. "There really wasn't a whole lot to prove that the dead guy was who they said he was," he recalled. Yet as far as the coroner's office was concerned, the case was closed. The man had died of natural causes. Hadn't Dr. Evancia Sy said so after conducting a thorough autopsy?

Stoutsenberger picked up the telephone and dialed the Glendale police department. He was stunned by what detective Jim Peterson told him. Yes, Peterson admitted, he too had come to suspect that there had been a mis-identification in the case. Yet Peterson seemed unprepared or unwilling to act upon that belief. "Until the coroner's office comes up with a cause of death," Peterson insisted, "we're not going to do anything."

Frustrated by Peterson's rigidity, Stoutsenberger was feeling further pressure because by then representatives of the various insurance companies, especially Mel Weinstein in Ohio, were clamoring increasingly for authorities in California to take some sort of action. Yet Stoutsenberger felt blocked by Peterson's unyielding attitude.

"Most of the stuff we get involved with is pretty much routine—to determine the cause of death and mode. We're not into prosecuting murders or looking for suspects and things like that," Stoutsenberger recalled later. "Typically, we go in, gather, protect, and preserve evidence. Take pictures. The basics. Prosecuting a murder case really wasn't the coroner's office's function," he said. "But we were getting nowhere with the Glendale P.D."

Peterson resolutely refused to budge from the position that, a likely mis-identification notwithstanding, there was no homicide, and so there could be no murder investigation—unless the coroner's office ruled that a homicide had occurred. In the meantime, the official cause of death—non-specific focal myocarditis—would stand. Peterson, in effect, booted the ball back into Stoutsenberger's lap. The detective was treating the case like a hot potato, Stoutsenberger thought.

Still, he had to admit that Peterson had a point. The government cannot simply change a cause of death on a certificate without ample documentation and proof. And in this case, any effort to revise the cause of death would be extraordinarily difficult, for the corpse in question could not be exhumed for additional forensics tests. John Hawkins had had it cremated almost right away.

Still, Stoutsenberger was determined to press on, meeting several more times with Peterson, as well as with other Glendale police officers, all to no avail. "There was plenty of circumstantial evidence that certainly justified a deeper look. But Glendale just wasn't wiling to do that," he recalled.

In the meantime, Stoutsenberger continued to keep Dr. Sy apprised of the progress of his investigation. She was one of the first people he had called after taking on the case, and from the start the physician was extremely cooperative—despite the fact that the fruits of Stoutsenberger's investigation might cast her in a less than positive light. In fact, almost immediately Sy was open-minded about eventually amending the cause of the death on the man's death certificate. And for that Stoutsenberger breathed a sigh of relief. It was one less battle that he might have to wage.

Together he and Sy strengthened their suspicions that foul play, and possibly murder, had been committed. And gradually they knew that it was now only a matter of time before Sy would have to go to her supervisors to say that the coroner's office must amend the death certificate. Such action, they both also realized, inevitably entailed a massive amount of red tape all the way up to Sacramento. Affidavits from all sorts of investigators, representing different agencies—many with competing interests and agenda—would have to be obtained, typed up, signed, and notarized. Fresh evidence had to be marshaled. Prosecutors would have to be brought on board. It would be a massive undertaking, but it had to begin with the basics.

Above all, Stoutsenberger knew he had to figure out who, if not Gene Hanson, the dead person was. Only then can a man's name, date and place of birth, the next of kin, along with all the other vital information be entered into the amended death certificate. "We knew it was just a matter time, and we wanted to do it all at once and not by piecemeal," Stoutsenberger said.

He set out in earnest to learn the true identity of the mystery dead man. And he wanted to do it quietly to avoid tipping off Dr. Boggs to his investigation. The arrogant doctor was going about his business as usual, seemingly unfazed by the curious case and the many new questions that it was arousing.

Stoutsenberger was barely underway when, much to his chagrin, distant rumblings from Columbus in late August forced his hand, leaving him little alternative but to immediately go and confront the doctor.

House Calls

In the summer of 1988, Mike Jones was clearly a young man on the fast track. After several weeks off, the burly criminal investigator was back on the job at the fraud bureau of the California Department of Insurance. Jones, thirty-one, had taken time off to study for and then take the grueling three-day California Bar exam. Then he underwent a back operation. To recover from both ordeals, Jones, his wife, Kim, and their son, David, had gone to visit Kim's family up in Northern California.

Back now at the office, Jones was looking forward to resuming his duties, which included undercover work to bust large rings that staged accidents throughout Southern California to bilk insurance companies. It would be months before Jones knew whether or not he had passed the difficult bar examination. Known as the toughest in the nation, the California Bar's pass-rate was less than fifty percent. But Jones didn't mind waiting it out. After attending night law school for five years, while holding down a full-time job, what's another few months?

In the meantime, Jones was again enjoying the work in the fraud bureau's six-member Los Angeles office. Aside from conducting investigations, Jones especially enjoyed the many paralegal duties his job entailed, such as going to court to obtain search warrants.

On his second week back, as the noon hour approached, Jones's telephone rang. The caller identified himself as Kurt Stoutsenberger, an investigator at the Los Angeles County coroner's office. And he needed help.

Having been bounced from one agency to another in a classic bureaucratic run-around, Stoutsenberger wasted little time getting to the heart of the matter, knowing that he had but a few minutes—if that—to interest Jones.

But after Jones heard the bare-bones outline of the case, he too was immediately intrigued—and shocked by the refusal of the Glendale police department to conduct a thorough investigation. "I knew two things," Jones would recall. "Either they killed a guy or stole a body."

But stealing a body, Jones thought, seemed unlikely. Such a risky undertaking would have had to involve many people, and one of them surely would have snitched by now, what with the heat that authorities were beginning to apply. Still, Jones couldn't as yet rule out the possibility that Dr. Boggs, Gene Hanson, and John Hawkins had somehow obtained a corpse, perhaps from a hospital, and passed it off as Hanson.

It seemed far more likely the trio had murdered someone instead.

"We've got to put a finger on the doctor right now," Jones told Stoutsenberger.

Though it was lunch hour, Stoutsenberger readily agreed to meet Jones. You name the time and place, he said. The logical starting point was the Glendale police department. The investigators decided to pay detective Jim Peterson a visit.

The elated coroner's investigator could hardly believe his good fortune. Someone at last was interested in the case—indeed, excited. Only a day earlier, Stoutsenberger had felt a sense of urgency that bordered on panic. Word had reached him that a Franklin County Court of Common Pleas judge in Ohio on August 24 had granted Farmers New World Life a temporary restraining order that barred John Hawkins from spending any of the insurance proceeds. That ruling was immediately picked up by the *Columbus Dispatch*. Its story the next day was headlined: " 'Wrong' corpse at heart of insurance suit."

Stoutsenberger was dismayed to learn that the brewing scandal had gone public in Ohio. He had hoped to keep his sleuthing under wraps until he had at least learned the identity of the dead man. But now the news from Ohio might very well prompt Dr. Boggs to destroy any incriminating evidence—and possibly even flee.

"At that point we didn't really know for sure if Boggs was aware that there was now a criminal investigation going on," Stoutsenberger recalled.

He realized right away that he needed to consult a prosecutor about making a move against the doctor. "It wasn't like we suddenly decided that we had the case all wrapped up," Stoutsenberger said.

He didn't know any Los Angeles County prosecutors, but his partner, Ranney Pageler, had recently been involved in helping prosecute a case out in San Fernando Valley. And so Pageler called the deputy D.A. with whom he had worked for advice. After outlining the case, the prosecutor told Pageler and Stoutsenberger to call the medical-legal division in the 800-lawyer D.A.'s office.

But when the two investigators called there, the prosecutor in charge told them that it sounded more like a case for the major fraud section instead.

Finally, Stoutsenberger reached a deputy district attorney named Albert MacKenzie, a low-key but experienced white-collar crime prosecutor. Stoutsenberger spared few details as he laid out the still unfolding case for MacKenzie.

"What should we do?" he asked when done.

Go talk to Dr. Boggs immediately, MacKenzie advised noncommitally. The prosecutor also suggested that Stoutsenberger call Hal Huber, a supervisor that MacKenzie knew at the California Department of Insurance's fraud bureau across town.

Stoutsenberger took MacKenzie's advice on both counts. "But when I called the doctor's office, I got three different stories for where he was," he recalled. The run-around only further strengthened Stoutsenberger's determination to unravel the case.

His next call was to Mike Jones, placed at Huber's

suggestion. Jones immediately sensed Stoutsenberger's utter frustration and uncertainty about what to do next.

"Let's just go over there," Jones now was telling Stoutsenberger.

"I'll see you there in a half hour," Stoutsenberger replied exuberantly.

Already hooked on the case, Jones badly wanted to get an immediate look at the doctor as well as to acquire a sense of what evidence might still be available at the doctor's office. For one thing, Jones wanted to confirm, by seeing for himself, the existence of a medical file for Gene Hanson. Such a document would be among the top items that Jones would list on any request for a search warrant.

At the two-story headquarters of the Glendale police department. Jones told detective Peterson that he and Stoutsenberger strongly suspected that a million-dollar insurance fraud had taken place, possibly involving first-degree murder. But, just as Stoutsenberger had predicted, Peterson reacted with bemused tolerance.

"That's not what the coroner's office found," the detective said with a chuckle. "Until we're told that we have a homicide, we don't have a homicide," he added. Turning now to Stoutsenberger, Peterson said: "You're the ones who make the determination."

Still, the investigators invited Peterson to help them delve into the matter. They told the detective that they were heading for Boggs's office and asked Peterson if he would like to join them. But the detective begged off. He had too much work to do.

It was late in the afternoon by the time Jones and Stoutsenberger arrived at 540 North Central Avenue. After they identified themselves to Jean Walker, the receptionist said curtly that Boggs was not in and furthermore she didn't know when he would be back.

Jones and Stoutsenberger decided to take a seat in the deserted waiting area. Studying the tattered lounge, with its well-worn furniture and dog-eared magazines, Jones knew that this was the office of a down-and-out physician—not at all unlike those he had seen dozens of times over the past few years while investigating medical-insurance frauds all over Southern California. But one big difference was that the other clinics typically were located in ghettos and other low-income areas. But this was ritzy, upscale Glendale. Something didn't seem to quite add up. Still, judging by the shabbiness of the office, Jones was convinced that Boggs had to be surviving on scams of one sort or another. The doctor clearly wasn't making a living treating patients.

Jones and Stoutsenberger waited and waited, but there was no sign of Boggs. Finally they gave up. Next, they drove over to the doctor's home on Belmont Street. But he wasn't there either. The two investigators decided to return the next day—with a subpoena.

Much to Stoutsenberger's amazement, by the time he got back to his office in downtown Los Angeles, Boggs had already telephoned his boss, Carl Harris, saying angrily that he had friends on the Los Angeles County Board of Supervisors and that he could cause a lot of trouble for the coroner's office, which already was under fire for shoddy management practices unrelated to the Hanson case. At last, Stoutsenberger thought, the doctor was beginning to feel the heat.

Early the next morning, armed with a mugshot of Gene Hanson that Stoutsenberger had obtained from the California Department of Motor Vehicles, the two investigators returned to 540 North Central. They went straight to Riley's Pharmacy on the building's ground floor and began interviewing its employees. One of them, Brian Archambault, had worked there for six years, and he said he was very familiar with both Boggs and one of the doctor's long-time patients, Gene Hanson.

Then Jones discreetly pulled Archambault to the side and showed him what cops call a ''six-pack''—mug shots of six different people, used for purposes of identification. Among the six-pack that Jones now held was one taken of the dead man whom Boggs had identified as Gene Hanson.

"Do you recognize anyone in these photographs?" Jones asked Archambault.

The druggist did not. No, he said, Gene Hanson is not in this group.

Next, Jones pulled out a second, different six-pack. This time there was no photograph of the dead man. Instead, among the six mug shots was the one of Gene Hanson.

"That," Archambault said without hesitation, pointing to Hanson's mug shot, "is Gene Hanson." Archambault was dead certain: The man who had died in Boggs's office was not Gene Hanson.

By now Jones was eager to get at the doctor—especially after a second Riley's employee corroborated everything that Archambault had said. Jones and Stoutsenberger thanked the druggists and then quickly went upstairs. On the way, Jones patted his jacket pocket to make sure the subpoena was there. In another pocket were the two six-packs. As they rode up in the small elevator, Jones no longer harbored an iota of doubt that Boggs had been in on the insurance scam, quite possibly involving murder.

Even earlier that morning, before Jones and Stoutsenberger had arrived at the medical building, the coroner's investigator had called Boggs, managing to reach the doctor at his office. He told Boggs that he and Jones needed to speak to him right away, and in person.

"Let me check my schedule and I'll call you back," Boggs replied, business-like.

About twenty minutes later, the doctor called to say that the best he could do was to meet with them at four that day. That's fine, Stoutsenberger agreed.

Instead, however, he and Jones decided to show up early, dropping in on Boggs at two. This time they found Boggs. Just minutes earlier, the doctor had finished seeing his only patient of the day. Had he and Stoutsenberger waited until four, Jones suspected, the doctor probably would not have been around.

Initially, Boggs seemed cooperative about turning over

Gene Hanson's file. "I'll get it copied and get it to you," Boggs said. "I don't want you to take the file."

No, Jones replied. "We have a subpoena for the file and we're not leaving without it."

Boggs, peeved, once more telephoned Carl Harris at the coroner's office to complain. Harris listened politely and then asked to speak to Stoutsenberger. "How do you feel about Boggs? Do you trust him?" Harris asked.

No, Stoutsenberger replied. "If we leave without it, God knows what he will do with it."

"Okay," Harris said. "Don't come back without that file."

Harris's support was reassuring, though hardly surprising. And Stoutsenberger hardly needed to relate Harris's order to Jones or Boggs, who were right there during the entire conversation.

Finally the doctor gave in. But his Xerox machine was broken. So he and the investigators went to the medical suite next door and, page by page, laboriously copied the half-inch file. Jones was grateful to have the extra time simply to observe Boggs. Afterward, they returned to the doctor's office and sat in the empty waiting room for an interview. Over the course of the next hour, the doctor once more went over the events that he said had taken place in the early morning hours of April 16. But Jones found the doctor not at all convincing—seeming to feign memory lapses whenever convenient.

Finally, Jones pulled out his two six-packs.

"That's Gene Hanson," Boggs said without hesitation, pointing at the mug shot of the man who had died in his office more than four months earlier. It was, of course, the man that the druggist downstairs had said was not Gene Hanson.

"You're full of shit," Jones snapped at the doctor, barely concealing his contempt.

"How can you say that's Gene Hanson when others say *this* is Gene Hanson?" Jones added, pointing now to the second six-pack, jabbing at the California DMV picture of Hanson. *"That's* Gene Hanson, Doctor," Jones said.

"No comment," Boggs said, somewhat flustered as he averted his eyes. Quickly the doctor seemed to realize that he had erred.

"Then why," Boggs thundered, pointing at the picture of the dead man he had identified as Hanson, "has this person been coming here for seven years as Gene Hanson?"

Jones and Stoutsenberger stared back at Boggs, saying nothing.

Becoming defensive, the doctor suggested that the investigators track down Gene Hanson and John Hawkins and interview *them*. "If there's been a scam, I'd like to know about it too," Boggs said with exaggerated irritation.

Jones knew it was time for some straight talk.

"I know, and you know, that you guys pulled a scam," he told Boggs, staring coldly at the doctor with unblinking eyes. "And this is your only opportunity to tell me."

For a split second, fear seemed to flicker across the arrogant neurologist's face. Then he became defiant once more.

"You are a stubborn asshole," he told Jones.

The investigator didn't bother to reply. Instead, Jones vowed to proceed methodically to nail the doctor and put him on Death Row in San Quentin.

As the investigators left Boggs's office, Jones stopped at the door. Turning back to the doctor, he said, "I'm going to get to the bottom of this. I'm not going to set this aside—like the Glendale P.D. You'll be hearing from me again."

Now it was Boggs who said nothing. Standing there in the empty waiting room, in his rumpled trousers that were torn in the back, Boggs for the first time looked downright frightened. Then he turned his back on the investigators and went back into his office.

Back at his own office, Jones began drafting an affidavit for a search warrant. There would be no more pretense. Richard Boggs was now a prime murder suspect.

But just whom had he murdered?

A Perfect Match

Mike Jones felt guilty every time he looked at the tall stack of missing-persons reports sitting neglected on a corner of his desk. For weeks he had been pestering Kurt Stoutsenberger to figure out a way to retrieve the reports through a computer, hoping to find in them some clue as to the identity of the dead man found in Dr. Richard Boggs's office.

But for days after Stoutsenberger finally got them to him, Jones had been unable to find time to go through them with a fine-toothed comb. Despite his abiding interest in the Boggs case, Jones had other duties at the fraud bureau, including participating in a federal task force that was investigating a huge ring of doctors and mobile laboratories that was bilking insurers out of millions of dollars by submitting bills for phony and unnecessary lab tests. And that wasn't all. Jones also was investigating a similar but separate ring, comprised mostly of doctors who were Russian emigres.

What really turned Jones on, though, was going undercover. And in the summer of 1988, Jones participated in a bureau investigation that was looking into a huge ring that was bilking insurance companies by staging auto accidents and then submitting vastly inflated repair and medical bills.

The fraud bureau first got involved when an informant approached it. Because the informant was a female, investigator Kathy Scholz was assigned to the case, posing as a girlfriend of the informant. Then to further maintain Scholz's cover, Jones volunteered to pose as Scholz's boyfriend.

Together, and wired for sound, Jones and Scholz

quickly managed to infiltrate the ring, which included not only body repairmen, mechanics, and drivers who actually staged the accidents but also doctors and lawyers. Typically, a newcomer such as Jones would receive $3,000 for allowing his car to be used in the scam, depending on the particulars of his insurance policy. The contrived damage usually was maxed out to the full extent of one's coverage. Often the schemes also involved fake "soft tissues" injuries that were hard to prove, netting additional sums in "pain and suffering" for the perpetrators.

It was such derring-do that Jones most enjoyed about his job. "Uncovering fraud is interesting. You have to think," he explained. Thus he volunteered frequently for such undercover operations. Indeed, such a spirit and willingness to help out permeated the closely knit fraud bureau. And thus it was that one late September evening, when Jones decided to stay late to go through the missing-persons reports, his "girlfriend" in the sting operation, Kathy Scholz, volunteered to help him.

Grateful, Jones readily accepted her offer. Despite his guilt, in the past few days he had managed to comb through some of the reports, weeding out those that obviously had no connection to the dead man found in Boggs's office, such as race or age, while highlighting portions of other reports that seemed to merit a closer look.

Jones took a stack for himself and handed Scholz another. They began methodically going through the reports, looking for details and descriptions that might match those of the dead man.

It had not been an easy job getting the reports in the first place. After both Jones and Stoutsenberger became convinced that the dead man was not Gene Hanson, they reckoned that somewhere, someone must have filed a missing-persons report on the man who died in Boggs's office. If they could only come up with his name . . .

They both knew of the National Crime Information Center, a vast computer network operated by the federal government that supports a variety of law enforcement activities throughout the country. One of its functions is to serve as a clearinghouse of information on missing persons and unidentified bodies.

But in 1988, the Los Angeles County coroner's office was so overwhelmed with work that the computer linking it into the NCIC was just sitting there, rarely used by anyone at the office.

Indeed, one of the goals of the office's newly created special operations unit was to get that system up and running. And now Jones and Stoutsenberger, investigating a possible homicide involving an unidentified body, desperately needed to tap into the network. It was, they figured, a last shot at learning the identity of the dead man. "I didn't know the system that well, and I frankly didn't have much faith in it. I mean, it was so massive," Stoutsenberger recalled. "But we had tried everything else. So I just thought, what did we have to lose?"

No one in the coroner's office even knew how to gain entry into the electronic network, so Stoutsenberger himself had to sit down at the long-neglected computer terminal and spend the better part of several days laboriously consulting a manual and slowly figuring out how to do it. "It was all so precise," he said. "You had to have the exact codes and commands." But his persistence paid off. He finally managed to gain access into the network and entered all the information he possessed on the nameless dead man—his apparent age, clothing, and all the physical characteristics, from hair and eye color to teeth condition.

To Stoutsenberger's delight, within twenty-four hours he had a long printout containing the descriptions of all the missing persons who fit the general description of the dead man in L.A. There were seventy-six in all. "They were from all over, and I mean all over. Not just the West, but the East and the South—even Canada," he recalled.

The prospect of going through them one by one was a bit overwhelming as Jones and Scholz sat down at their desks. But before long, Scholz hit paydirt.

One thing that the investigators had going for them was the unusually detailed information they had on the dead person. The corpse had not been decomposed when it was photographed. As a result, Stoutsenberger was able to describe it to a *T*—the man's pants, the shirt right down to the stripes, the cowboy boots, even a detailed physical description.

It turned out that of the seventy-six missing-persons cases in the printouts, only one subject had been reported missing the night of April 15—and only about eight hours before a body was found in Dr. Boggs's office. "This one looks good," Scholz told Jones. Looking up, Jones quickly scanned it and agreed. He felt his excitement mounting. According to the missing-persons report, the subject had last been seen in North Hollywood.

"That," he said, "is just too coincidental!"

The report had been filed jointly with the Los Angeles police department by a North Hollywood woman named Cleo Fasulo and a Burbank certified public accountant named Parker Martin—the aunt and the employer of Ellis Henry Greene, the missing man. The two had told police that Greene was last seen alive by a friend, Chip Suntheimer, entering a bar called The Bullet on the night of April 15.

His fingers trembling, Jones quickly punched in Stoutsenberger's number at work. The young investigator also was working late. Jones asked him to get the snapshot of the dead man in Boggs's office.

In a few seconds, he told Jones, Okay, go ahead.

Then Jones began reading from the missing person report filed by Fasulo and Martin. As he did, it was as if he had been looking at the snapshot over Stoutsenberger's shoulder.

It was a perfect match.

At long last, Jones realized, they had learned the identity of the dead man that Dr. Boggs had misidentified as Gene Hanson, a longtime patient, and that John Hawkins had so hastily cremated.

As Jones hung up, he noticed Ellis Greene's date of birth: September 29, 1956. It would have been

Greene's thirty-second birthday. "Happy birthday, Ellis," he said.

Just to be certain, Jones also ordered up a fingerprint comparison. It too confirmed that the dead man was Ellis Greene.

When Cleo Fasulo saw the pictures of the dead man taken at the crime scene, she broke down and wept. Yes, she said, that was Ellis.

Last Call

It was nine-thirty on a Friday night, and on any other night of the year the post office would have been deserted. But this was April 15—the annual tax-filing deadline, and the Van Nuys post office was a bustle of activity as taxpayers streamed into the little building to mail their forms before midnight. Amid the gridlock out front, virtually unnoticed, was a young bearded man who had set up shop on the trunk of a car, helping an older woman finish her tax return.

That was just like Ellis Greene—always willing to help someone in distress, even strangers.

He had accompanied a buddy, Chip Suntheimer, to the post office so Suntheimer could mail his return—which Greene had just finished typing up. At the post office, Greene waited outside with a third friend as Suntheimer went in to mail his returns. While hanging out, Greene had casually struck up a conversation with the woman and then discovered that she had mistakenly prepared two federal returns but no state return.

No problem, Greene told her. With a flourish he took the woman's returns, pulled out assorted pieces of scrap paper, and began preparing a state tax return for her on the spot. "He set up a desk on the back of my car and did her whole state return from beginning to end," Suntheimer recalled, marveling at the memory.

Greene had always been an outgoing, caring person. "He'd give you the shirt off his back even if he knew he was going to starve tomorrow," said Darlene Greene, his mother.

Ellis Greene never starved but there had been some

pretty lean times. Greene was no drifter, but his family members, mostly back in Ohio, did not always know where he was or what he was going to get by. He seemed aimless, unsure about what he wanted to do or become in life—especially after his divorce, when he came out of the closet as a gay.

Greene and his twin brother, Basil, were born in San Diego. But before they had entered first grade, their parents, Harry and Darlene Greene, moved to Powhatan Point, Ohio, a sooty blue-collar community in the forlorn Ohio River valley, where Harry Greene took a job with U.S. Locks in nearby Clarington.

Ellis Greene was no scholar either. By 1973, while a junior at River Local High School, he dropped out and joined the Army. "Ellis was a boy who couldn't be content, but he wasn't a bum," his mother said. After he got out of the Army, Greene returned to Ohio and worked as an accountant at several medical facilities and at the Ohio Payroll Processing Company in Columbus.

In 1979, he married a southern Ohio woman and they moved out to California, where he held down a job at Western Medical Enterprises. But just three years later, they separated and eventually divorced. After that Greene seemed to lose direction in his life, and he began bouncing back and forth between Ohio and California, at one point performing menial tasks at a temporary medical service firm in Belmont County, Ohio.

By 1987, Greene was back for good in his native Southern California. If he arrived without a drug or alcohol habit, it didn't take him long to develop both. Once, high on speed, he was up for three days straight. Shortly after that, Greene had to be taken to a detoxification clinic in West Hollywood.

In Los Angeles, he lived alone in a little bungalow owned by his mother's older sister, Cleo Fasulo, in North Hollywood. The house was nestled right behind Fasulo's, on the same lot. But in early April 1988, Greene had to move out because Fasulo was about to sell the property. Her husband had recently died after a long illness and she needed the money. "There were a lot of expenses," Fasulo recalled.

After Greene moved out, she never saw him again. By then he had been working part-time for several months for Parker Martin, a certified public accountant in Burbank. And so Greene simply took his meager personal belongings over to Martin's office and used a back room there as his temporary home.

Martin didn't particularly mind that, for spring is always a busy time for any accountant and Greene was a hard worker, cheerfully going about doing his clerical work, answering the telephones, Xeroxing returns, and running general errands. Indeed, things became so hectic by early April that Greene began working full-time, putting in grueling hours just as Martin did. And so it hardly seemed unnatural for Greene simply to bring his personal effects over to the office.

In the short time that Greene had worked for Martin, the two men had developed a good rapport, though they had already known each other socially for two years before then.

By mid-afternoon on Friday, April 15, Martin and Greene were done. They had finished every last return for their clients, and it was time to celebrate the end of another tax season—and the start of the weekend. After paying Greene $240 in cash, Martin and his secretary, Jill Halstead, left for the Rawhide bar on Burbank Boulevard, inviting Greene to join them after picking up a bit at the office.

A little over an hour later, Greene walked through the back door of the North Hollywood bar, his ever present backpack slung over a shoulder. As usual, he was casually dressed, wearing a pale blue cotton pullover, jeans, and sneakers.

Being the middle of a Friday afternoon, there were only a half-dozen customers inside the pleasant country-and-western bar. And so Greene easily spotted Martin and Halstead having drinks at a corner table. The Rawhide was a bright, airy bar with lots of bleached wood, fern plants hanging from its high ceiling, and parquet floors that were sprinkled with sawdust. Once a neighborhood dance club, over the years it had been increasingly taken over by suburban gays. But still, many of the Rawhide's longtime clientele continued patronizing the bar, especially on weekends, doing the two-step with their spouses side by side with male couples in easy coexistence. The only thing they seemed to have in common was their cowboy gear, ten-gallon hats and all.

At their corner table, Ellis Greene declined to join Martin and Halstead in a drink, telling them that he later would be heading to Long Beach with a friend for the weekend. About five minutes later, he left.

His employee had seemed somewhat preoccupied, Martin later thought, and he got the impression that Greene had dropped by the Rawhide simply to be polite. Again, that was just like Ellis Greene—he didn't like to hurt people's feelings.

After that Martin never saw Greene again.

A few hours later on that same day, at another North Hollywood bar, Chip Suntheimer also had taxes on his mind as he and a friend, Billy Ray, stood idly in the Bullet, watching a pool game.

Suntheimer had already prepared his returns, but he had yet to mail them. And it was now going on eight o'clock, only a few hours away from the filing deadline. Suntheimer was thinking about leaving to head over to the post office when Greene, his longtime buddy, entered the cozy one-room bar.

When Greene discovered that Suntheimer had prepared his returns by hand, he insisted that it should be typed, and he offered to do it. And so the three of them piled into Suntheimer's car and drove the two miles down Burbank Boulevard to Martin's office.

When they arrived, the office was dark and empty, but Greene had a key. Inside, from a miniature refrigerator, he produced three cold beers. Time passed quickly as Greene prepared Suntheimer's returns on an electric typewriter, chatting all the while. Less than an hour later, he was done. After making Xerox copies, they drove to the post office in Van Nuys, and Suntheimer went inside to mail his returns.

When he came back out, Greene was nearly done helping the older woman fill out a state return. Then the three men went to a nearby Arby's, where they each had a soft drink and two sandwiches. Suntheimer picked up the tab.

From there they went to the Mag, a homey, hole-in-the-wall bar with an easy-going, low-key clientele tucked away in a corner of a North Hollywood mini-mall anchored by a Lucky Supermarket. After just one beer each, Suntheimer was ready to call it a night. As manager of the L.A. Wrecking Company, a building-demolition firm, Suntheimer had to work early the next morning. And it was already eleven.

So he and Billy Ray took Greene back to the Bullet. Before leaving Greene there, Suntheimer borrowed $20 from him, and then watched to make sure that Greene had safely entered the bar before driving off. The Bullet, Suntheimer knew, was not located in the best part of North Hollywood, and often large, powerful motorcycles are seen parked right out in front on the sidewalk. And while the atmosphere inside the bar is usually quite relaxed and friendly, the surrounding areas just outside the bar often seem menacing at night.

Greene entered the Bullet without incident, waving a casual good-bye to Suntheimer. It was the last time Suntheimer ever saw his friend.

By midnight, Suntheimer was home in bed. And he was just about to doze off when the telephone rang. The answering machine picked up after the first ring.

It was Greene. "Chip," he said, sounding distressed. Then the line went dead.

Groggy, Suntheimer replayed the tape, and when he heard Greene's tone of voice and the sudden disconnection, he became instantly concerned. Greene clearly sounded as though he was in some kind of trouble.

The two friends had known each other for more than five years, and Suntheimer knew that his friend enjoyed marijuana, cocaine, and methamphetamine in addition to booze. And it wasn't unusual for Greene to occasionally call Suntheimer at home, asking for a ride home. But Greene had never sounded this way before, and the abrupt disconnection . . .

Alarmed, Suntheimer quickly got dressed and returned to the Bullet to look for his friend. By then there were few customers left at the bar, and Suntheimer could plainly see that Greene was not among them. And so he didn't even bother to ask Tony White, the bartender, about Greene before heading for several other neighborhood bars in search of Greene.

In fact, however, shortly before Suntheimer had returned to the Bullet, bartender White had refused to serve Greene a mixed drink because he clearly was already drunk—slurring his words and stumbling around. Instead, White had given Greene a Coke on the house.

With only one or two other customers sitting at the long bar, Greene took a stool at the far end, nursing his cold soda and stewing for the better part of an hour over White's refusal to serve him booze. At one point Greene threatened to go to a nearby bar, the Oak Room, where he said he was sure a man could buy a drink. That would be just fine with me, White thought to himself, although he remained silent.

Greene didn't make good on that threat. Instead he went to make a phone call in the hallway. Back at the bar a few minutes later, he handed White a Checker Cab card and asked White to call him a cab, using the number on the card, which also bore the name "Russ." White was happy to oblige. It was always nice getting rid of a drunk.

It was nearly midnight when Russell W. Leek, a stocky, bearded man with long hair, walked into the Bullet to pick up his fare. By then there were only two or three customers left in the bar. "It was tax time and it was a very slow night," White recalled.

It was clear to him that Leek and Greene knew each other. Greene often called the Checker Company late at night from some bar and asked specifically for Leek, for he allowed Greene to run up a tab. "When he was broke, I would still get him home.'' the fourteen-year cabdriver said. ''I drove him back and forth to the bars and then back to his office a lot of times.''

Mostly, though, it was the Bullet and no other bar. ''I would usually pick him up right at closing time or shortly afterward,'' Leek recalled. Almost without variation, he would take Greene back to Martin's office. The only departures from that routine were the rare times when Greene had Leek stop at the Jack-in-the-Box so he could pick up a snack on the way back to Martin's.

But years later, Leek could not recall specifically where he had dropped Greene off on what proved to be the final hours of Greene's life.

Interestingly, just days before his disappearance, Greene had a telephone conversation that later aroused great interest among investigators. Excitedly, he told Basil, his twin brother in Portsmouth, Ohio, that he had recently met two men who were interested in investing in a pet project of his: a cheesecake company that would market his special recipe. At the same time that he was working for Martin, Greene also was trying to start a catering business, occasionally borrowing the kitchen of a friend who was a licensed caterer.

It was also about the same time that Greene spoke proudly to both Martin and Suntheimer of a new friend he had made. Greene didn't mention a name, but did say that his new friend was a doctor.

Shortly after Greene's disappearance, Martin's office got a number of telephone calls from someone who refused to identify himself, asking for Greene. Could it have been one of the killers calling, perhaps trying to find out if Greene's demise had been noticed?

A full week passed before Parker Martin and Cleo Fasulo filed a missing-person report with Los Angeles police.

Sobbing years later, long after it became known that Greene had been murdered, the tiny, white-haired woman would say of her nephew: ''He loved everyone and trusted everybody. You could be a total stranger and he would do just as much for you as if he had known you all his life. He's just a good kid. He was a good and hard worker. He didn't steal. And if he had food, then everybody had food. Ellis never turned anybody down.''

"Gene's Alive"

One slightly muggy mid-summer evening, a sleek, white limousine quietly pulled up at a swanky town house in Columbus, Ohio. The limo had a uniformed driver and a well-stocked bar—both nice touches befitting the city's newest millionaire. And even before the stretch limousine had pulled out into the evening traffic, John Hawkins and his best pal, Erik De Sando, each had a drink in hand, passing a joint back and forth.

It was a Friday night, July 15—precisely three months after Ellis Greene had vanished and a week after Hawkins had received his $1 million check from Farmers New World Life. And now Hawkins was ready to party.

He and his roommate were going barhopping on the North Side, as they did several nights a week, although usually not in such elegant style.

De Sando, as equally well-tanned and muscular as Hawkins, worked for a local contractor, building outdoor decks. During the previous winter—a slow time for outdoor construction but a hectic one for Just Sweats—De Sando had begun doing odd jobs for Hawkins's company. In December 1987, for instance, when Just Sweats found itself desperately short-handed, De Sando willingly pitched in by driving truck loads of merchandise to the company's stores in Kentucky. For performing such chores, however, De Sando received only two Just Sweats paychecks. He also didn't get paid for his appearances in Just Sweats television commercials that aired in early 1988. Instead of paying De Sando cash for his work, Hawkins frequently took him along on out-of-town trips, all expenses paid. They went to the Bahamas for a long weekend. They went to Las Vegas several times. And then there was the Christmas vacation to Hawaii in 1987. Hawkins, in De Sando's words, "took care of me."

And certainly on this promising July evening, as their limousine cruised toward the city's lively North Side bars, De Sando fully expected to be taken care of.

Whenever they went barhopping, the usual routine was to stop first at a Just Sweats store—any one would do. Inside, Hawkins would quickly greet the employees, spread some good cheer, and then head straight for the cash register—leaving with a pocketful of money. And then off they went. Hawkins treated the stores' registers as if they were his personal till. During particularly good times for the business, Hawkins would hire a limousine and leave the driving to the chauffeur as they partied. When they were entering a bar, Hawkins would tell the driver to stand by outside while he and De Sando playfully competed with each other to see who could get a girl into the limousine's backseat first.

On this mid-July Friday night, there was clearly no need to get cash. Hawkins was rolling in it. Yet he didn't seem quite himself all night long, appearing distant and preoccupied, De Sando thought. Hawkins that night just wasn't the party animal that De Sando had become used to. Still, the two of them managed to put away a fair amount of booze and spread their charm liberally among the women.

And so it wasn't until almost one in the morning, when Hawkins and De Sando arrived at the R 'n' R Bar that De Sando realized his buddy was not only very drunk but extremely upset over something.

The club was still rocking, but Hawkins almost immediately took De Sando aside. "I've got something to tell you," he told De Sando. "I'm leaving tomorrow and I'm never coming back," Hawkins said. "You're never going to see me again."

De Sando was puzzled.

Then Hawkins added conspiratorially: "Gene's alive."

Looking Good

Over the din of the jukebox music and the loud conversations at the R 'n' R, Erik De Sando couldn't be sure that he had heard John Hawkins accurately. But then his friend elaborated.

"Gene's alive and well—in Florida," Hawkins said, carefully watching De Sando to gauge his reaction. "The insurance money is a scam," Hawkins continued. "And I'm leaving tomorrow—forever. I'm never going to see you again."

Stunned, De Sando was still trying to digest what his friend was saying, but Hawkins raced on. While in Florida to see his father two weeks before, Hawkins said, he also had visited Hanson down in Miami.

"Gene looked good," Hawkins said. "He had some cosmetic surgery done and is doing quite well." The face-lift had cost Hanson more than $20,000, Hawkins said.

It finally dawned on De Sando that Hawkins and Hanson had pulled off a million-dollar insurance scam.

But then who, he finally asked Hawkins, was the dead man?

"We got the body from the morgue. We paid somebody off at the morgue," Hawkins replied. "From what I understand, it looked just like Gene."

Initially they had had trouble locating a body that matched Hanson's physical characteristics. But finally they found one. The body, Hawkins said, was "almost fresh from a hospital"—that of a man who had died of a heart attack while on the operating table. "And then they brought him over, put him in the doctor's office," he continued.

According to the plan, once the fake death scenario was played out in Boggs's California office, the morgue was supposed to return with an ambulance and transport the body back. But then the morgue got backed with three hours worth of work, and so two Glendale police officers responded, Hawkins said, somewhat inaccurately. And it was those two cops that called in the L.A. County coroner's investigators, who conducted something of an inquiry, including taking fingerprints of the corpse.

Had the morgue been able to respond quickly to Boggs's office, Hawkins rued, the plan would have sailed through smoothly without detection. It would have been a perfect crime.

"Anyway, that's how it transpired," he concluded. "That's why it took so long for Gene to die."

"Why do you have to leave?" De Sando asked his friend. "Why don't you just return the money and stay? There's a good chance, you know, that you could get off really light on this. It's better than having to run the rest of your life."

No way, Hawkins said. "Boggs has tapes that incriminate me. He taped all our telephone conversations. We're all in this together," Hawkins replied, adding that Boggs had $100,000 coming for his part in the scheme.

Incredulous at his friend's stupidity, an incensed De Sando screamed at Hawkins over the din, calling him idiotic and greedy. "You dumb ass," De Sando snapped.

Hawkins sheepishly accepted his friend's harsh rebuke, conceding that he had made a disastrous blunder.

And then, as far as De Sando was concerned, that was the end of it. The night was still young. There were scores of pretty women at the nightclub having a good time, and De Sando was not about to miss out on all the fun.

A short white later, Hawkins went home alone.

Later, when De Sando finally arrived back at the condominium after getting something to eat, he found

Hawkins curled up on the living room floor in a fetal position. He was sobbing.

Still livid at his roommate, De Sando stepped over Hawkins and went straight to bed without saying a word.

But Hawkins quickly recovered, and he did what he usually did when there was trouble on the horizon. He called up his best girl.

A Mad Dash

Margaret Moulson got home from a late date only to find a message on her answering machine from John Hawkins. Sounding desperate, he said he wanted her to come over to his place right away. "I'm leaving town and I don't know when I'll be back," he said.

Two nights earlier, when the two of them had gone to an early dinner and then a movie, Hawkins seemed unusually quiet and subdued throughout. And after the movie he simply took her home. Moulson was still puzzling over Hawkins's uncharacteristic behavior on Wednesday night as she listened to his pleading voice on her answering machine.

Concerned, Moulson quickly threw on some jeans and drove to Hawkins's town house on Ellerdale Drive, just a few minutes away. By the time she arrived, Hawkins was no longer maudlin, and the two of them sat up until nearly dawn, with Hawkins doing most of the talking. He told her that he was tired of it all, particularly the stress of the merchandising business, and that he therefore had sold Just Sweats for $1 million. Then Hawkins began speaking dreamily once more about Hawaii.

Moulson was noncommittal when he asked her to join him after he had re-established himself, most likely in some tropical paradise. Then they both drifted off to sleep, with Moulson thinking to herself that she was really going to miss Johnny.

The next morning, Erik De Sando was surprised to see a cheerful Hawkins bound into his room. "I feel a lot better this morning," Hawkins announced. "Things are going to work out fine."

De Sando got his second surprise of the day when he saw, over Hawkins's shoulder, Moulson in the dining room having coffee.

Hawkins was in an ebullient, talkative mood. He told De Sando that he was leaving town for a while—"to talk to somebody who knows what I should do." De Sando knew right away that Hawkins was referring to his mom out in Las Vegas.

De Sando also knew that he couldn't turn Hawkins in. And so he wisely kept his mouth shut, feeling more sorry than mad for his friend. Then, much to his astonishment, Hawkins began talking about the scam once more, providing shocking new details.

Gene Hanson's embezzlement of $1.8 million from Just Sweats six months earlier also had been a part of the plot, Hawkins told De Sando. Hanson was to take that money and disappear for good. In the meantime, Hawkins and Boggs would fake Hanson's death—with Hawkins then collecting the $1.5 million that Hanson had in life insurance.

As Hawkins talked on, it all became clear to De Sando: When they were unable to locate a Hanson look-alike shortly after Hanson's disappearance, Hawkins had no choice but to go out to California and bring back the money, along with his contrived tale of tracking down Hanson in Los Angeles.

"Please, Erik," Hawkins finally said, "don't say anything to anybody about what I told you last night. And please don't tell my mother. You know, I never should have told you what I did last night. You can't tell anyone—especially my mother."

De Sando again pleaded with Hawkins: "Look-it, John, I know you're in some trouble. But you never identified the body. And, you know, it seems to me that you should be able to work out some kind of deal if you give the money back and turn in the other guys involved."

"Erik, I can't do that," Hawkins replied, again reminding him of the tapes that he said Boggs possessed. "He would give those tapes to the authorities."

Then Hawkins went back into his room and began

packing. A short time later, he and Moulson left, driving away in their own cars.

Casually dressed as usual in a T-shirt, shorts, and sneakers, Hawkins looked like any other working stiff in Columbus setting out to run Saturday errands. But Hawkins didn't have a list of chores, though. All he needed was his Just Sweats checkbook. He also had with him a sheet torn out of the Yellow Pages that listed every branch office of the Fifth Third Bank of Columbus.

It was time to cash out and then run.

Eight days earlier, after receiving the $1 million check from Farmers New World Life, Hawkins had deposited it immediately—all in his personal account at Fifth Third Bank. On the following Monday, he withdrew $30,000. Two days later, he transferred $500,000 into the company's account, also at Fifth Third. It was after that that Hawkins learned that authorities had wised up to their insurance scheme. And by then Hawkins had obtained another $322,000 in cash, writing an assortment of checks on the different company and personal accounts, at Fifth Third and other banks.

And now, on his final day in Columbus, Hawkins drove from one Fifth Third branch office to another, asking how much cash each one had in hand. Then he would pull out his checkbook, writing out a check for that amount. The branch tellers gave him all the cash they could muster and then issued him cashier's checks for the balance.

By the time Hawkins got back to the condo, his duffel bag was bulging with cash.

"Everything's gonna work out," he told De Sando. "I know it will. There's even a good chance," Hawkins said with expansive intimacy, "that I'll be back."

Then he slung the duffel bag into his blue Mercedes and drove to the airport.

Sweating it Out

It was late Friday afternoon, July 22. Ed Laramee sighed with relief, grateful that he and the others had somehow managed to get through the week amid utter chaos. All week long, the company's owner, John Hawkins, had been nowhere to be found. All kinds of company decisions had to be put off until his return. Yet no one knew he would be back—or where he had gone.

But Laramee's sense of relief proved premature.

Virtually at the stroke of five o'clock, a Fifth Third bank representative appeared at Just Sweats headquarters to hand-deliver an envelope. It was addressed to Hawkins.

Laramee looked at the messenger and the envelope with great trepidation. "I had been around long enough to know that when you get a hand-delivered note from your bank at five o'clock on a Friday, you open it," he said.

The letter made the hairs on the back of his neck stand up. The bank, fed up with Just Sweats' financial management practices, was calling in three notes, totaling about $450,000. That threatened to put the already cash-strapped company out of business.

In the space of less than two weeks, the company's future had first taken a turn for the better and now this. Laramee cursed the day he had accepted Hawkins's job offer.

When Hawkins put half of his life insurance proceeds into the company's account on July 13, it seemed as if Just Sweats had at last put its financial problems behind, problems that stemmed from Gene Hanson's

clumsy embezzlement attempt back in January. The
fresh infusion of a half-million dollars was going to
allow Just Sweats to finally settle all its bills and then
to begin stocking up on vital fall merchandise. Everyone was sorry about Hanson's untimely demise, but
the company that he had left behind seemed poised to
make a nice recovery—in large part because of his
death.

Yet the following week it all began to unravel. One
day treasurer Paul Colgan got a call from an official at
the Fifth Third Bank. She said Just Sweats had no
funds in the bank to cover some $68,000 in checks
that the company had issued.

Until then Colgan had known nothing about Hawkins's massive withdrawals of company funds the previous week. And now he had no idea where Hawkins
was, and neither did anyone else. All Hawkins had
said was that he was going on a buying trip, and nobody had bothered to ask for more details.

Still, the bank official didn't sound overly concerned
at that point. She simply asked if Just Sweats funds
would soon be deposited to cover those checks. Colgan innocently said he assumed that that would be the
case.

But when Laramee learned of the bank's call, and
of the huge, unexplained cash withdrawals by Hawkins, he felt stricken. Something didn't add up.

Nobody knew how to locate Hawkins. He had already missed a crucial meeting on Monday afternoon
with the new president of the Fifth Third Bank, Tom
Fischer.

Now looking at the demand note from Fifth Third
on late Friday afternoon, Laramee walked it over to
Colgan. When Colgan read it, the blood drained from
his face. Looking up, the treasurer said grimly, "If we
don't hear from John by noon Monday, we've got to
call in the lawyers." Laramee agreed.

Over the weekend, Laramee directed a frantic effort
to locate Hawkins, but to no avail. Some at the office
told Laramee not to worry, saying that Hawkins was
sure to turn up by Monday. "Hell, we all thought he

had just gone somewhere to blow off some steam,''
recalled one senior Just Sweats official. But Laramee
was unconvinced. After a miserable weekend, Monday arrived with still no sign of Hawkins. It was point-
less to wait until noon.

''We were dead in the water, and it didn't feel very
good,'' Laramee recalled. He wasted no time calling
Dick Curtin and Austin Wildman.

The one immediate question at hand was who, in
Hawkins's absence, had the authority to act for the
company. Seeking guidance, Wildman retrieved the
company's corporation charter. It had no such provi-
sion. The company once more was on the brink of
ruin, and this time there would be no turning around.

Talking Numbers

No one at Just Sweats now expected John Hawkins to return, certainly not in time to avert catastrophe for the company. And so, led by Ed Laramee, they agreed that it was time to confront Erik De Sando, sure that Hawkins's pal and roommate knew something about his sudden disappearance.

When Laramee, Paul Colgan, and Melissa Mantz pulled up at the Ellerdale Drive town house, a smiling De Sando met them at the door. Once they sat down in the basement family room, the three officers spoke bluntly: "We know you're not telling us everything."

De Sando conceded the point, saying only that Hawkins was in "bad trouble" and that he had gone away for a while. As the conversation droned on, Mantz unobtrusively slipped away and began wandering around the town house.

On a bulletin board by the entry, she picked up Hawkins's telephone messages. Many of them were from Dr. Boggs out in Glendale, California.

On their way out, Mantz spotted a notice of attempted delivery of a piece of certified mail, addressed to Hawkins. She, Laramee, and Colgan decided to go retrieve the letter at the post office. After getting directions at a neighborhood gas station, they finally located the post office.

Mantz went inside to get the mail. She emerged ten minutes later with a large envelope that had been sent to Hawkins at his old Bush Boulevard address. The notice of delivery eventually found its way to the Ellerdale Drive condo, but De Sando simply had not found the time to go to the post office.

When Laramee saw that the sender was the Golden Rule Life Insurance Company, he immediately knew what was inside. He also knew that the check for nearly $500,000 was no good anymore.

It was quickly shaping up to be another demoralizing week for the Just Sweats trio. It had begun with the arrival of Mike Guglielmelli, who held the honorific title of vice president of Just Sweats—bestowed simply because he had invested $50,000 in the company to help it get started three years earlier. Even after Hawkins and Hanson moved to the Midwest in 1985, they had maintained contact with many acquaintances in the New York–New Jersey area. One such person was Mike Guglielmelli, the credit manager for a large textile firm that was a Just Sweats supplier. At the time Guglielmelli had been looking to invest $50,000 of his own money in some sort of a retail outlet.

And when Just Sweats from the very start grew by leaps and bounds, Guglielmelli wanted in on the action. He proposed opening a Just Sweats franchise in New Jersey, where he lived. But Hanson and Hawkins did not want to franchise their stores. In the end, Guglielmelli invested the $50,000 in HHG, the parent company of Just Sweats, and was given the title of vice president. Hawkins was president and Hanson secretary-treasurer. But Guglielmelli never participated in the running of the company. He was truly a silent partner, though that seemed certain now to change with both Hawkins and Hanson gone from the scene.

Attorney Austin Wildman offered to call Guglielmelli to deliver the bad news and to ask him to come out to Columbus on the next available flight.

In the meantime, Laramee and Colgan began combing through the company's ledgers, trying to figure out how much money Just Sweats still had, if any, and how much was missing.

After Guglielmelli arrived in Columbus, he got a full briefing from the lawyers and company officials. Then he joined them in a meeting with Fifth Third

Bank officials. They came clean with the bankers, telling them everything they knew about the insurance scam, sparing nothing.

When the conversation focused on the company's dire financial situation, Colgan disclosed that Just Sweats owed more than $160,000 in back sales tax to the state of Kentucky.

An even more pressing matter, Laramee added, was an impending payroll. He said he was prepared to transfer sufficient funds from the previous weeks' sales receipts to cover the payroll—as long as Fifth Third would agree to honor the checks. The payroll account had always been kept separate from the operating account. Much to Laramee's relief, the bank agreed.

Laramee also assured the bank that Just Sweats would not accept future shipments of merchandise, and thereby incur additional debt, until the firm's murky financial situation became clearer. "We were," Wildman recalled, "a rudderless ship."

As the conversation rambled on, Laramee did a quick mental calculation, arriving at the conclusion that the company owed various creditors, including the government, a grand total of more than $1.5 million. Finally he uttered the unspeakable: "The handwriting for Chapter 11 is on the wall," he said. "I don't see anything else but that." No one argued with him.

And so he instructed Wildman and Curtin to draw up a list of bankruptcy law experts. With grim resignation they all realized that they were about to sail into uncharted waters.

Wildman also pointed out to Guglielmelli that should he end up wanting to take legal action against Hawkins, he needed to hire a different law firm for the task, since Hamilton, Kramer, Myers & Cheek had been too actively engaged in representing Hawkins, Hanson, and Just Sweats. Guglielmelli understood, and he appreciated Wildman's candor. But he said that would probably be unnecessary.

After the meeting at the bank broke up, Laramee drove Guglielmelli to the police station so Guglielmelli could file an official report stating that Hawkins had committed grand larceny, making off with hundreds of thousands of dollars in company funds.

Back at the office, the two men chatted for a while before Guglielmelli left for the airport to catch a flight home. As they talked, Laramee was dumbstruck by the fact that the company's only remaining officer hardly seemed interested in confronting the crisis, and now he was about to leave town without mentioning any plans he had for the company—or even saying when he would return.

Laramee was further astounded when Guglielmelli, getting up to leave, asked about being reimbursed for his travel expenses. "Here's this company, missing its majority owner, having just gotten over a large embezzlement, with no cash to pay the bills, $500,000 in bank loans due, and with the employee payroll threatened, and he's worried about his travel expenses!" Laramee thought to himself. He cursed the day he had joined the company.

Power to Act

United by the deepening crisis, Ed Laramee, Paul Colgan, and Melissa Mantz worked day and night, even coming in on weekends, struggling valiantly to hold things together—mostly by finding artful ways to keep angry creditors at bay. "We weren't sure what to tell them," Laramee recalled. "We were dead in the water." About the best they could do was stall for time, hoping against hope that John Hawkins—and the money—would somehow turn up.

On the last Saturday morning in July, two weeks into the crisis, the telephone rang at the Just Sweats headquarters. It was Erik De Sando. A package from Hawkins had arrived at the apartment, he told Mantz, and it was for her. Mantz and Colgan dropped everything and went straight to De Sando's town house to fetch it.

On the outside of the package, there was no indication of its origin. The package didn't have any postal markings at all. So Mantz and Colgan assumed that it had probably arrived in a larger container that held other contents, probably addressed to De Sando.

In any case, inside was an official blanket power-of-attorney, conferring upon Mantz the authority to act on Hawkins's behalf. The legal document had been notarized in Baltimore, they all noticed. De Sando said nothing.

The Just Sweats folks were immensely relieved. With Mantz now in charge, the company at last could move forward and try to extricate itself from its latest quagmire.

The power-of-attorney was not entirely unexpected,

for shortly after his disappearance, Hawkins had begun to call the office, mostly speaking only to Mantz. But even then he refused to tell her where he was.

Livid as they all were at Hawkins, Laramee, Mantz, Colgan, and Wildman controlled their tempers when they spoke to him, especially at first. They knew that their best hope—really, their only hope—was to persuade Hawkins to cooperate with them, if not by returning with the money, then at least granting them the legal authority to act.

With each passing hour the company's affairs became increasingly desperate. "You people had better get your asses over here to explain what the hell's going on," a banker at Fifth Third had thundered, abruptly terminating a conversation with Dick Curtin. Yet no one at the time had had the authority to act as a company officer on behalf of Just Sweats.

When Hawkins first called Mantz, he had launched into an inquiry about various merchandise shipments. Astonished, she demanded to know where he was and why he had so abruptly fled, taking all the company funds and leaving the crew in such a terrible lurch. Hawkins held fast, evasively talking about his need to take some time off and recover from his "stress." Quickly changing the subject and speaking as if it were business as usual, Hawkins then began asking about orders and sales. The call left Mantz flabbergasted.

Hawkins later also called Curtin and Wildman, ostensibly to talk about the company's legal affairs. But Wildman didn't let Hawkins off the hook so easily. "What the hell is going on?" he railed at Hawkins. "The people in the company are madder than hell. You've left the company with no corporate officers!"

Wildman finally appealed to Hawkins's sense of commitment to the people at Just Sweats, urging him to immediately send back a power-of-attorney document empowering someone in Columbus to act legally for the company in his absence. Hawkins agreed to do so, but Wildman was not optimistic. Disgusted, the lawyer now also rued the day that he met Hawkins and Hanson.

In addition to the power-of-attorney, the package that arrived at the end of July also contained a personal letter from Hawkins to Mantz. It read, in part:

Dear Melissa,

This is undoubtedly the toughest letter I've ever had to write. There is no other way I could do what I'm doing except through a letter. The pressures of running the business have totally driven me almost crazy. I know you think I'm a wimp for running from the responsibilities like this, but my happiness is more important to me than the power and prestige Just Sweats gave me.

I am going to ask a very important thing of you. I need you to take care of everything for me until I return. You are the only friend I have who is responsible enough to handle what I am going to ask. The enclosed power of attorney will give you the ability to do everything I want. . . .

I have $150,000 in a money market account at Blunt, Ellis & Loewi. . . . I want those funds [invested] in tax-free bonds and transfer ownership to a joint account of mine and my mom's. There is $450,000 owed to me by another insurance company. . . . When the check comes in, have the money invested the same way. I also have an account at Fifth Third Bank which has approximately $109,000 in cash. You may use those funds as collateral for Just Sweats to borrow money against for one and a half years. After that time, I want my mother to have the money. As with Just Sweats, it's yours to do as you please. With what you are about to go through, it's the least I can give you.

Missy, I'm very sorry I'm dumping all of this on you. You have no idea how bad I feel. I'll make it up to you someday and that's a promise. I miss you guys already, but the only way I can get my sanity back is to walk away from all the pressures for a while. I'll call you, but it's going to be at least six months. I have a friend in London, England, and I plan to stay there for a while. You can't let anyone see this letter as they will try to take the power of attorney away from you, saying I wasn't sane at the time of writing it. You will be asked repeatedly where I am and why did I leave. The best response will be that I wanted to take some time off and enjoy the insurance money. Good luck, Miss! I'll love you always.

John

Through the rest of the summer, Hawkins continued calling Columbus almost every other day. But from where, nobody knew. "I didn't ask where he was, no. I didn't want to be insulted by being lied to," Wildman recalled. In retrospect, he surmised, Hawkins was calling so frequently probably because he knew that Wildman was talking to the authorities, and Hawkins hoped to learn what Wildman and the authorities knew.

In one of the those telephone conversations with Wildman, Hawkins casually mentioned that he might return to re-assume control of the company. That really set Wildman off. Returning, he told Hawkins, would not be a smart move at all. "Those people would tear you to shreds," Wildman said. Hawkins seemed genuinely hurt by the thought that he was now viewed with disdain by everyone at Just Sweats—his company!

In a later conversation that autumn, Wildman had some interesting news to pass on to Hawkins. Authorities out in California had finally identified the man whom Hawkins had cremated. It was most certainly not Gene Hanson.

Hawkins stopped calling.

A New Start

The arrival of the power-of-attorney document meant, among other things, that Melissa Mantz, Paul Colgan, and Ed Laramee no longer had to worry about Mike Guglielmelli. But at the same time Laramee feared that they would still be operating on tenuous grounds because the legal document seemed to state that Hawkins could revoke the power-of-attorney at any time—as he had intimated more than once in his long-distance calls. But according to Wildman and Curtin, Hawkins's accompanying letter to Mantz, written in longhand, gave her sufficient room within the power-of-attorney to vote his shares.

Backed by that opinion, Mantz submitted Hawkins's resignation as president. Then she transferred all of his company stock to herself and to Laramee, dividing the shares equally. Next, she named Laramee president and treasurer and herself vice president and secretary. But that was hardly anything to celebrate about. "There was no money and very little merchandise," Laramee recalled. "So forty-five percent of that was still just about nothing." Still, he and Mantz were determined to make a go of it.

Laramee had not been surprised that Hawkins assigned his power-of-attorney to Mantz. He knew Hawkins didn't have full confidence in Colgan. And Laramee himself had been with the company only four months. Mantz, clearly, was the logical choice. She and Hawkins went back three years, to the day when she strode confidently into the Just Sweats store on High Street, across from the Ohio State University campus. Hawkins didn't say so, but Laramee also suspected that Hawkins believed he could control Mantz. If so, Laramee knew, Hawkins had made another miscalculation.

With Mantz and himself now in undisputed control of Just Sweats, the ensuing series of business meetings with banks, suppliers, and other creditors once again had real meaning. One afternoon Wildman accompanied Mantz to the brokerage firm of Blunt, Ellis & Loewi downtown to verify Hawkins's claim that he had $150,000 in an account there. "It was absolutely imperative to gain access to John's Blunt, Ellis account," Laramee explained. "No money, no work, no jobs—and no company." Luckily, the money was there.

Next, they went to the Fifth Third Bank, where the bank's senior officers met Mantz for the first time. She and Wildman produced copies of John Hawkins's power-of-attorney and then quickly brought them up to date on the latest developments. They also asked the bank officials about any other assets, if any, that Hawkins had in secret accounts at the bank, with the idea that any such funds could be applied to the outstanding loans in which Hawkins was a personal guarantor. The bank officials acknowledged the existence of a personal Hawkins account, but they refused, for legal reasons, to divulge its balance. The parties agreed to meet again soon. "Who the hell knew where the money was in those days?" Wildman recalled years later.

In the meantime, Fifth Third agreed to let Mantz open a new, separate Just Sweats account, using the $150,000 from Blunt, Ellis. That allowed the company to pay a few bills and meet the payroll.

Throughout the muggy Ohio summer, Laramee, Mantz, and the company's lawyers struggled mightily to stave off disaster. But inevitably they realized that it was all for naught. It was becoming clear that a Chapter 11 bankruptcy was not only unavoidable but imminent.

"The debt was just too big a hill to climb," Laramee recalled. The company needed fresh capital. It needed new inventories. It needed to reestablish its credibility and regain, if possible, the trust of the city's lending institutions. And all of those seemed impossibly out of reach. Laramee and Mantz began drawing up a list of Just Sweats stores to close down.

One night a meeting at Wildman's office didn't break up until eleven o'clock. Then Laramee and Mantz returned to their office to work some more. And as they idly lapsed into a conversation about Hawkins's disappearance, Mantz suddenly wondered about Hawkins's cherished Mercedes. It seemed unlikely that he would have taken it with him if his intention was truly to vanish. A car is so easy to find.

A couple of hours later, Laramee and Mantz finally emerged from their office into the steamy Ohio night. Laramee was more than ready to head straight for home. But Mantz was overcome by curiosity about Hawkins's car. She drove straight to the Port Columbus International Airport. There, she pulled into the short-term parking lot, which was closest to the passenger terminal.

Hawkins's car wasn't hard to spot. And not just because it was parked illegally. Columbus had experienced several weeks of drought, but over the weekend there had been torrential rainstorms that dumped several inches of rain on the area. Finding a car parked with its top down was most unexpected. Even more surprising, the keys were on the seat, in plain view. It was as if Hawkins had wanted someone to drive it away. Or else he had been in a terrible hurry. When Mantz opened the car door, a cascade of rainwater gushed out.

On the backseat was a partial page that had been ripped out of the Yellow Pages. It contained a list of all the Fifth Third Bank branches in the Columbus area. A parking lot attendant came over and helped Mantz put up the top and secure the car.

If there were any lingering doubts that Hawkins, Hanson, and their physician friend in California had pulled off an audacious insurance scam, possibly involving murder, they were dispelled by a piece of paper that Mantz came across one day while going through Hawkins's desk at the office. In the center drawer was a note in Hawkins's handwriting, with the figure 145,000 written at the top. Below, in a neat column were the notations: 30 F, 100 M, 85 B, 50 ME, and 500,000 JS.

It didn't take Mantz and Laramee long to conclude that the numbers stood for dollar amounts. The numbers didn't quite add up. But they knew the initials stood for Father, Mother, Boggs, Melvin Eugene (Hanson), and Just Sweats.

Bankrupt

One late August afternoon, Ed Laramee looked up from his desk as a somewhat shabbily dressed businessman came through Just Sweats' front door. The gray-haired visitor, the owner of a luggage store on High Street, looked very angry. He had a check in hand and said he was looking for John Hawkins.

The merchant told Laramee that he had recently sold Hawkins a $70 duffel bag, but Hawkins's check had bounced. Laramee was barely able to hide his bemusement, thinking to himself: Get in line, pal. Hawkins had even stolen the bag he used to carry away the loot.

Looking up at the irate merchant, Laramee could only offer the man sympathy. Just Sweats was about to file for bankruptcy.

Chapter 11 of the U.S. Bankruptcy Code allows a company to continue operating as a business while restructuring its finances under court supervision. Such a filing also would protect Just Sweats from all creditors, thus allowing the firm to use its income to make regular payments to vendors and suppliers and to meet the payroll and other operational needs.

This was precisely what Just Sweats needed. Its assets were down to $1.4 million, while its liabilities had reached $2.3 million and were still climbing fast. "They didn't have a sense of business controls," Laramee said of Hawkins and Hanson. "Rapid expansion was part of the problem. You can expand rapidly, but you have to stop and gather your senses. They just lost their sense of direction."

A few weeks later, Mike Guglielmelli formally relinquished his minority share in the company. "I truly feel that my professional judgment and reputation are tarnished," he rued. "I am abashed at being so easily hoodwinked in an industry where I am supposed to be knowledgeable. I feel it would be best to take my lumps and try to repair my career without further association with HHG Inc."

His ten percent of the company stock was worthless, Guglielmelli admitted. "Please tender it back to the corporation," he wrote, signing the letter:

"A sadder but much wiser Michael Guglielmelli."

Closing In

Jean Walker looked at the six mug shots that investigator Mike Jones put before her. It took her no time to spot among them the one of Gene Hanson. He was, after all, a longtime patient of the doctor's.

"That's him right there," Walker said cooly, pointing with her index finger. Ever the loyal employee, Walker was aloof but correct after she arrived for work that late August morning and found Jones, Kurt Stoutsenberger, and two other investigators rummaging around the doctor's office. They had come with a search warrant, and there was little Walker could do but go along.

After she picked out Hanson, Jones showed Walker another set of three mug shots. These were photographs of three dead people, among them a head shot of Ellis Greene, although no one as yet knew his identity.

"I don't know any of them," Walker said, very businesslike.

"Are you positive?" Jones politely asked.

"Yes, I'm sure of it," she replied.

"This person here," Jones said, pointing at the mug shot of Greene, "is the person that was found here, who Dr. Boggs identified as Gene Hanson."

It was as if Jones had slugged her in the stomach. Walker gasped. Speechless, she began shaking. Jones thought she was on the verge of passing out.

"Oh, my God," the woman said when she finally recovered, tears in her eyes. "What has he done?"

From that moment on, Walker's demeanor changed. She began cooperating fully with the investigators, showing them where the medical files were, explaining how the appointments books were kept, and generally answering any questions the men had about the workings of the office.

When Jones and Stoutsenberger had left Boggs's office the previous Friday afternoon, they had both been convinced of the doctor's complicity—and of the urgent need to search his office more thoroughly. And so on the following Monday, the two of them met in Jones's office and together drafted an affidavit for a search warrant. It wasn't until after five o'clock that they obtained a judge's consent.

Before ten on Tuesday morning, Jones and Stoutsenberger, joined by Hal Huber and Larry Spada, their respective supervisors, were at 540 North Central with the search warrant. Jones was disappointed to find no one in yet, for he had hoped Boggs would be there so that the severity of the situation might dawn on him. The building manager let the investigators in with his pass key. A short time later, Walker appeared. She was soon followed by Dana Boggs.

The doctor's son reacted angrily to the presence of the investigators, belligerently demanding to know why they were there. Shown the search warrant, the young man was somewhat mollified. Still, he was not about to cooperate with the search team. And when Jones showed him the photo lineups, Dana was deliberately vague and acted disinterested. But Jones saw no need to push the young man, who was clearly going to remain loyal to his father. He asked Walker and Boggs to wait in the lounge while the investigators finished their work.

Jones was shocked by the condition of the doctor's inner offices. There were used syringes everywhere. Old, discarded bandages had not been picked up. The equipment looked old or dysfunctional. Most of the rooms needed a good scrubbing as well as a fresh coat of paint. The entire place felt unsanitary. It was a hovel. And why anyone would come here for medical treatment was beyond Jones's comprehension.

The doctor also proved to be a pack rat. Throughout

his personal office were piles upon piles of business papers, legal documents, telephone messages, and other assorted papers, many of them dating back ten years or more.

Methodically the four investigators picked through the papers. While they were there, the office phone rang and Dana Boggs sprang for the phone. It was his father, and he had a message for Jean Walker. "That was the doctor," Dana said as he replaced the receiver in the cradle. "He doesn't want you to say anything."

It didn't matter. The searchers were about done anyway—for now. It hadn't taken them long, for they were primarily interested for the time being in finding out who Boggs had been seeing and talking to.

Among the documents that Jones and company left with were Boggs's appointment books, stacks of carbon copies of telephone message pads going back many months, and the original of Gene Hanson's medical file. One of the telephone messages was from someone named Wolfgang; he had left a telephone number in Miami. Another was from John Hawkins. It said: "I have idea re. project we're working on." It was dated only two weeks before the doctor had attacked Barry Pomeroy with a stun gun in his office.

But the most tantalizing piece of evidence was found within Hanson's medical files. They consisted of three EKG strips dated November 27, 1987, March 5, 1988, and March 22, 1988. At first glance, there was nothing remarkable about the strips. Each bore the jagged peaks of an electrocardiograph, a high-tech diagnostic machine that measures changes in the electric potential produced by each heart contraction. To a trained physician the three strips merely portrayed a man with a worrisome heart condition.

But at the Los Angeles County sheriff's crime lab, where Robert H. Takeshita put the three strips under a microscope, at first individually and then together, a far different picture emerged.

Takeshita was a senior criminalist assigned to the physical evidence section. It was his job to analyze evidence such as hairs, fibers, and clothing from crime scenes, looking for physical similarities—for instance, matching a murder suspect's hair with a strand found in the home of the victim. ''The term 'physical match' means that a particular object when broken, torn, or fractured can be placed back together again in a way that you know that it only could have come from that particular object. In other words, if you break a piece of plastic, when you put it together, it forms a physical match,'' Takeshita explained.

That was precisely what happened when he put the three EKG strips end to end under the microscope. The irregular, serrated edges matched up perfectly—forming one long, continuous strip. This meant that at one time all three strips had been connected—as one.

Despite the different dates recorded on each EKG strip, all three readings had been made at one time, Takeshita told Jones. ''I could physically match them together,'' he said. ''And I was able to do that by placing them together, checking the way it was cut, the irregularities, the grid pattern and the color and the width. . . . They all matched up perfectly—a lot like a jigsaw puzzle would.'' In addition, Takeshita noted, all three strips had a red line running along one edge—a paper manufacturer's way of alerting users that the end of a roll was approaching.

Now they had caught the doctor in a blatant lie.

The Right Man

It hardly surprised Mike Jones's bosses at the fraud bureau that he had managed to unearth important evidence against the doctor in only a matter of days. Ron Warthen and Jerry Treadway knew that Jones was one smart, dogged investigator who worked fast. But they had selected him for the job for another reason as well.

Jones was the consummate team player. Even more important, he had a winning way with people. Both traits, Warthen and Treadway knew, would come in handy in the fast-unfolding, multi-jurisdictional investigation. The two supervisors had been aware even as Kurt Stoutsenberger outlined the nebulous case in late August that the probe would demand unprecedented cooperation and coordination among many law enforcement agencies, but this case would be all the more difficult because the various agencies are scattered all over the country. Investigators tend to be secretive in the first place, distrustful of strangers, even other cops, and are loath to share information. This loomed as another serious management challenge. What's more, not all the agencies could be counted on to conduct the investigation with the same goals and agenda in mind. The Glendale police department, for one, seemed still more interested in covering its ass than getting to the bottom of the mystery, although there were signs that some within the red-faced department now were pushing for a full investigation in order to redeem the agency.

Above all, Warthen and Treadway knew they had to act quickly. More than four months already had passed since the suspected murder had taken place, and the trail was only getting colder. If toes had to be stepped on, then so be it. For all his tact, Jones was not one to let the task at hand be subverted by clashing egos or bureaucratic inertia.

Indeed, the two supervisors could not have chosen a man more suited for the job than Mike Jones.

The stocky, curly-haired investigator had been the quintessential military brat. His father was an air traffic controller in the U.S. Air Force, and the family moved so often from airbase to airbase that Jones went to a different school every year of his life until he was about to graduate from high school.

As a result, Jones even now had few deep-rooted friendships. Instead he was quick to make new friends wherever he went. The art of meeting strangers and winning them over was one that Jones had begun mastering as a child. It was a talent that would serve him well in life. And now, embarking on the most challenging assignment of his career, as events would prove, Jones was going to need every last ounce of it.

One of five children, Jones had been born three days before Christmas in 1956, on the March Air Force Base in Riverside, California. As a child he lived in Florida, New Hampshire, Washington, Mississippi, Georgia, Delaware, even in the Philippines.

Neither of his parents had gone to college, but they worked hard to provide a nice life for the kids, giving them what Jones would call "an All-American upbringing." His father was a country boy from Georgia. While stationed in Southern California, he fell in love with a Mexican woman who was living in the California desert community of Colton. She was a nursing assistant.

Although they moved around frequently, the couple went out of their way to be supportive of their four sons and one daughter, all of whom were active in sports and other extracurricular activities. And everywhere they landed, the family went out and explored the region. The Joneses were no couch potatoes.

By the time Jones was a senior at Walla Walla High School, it appeared that he might become the first in his family to attend college. But there was no money. Instead he went to work full-time at the local Safeway, where he already had a part-time job as a bag boy. A year later, he enrolled at Southern Utah State University. There he showed up one day, uninvited, for football practice and went on to earn a spot on the team as a linebacker. But his true love was wrestling.

In 1976, a life-threatening digestive disease sidelined him for nearly a year. Afterward, he transferred to Lassen Junior College in Susanville, California. At a party in that picturesque Northern California town, he met his future wife, Kim, a pharmacy technician. In 1978, he enrolled at the four-year Sacramento State University.

In high school Jones had acquired an abiding interest in science. Now in Sacramento, he discovered forensic sciences and began taking classes in criminal justice and law enforcement. He was at once intrigued and appalled by the new technologies that were rapidly becoming available to both law enforcement and criminals, from DNA analysis to sophisticated white-collar computer crimes.

After earning his bachelor's degree in criminal justice in 1980, Jones wanted to go on to law school. But again money forced a postponement. He had thousands of dollars to repay in undergraduate student loans. So he went to work for a company in Sacramento called Attorney's Aid, serving legal papers, retrieving legal documents, and generally running errands for lawyers. After two years he got a job with the Employment Development Department in Los Angeles to investigate fraudulent disability and unemployment claims.

He and Kim enjoyed living in Southern California, and when he began focusing on his long-term career goals, he realized that most of his peers in the office had either an advanced degree or at least some additional schooling beyond a bachelor's degree.

Jones had never forgotten his deferred dream of becoming a lawyer. And one night he came home and told Kim, "I want to go to law school." She was immediately supportive. "Well, it's up to you. If you think you can handle it . . ."

He enrolled at the Western State University College of Law as a night student, going to class on his way home from the office every day. It was going to take him four years to get a law degree, but he was determined.

While attending night law school, he again changed jobs, this time becoming an officer for the state Alcoholic Beverage Control agency. As a job prerequisite Jones had to attend a peace officers' training academy, and while there he developed several friendships that would soon shape his career.

At the academy, Jones sat next to Ken Kensler, an investigator with the state Insurance Department fraud bureau. Soon they became fast friends. Another academy pal was Dan Koenigsberger, who worked at the Employment Development Department.

At the ABC office in Long Beach, it didn't take Jones long to work his way up the ladder, and within two years he became a senior investigator. He also became a widely recognized expert on an emerging problem that would curse Los Angeles in the years ahead: youth gangs.

During semester breaks in law school, Jones worked overtime and double shifts to earn extra money. It was an extraordinarily busy time for him and Kim, but the couple still managed to have a son during it all.

One day in early 1987, a quiet, mustachioed man named Jerry Treadway walked into the ABC office and asked to speak privately to Jones. Treadway had heard nothing but good things about Jones, including from Kensler and Koenigsberger. Shortly after finishing the academy, the latter had left the Employment Development Department and became a fraud investigator for the state Insurance Department in Los Angeles.

Treadway was aware that Jones was only a year short of getting his law degree, but that didn't matter, he said.

Elated, Jones jumped at the chance to go to work for a full-time criminal investigative agency. He would have a car that he could take home at night and, far more important, he would no longer be saddled with administrative duties, which he found boring.

Above all, what Jones quickly came to appreciate was the dedication, talent, and esprit de corps of his colleagues at the six-person fraud bureau. Everyone kept his ego in check and went out of his way to help one another. Indeed, before the Boggs investigation was all over, nearly everybody in the bureau would play a part.

Drug Den

Well after dark on a Friday night, two separate teams of investigators, each armed with a search warrant, descended simultaneously on Dr. Richard Boggs's home and office in Glendale. It was September 30—barely twenty-four hours after Mike Jones and company had learned the identity of the dead man found in the doctor's office.

With that crucial piece of information at long last, and with both John Hawkins and Gene Hanson now on the lam, authorities in California had good reason to step up their investigation. Their most obvious target, and perhaps the only one, was Boggs.

Jones now was convinced that Boggs was the primary murder suspect—especially after his interview a week earlier with Barry Pomeroy, the man Boggs had attacked with a stun gun on April 1. In one of their many conversations, detective Jim Peterson had casually mentioned the Pomeroy incident to Jones. Astonished that Peterson had done so little to investigate the incident, Jones immediately arranged to talk to Pomeroy.

As soon as Pomeroy walked into Denny's, just around the corner from his apartment, Jones was struck by his resemblance to Gene Hanson. In fact, Jones thought Pomeroy looked more like Hanson than Ellis Greene did!

But two pots of coffee and a pack of cigarettes later, Pomeroy had little to say about the incident that Jones didn't already know. Still, it wasn't until after meeting Pomeroy that Jones accepted without reservation his account of being attacked by Boggs—and then, incredibly, accepting sedatives from the doctor and a ride home afterward! Pomeroy struck Jones as a jittery but easy-to-dominate person—''the fish that got away.''

Jones was determined not to let Boggs get away—with either the attempted murder of Pomeroy or the killing of Ellis Greene.

There was one other person Jones badly wanted to interview—another prime murder suspect in his mind: Hans Jonasson, the doctor's young Swedish lover. In late August, when Jones had last been in Boggs's office, Jonasson hadn't been there; he had gone home to visit relatives in Sweden.

And so on this cool Friday night, as the two search teams split up, one heading for Boggs's office and the other for his apartment, Jones opted to go with the second group. The doctor was more likely at that hour to be home than at work.

Heidi Robbins, a senior criminalist at the Los Angeles County coroner's office, led the search at 540 North Central. After being let in by the building manager, she found Suite 201 to be a veritable drug den. In one back room were large vials full of sulfuric acid, concentrated hydrochloric acid, ethyl ether, and a host of other chemicals. The room was also filled with large laboratory glassware and various unlabeled containers, many of them connected to one another amid a jumble of Rube Goldberg-like contraptions.

Robbins initially was puzzled. ''I was real perplexed as to why these things would be in the doctor's office,'' she recalled. But there was no doubting the evidence. The smorgasbord of chemicals had no purpose other than the manufacture of methamphetamines.

It was time to summon the Los Angeles County sheriff's department narcotics bureau. That unit, Robbins knew, had far more experience in the safe handling of potentially volatile drug-making ingredients than insurance-fraud detectives or coroner's investigators.

Then Robbins joined Jones at the doctor's apartment on South Street, only a mile away. There, investigators found another elaborate illegal drug dispensary, this time including a book containing recipes for making illicit drugs. Among the many controlled substances they found was amyl nitrate, a vasodilator popular among homosexuals because of its reputation as an agent that enhances orgasms. And in a little safe inside a walk-in closet, investigators found a large amount of various opiates.

That was just for openers. Also in the safe was a .38-caliber revolver. It was loaded. And when Larry Spada, Kurt Stoutsenberger's supervisor, reached into a blue denim jacket in the same closet, he found a stun gun.

Upon arriving at the two-bedroom apartment on South Street, Jones had been disappointed to find no one home. But soon after the apartment manager let them in with a master key, the doctor and his young lover returned, pulling up in a battered 1979 Chevy pickup truck. The doctor's Cadillac had been repossessed.

Jones had no trouble recognizing Jonasson. For, moments earlier, investigators had uncovered in another closet an array of sado-masochistic, sexually oriented paraphernalia, including chains, whips, assorted restraints, and a Batman-like black mask. Along with a large collection of hard-core gay porno films were some equally risqué snapshots of Jonasson.

Boggs, outraged by the presence of law enforcement personnel rummaging through his home, angrily demanded to know why they were there. When Jones produced the search warrant, the doctor put on his glasses and carefully read the document.

"Who the hell is Ellis Henry Greene?" he demanded, whipping off his glasses.

"Ellis Henry Greene," Jones replied evenly, "is the guy you killed."

Boggs just stared at Jones.

"Doc, we've got you," Jones added.

Boggs went to the phone to call a lawyer.

In the meantime, Jerry Treadway searched through

the briefcase that Boggs had brought home. Inside was a second stun gun.

Unable to reach a lawyer after several attempts, Boggs plopped onto the living room couch next to Jonasson, as the other agents continued their methodical search. For all they knew, the tiny apartment had been the scene of Greene's murder. What the investigators were hoping to find was evidence to link Boggs, Hanson, and Hawkins to one another—and to Ellis Greene and Barry Pomeroy.

It was nearly three o'clock in the morning by the time the investigators were done. In all, they had taken about seven hours to go through Boggs's home. They carted away several boxes of materials.

That night, every pertinent law enforcement agency in California, from the coroner's office to the district attorney's office, had been represented except the Glendale police department. And it had been no accident. By then Jones wanted to have nothing to do with Peterson and as little as possible with the rest of the Glendale police. They had had their chance and they had blown it royally.

After the massive search of Boggs's home and office hit the local newspaper, a miffed Glendale police captain called Jones to complain about being excluded. "This is a Glendale P.D. investigation now," the captain asserted.

"Wrong," Jones replied. "This is a state investigation now—along with the L.A. district attorney's office."

Nowhere to Run

Dr. Richard Boggs asked Hans Jonasson for a favor. Someone in Ohio, he told his young roommate, was about to wire him a large sum of money, but he was afraid the Internal Revenue Service would get a hold of the money. Would Jonasson mind using his personal bank account to receive the wire transfer and then give Boggs the money? The doctor said he planned to use the money to settle up some old debts—including Jonasson's back pay.

Not at all, the young Swede said, smiling. He would be happy to help out. They could go down to the bank just as soon as they got dressed.

And so on this beautiful Southern California morning, the first working day after the Memorial Day weekend, some six weeks after Ellis Greene's murder, Boggs thought his ship had come in.

Earlier that morning, a young man in Columbus, Ohio, also had asked his roommate for a favor, and it too involved a trip to the bank. From his office downtown, John Hawkins called Erik De Sando at home, asking De Sando to meet him at a Huntington National Bank branch office. "He was having problems wiring the money through his own account, due to the fact that his driver's license had expired," De Sando recalled. Having little else going on that morning, De Sando readily agreed. When they met, Hawkins handed him a $6,500 cashier's check to deposit into his own account. Next, still following Hawkins's instructions, De Sando wired the entire sum to someone by the name of Hans Jonasson, in care of the Security

Pacific National Bank branch office in Glendale, California.

Several hours later, when Boggs got the money, he was both pleased and somewhat puzzled. Boggs was happy finally to get his hands on a wad of money, but it was far less than he had expected.

In any case, within days the $6,500 was gone, gone to pay some pressing debts, gone to booze, gone to drugs. But not to worry, Boggs told Jonasson. There would be more, lots more, where that came from. The $6,500 must have been just the initial down payment, the doctor thought to himself. But Boggs soon discovered that Hawkins had suddenly become extremely difficult to reach. In reality, Hawkins had no intention of paying the doctor one more penny—especially not after how he had blown his cool that Saturday morning six weeks earlier, bringing the heat down on them all.

In fact, authorities were baffled by Boggs's conduct throughout the summer of 1988. Why didn't he flee, as had his two fellow suspects? Instead the doctor seemed to carry on as usual. Most days he slept late, once in a while going to the office in the afternoon to see an occasional patient. Mostly, though, he continued cruising the gay bars in West Hollywood. But that was hardly a crime.

The reason Boggs didn't flee was because he didn't believe he would be caught. He also had no place to go. He was stone broke. But for a telephone calling card, Boggs didn't even own credit cards anymore. His credit rating was so abysmal that after they had been evicted from their Belmont Street apartment in the spring, he couldn't even rent a two-bedroom, $835-a-month apartment. Jonasson had to sign for it. Boggs by then was virtually living hand to mouth, surviving in large part by the grace of his few remaining friends and loyal patients.

One night he showed up at Chuck and Lee Reedy's house high up in the Glendale hills in his ten-year-old pickup truck. He asked to borrow $20. The doctor looked so unkempt and his hands were shaking so much that Lee was alarmed. She also felt embarrassed for him.

On a different occasion, Boggs asked another former patient, George House, for a $5,000 loan, saying that he had huge debts but that the banks would no longer lend him any more money. In this pathetic manner the doctor went from patient to former patient, tin cup in hand.

Boggs was so desperately broke that after killing Greene and passing him off as Gene Hanson, he even submitted four bills to Farmers New World Life, totaling $2,517.20—for having provided Hanson emergency treatment on the morning of April 16, the doctor claimed.

Tracks

Thirty thousand feet above the Gulf of Mexico, Gene Hanson sipped chilled orange juice from a stemmed glass as he tilted back his first-class window seat in an American Airlines jet racing from Miami to Los Angeles. In an expensive jogging suit with matching aerobics shoes, Hanson exuded the aura of a well-to-do businessman whose schedule granted him the freedom to dress so casually for a weekday, cross-country flight. That was just one giveaway. Another was the Lucien Piccard watch on his left wrist. And so was the thick twenty-one-karat gold chain around his neck. So was the morning *Wall Street Journal* that protruded conspicuously from his burgundy, French-made attaché case.

As the wide-bodied Boeing 757 passed over the bayous of Louisiana, Hanson settled back and lit a slender, dark brown cigarette.

"A newspaper or magazine to read, Mr. Hanson?" a pretty stewardess asked him.

"No, thanks," the traveler said.

The stewardess moved on, and Hanson inhaled deeply, allowing himself a thin smile that was barely discernible. Less than twenty-four hours from now, Melvin Eugene Hanson would cease to exist. After that it would be . . .

Wolfgang von Snowden! The name had been selected by caprice, but it seemed to suit him. Grateful that no one was next to him, Hanson pushed his seat all the way back and settled in for a long nap as the attendants darkened the cabin for the in-flight movie. Might as well get some sleep, he told himself. This promised to be a long day—and night—in Los Angeles. But it would be worth it.

Hanson slept right through the meal and did not awaken until the plane had begun its final descent over the Southern California desert. Crushing out one last cigarette in the narrow ashtray, Hanson felt a surge of adrenaline as he gazed down at the brown haze that hung over Los Angeles. Somewhere down in that smog was a man who looked just like him, innocently going about his affairs—perhaps even putting the finishing touches to his tax returns on this, the final filing day of 1988.

As the jet came to a stop at the terminal gate, Hanson realized that he was famished. Slinging his leather suit bag over the shoulder, Hanson was the first to emerge from the plane. There in the lounge, as planned, was a gray-haired gentleman nattily dressed in gray slacks, a blue blazer, and black tasseled loafers. It was Dr. Richard Boggs.

All around the Los Angeles International Airport, the Friday afternoon traffic was steadily picking up. Both directions of the heavily used San Diego Freeway were already gridlocked. And so they took the surface streets to West L.A. for dinner at one of their favorite Mexican restaurants, the Big Enchilada. Over a meal of fresh-ground corn tortillas and chicken tamales, Hanson and Boggs went over their plan once more. Unlike two weeks earlier, this time they were not going to use a stun gun.

En route to Glendale, they stopped for a quick beer at The Spike, the rough-and-tumble bar where Boggs had met Barry Pomeroy a month earlier.

Soon it would be time to go to work.

Ellis Greene was long dead by the time Hanson walked up to the reception desk at the Glendale Holiday Inn to check in around 6:00 A.M., registering as Wolfgang von Snowden. He was exhausted, but he knew sleep would not come easy. Instead he shaved, took a hot shower, put on fresh clothes, and went down to the coffee shop for breakfast. He tried to read the morning *Times*, but he wasn't able to concentrate.

Hanson's mind was still racing with the horrifying, unspeakable events of the past few hours.

As the California sun rose high over the San Gabriel Mountains, Hanson paid his breakfast bill and walked outside. The fresh air was invigorating. Lighting yet another cigarette, he began casually walking back toward the scene of the crime, the bright morning sun in his eyes. But when he turned a final corner and 540 North Central came into view, Hanson was stunned. Boggs's office building was surrounded by fire engines, an ambulance, various other rescue vehicles—even police cars. Something must have gone horribly wrong. Only a hearse from the county morgue was supposed to have come and take away the dead body.

Hanson's first impulse was to run. But he realized that at this early hour on Saturday morning, that might attract unwanted attention. Instead he walked deliberately past the building, staying on the opposite side of the street, trying to see what was going on without seeming conspicuous. He paused only to light a cigarette. The only other passerby was a homeless man pushing a shopping cart down the sidewalk, oblivious to the commotion, mumbling to himself.

A block away now, Hanson picked up his pace, heading back to the Holiday Inn. He was barely able to keep from breaking into a dead run. By the time he reached the sanctuary of his hotel room, Hanson grabbed for the telephone.

Afraid to call Boggs just yet, he instead tried to reach John Hawkins back in Columbus. But it was several hours before he finally reached him. Hawkins also was unsure what had transpired after Boggs, according to plan, called the paramedics shortly after seven.

All he knew, Hawkins told Hanson, was that the cops for some reason were there—because a Glendale police detective named Peterson had called him to ask about the supposed dead man, Gene Hanson. But not to worry, Hawkins said. The detective did not at all sound suspicious.

Hawkins otherwise had little real information either. But it took him a half hour to calm Hanson down.

Then Hawkins really had to go. He had a flight to catch—to Los Angeles to dispose of the dead man's body.

After they hung up, Hanson called American Airlines, telling a reservations clerk that he urgently needed to be on the next available flight back to Miami. Yes, of course, he would be traveling first-class.

Shortly after Hanson arrived home that evening, his phone rang. It was Boggs calling from California. Hanson at last got the low-down on what had happened that morning. Then he broke out in a sweat, and it wasn't from the Miami heat.

New Horizons

As a successful realtor in Miami, Malcolm Briggs was used to getting telephone calls out of the blue from wealthy strangers, many of them foreigners, who were interested in beachfront properties. Or said they were. Often they turned out to be less than serious prospects, or else they were so obviously toting drug money that Briggs wanted nothing to do with them.

That's why he hesitated slightly when a West German businessman named Wolfgang von Snowden called from North Palm Beach in late January 1988, saying he was interested in a luxury condominium in Miami Beach.

"Call me when you get here, Mr. von Snowden, and I'll be happy to show you around," Briggs told the caller.

A few days later, Hanson called Briggs back, saying he was now in Miami and staying at the Mutiny Hotel, a funky motel on South Bay Shore dressed up as a ship, with mock portholes and mirrored ceilings over the beds. One of the first things Hanson did after checking in was to get a safe-deposit box. He was flush with cash. But then, there were plenty of monied strangers running around Miami in those days, albeit mostly from South America.

From the Mutiny, Briggs drove his new client straight to the Bay Shores Condominium, an expensive high-rise that looks out on Biscayne Bay. After only a cursory look at an open unit, Hanson said the apartment was just what he was looking for. The visitor was so eager to take the apartment that he wanted to move in within a week. On the spot Hanson pulled out

$7,200 in cash to put down as the first six months' rent.

On his application form, Hanson identified himself as an inactive partner in Just Sweats and listed his previous address as 1620 East Broad Street, Columbus, Ohio—which was, of course, Gene Hanson's last address there. He also listed his Social Security number as 263-66-1924—just one digit off the number that the government had issued decades earlier to one Melvin Eugene Hanson (263-66-1923).

As personal references, Hanson listed John Hawkins and Richard Boggs. "I have known Mr. von Snowden for about seven years. He is a nice and friendly person," Hawkins wrote. The doctor added: "I have had the pleasure of knowing Mr. von Snowden for about ten years. During that time he has been a friendly gentleman and a very good businessman."

Hanson and Briggs, a tall, dapper man in his late forties, grew to enjoy each other's company, and they quickly learned that they shared many things in common. And one of Hanson's steadiest visitors in Miami was Cecil Tanner, who, it turned out, had gone to the same high school in Atlanta as Briggs. Another mutual acquaintance was Mark Abrams, a Coral Gables travel agent who had recommended Briggs to Hanson in the first place. For more than twenty years Briggs had owned the travel agency, and then he sold it to Abrams, who was from Columbus and handled many of Hanson's travel arrangements.

Once he settled into his bayside apartment, Hanson began living it up, heavily tipping the complex's security personnel to look the other away as a steady stream of male escorts showed up at his apartment at all hours, summoned from the escort listings in the local gay newspapers.

Hanson also became a regular at several gay bars, including Club Milord, an infamous Miami nightclub featuring nude muscle-boy dancers. Hanson actually became interested in buying the joint. At one point he even began counting customers and trying to tally the bar's income and overhead. But those plans fell through when the joint was closed down. After that, Hanson and Tanner spoke of opening a gay bed and breakfast place in Key West. Hanson seemed never to be without some get-rich idea.

Over drinks one early April evening in the lounge of the Foxes Restaurant on South Dixie Highway, Hanson told Briggs that he had a dear friend named John in Columbus who had conceived a great get-rich scheme—but that they were really pissed off because a doctor in California had "really fucked things up for us." Hanson did not elaborate.

He also continued traveling frequently, jetting back and forth between Miami, Los Angeles, and Columbus. Often when he returned from Southern California, Hanson was loaded with assorted prescription drugs. Uppers, downers—he had it all, and in vast quantities.

Gradually, Briggs began to wonder about his new, mysterious friend. One night the two of them went to dinner at a German restaurant owned by a friend of Briggs's. It would be a nice touch of home for Wolfgang, the realtor thought. But shortly after introducing Wolfgang to the restaurateur, Briggs's friend stopped by and whispered in Briggs' ear: "This man's not from Germany. He's from the Deep South." Herr von Snowden, it turned out, could not speak a single word of German.

Briggs's nagging doubts about Wolfgang von Snowden's shadowy past deepened one night when his friend left a message on the answering machine that began: "Hi, Malcolm. This is Gene Hanson—uh, I mean, Wolfgang von Snowden. Please call me back." On another occasion, Briggs overheard his friend on the telephone, identifying himself to Tanner as Gene Hanson.

By late spring, Hanson inexplicably was no longer traveling much to California; at the same time his supply of drugs seemed to be running out. In early summer, when Briggs was about to go on his annual vacation to Costa Rica, where he owns a house, Hanson desperately wanted to go along, saying he wanted to stock up on Percodan. He also was extremely interested in buying a second citizenship either in Belize or Costa Rica.

By now deeply suspicious about his German friend, Briggs departed alone for Costa Rica. Besides, he already had a friend at the house waiting for him.

When Briggs got back in late July, Wolfgang von Snowden—or whoever he was—had vanished, and he had left no forwarding address.

Sound of Mind

On a blustery winter morning in mid-February, an extraordinary court session was convened by a Franklin County Probate Court judge in downtown Columbus, Ohio. In a virtually empty courtroom, with a seemingly bored clerk looking on, a wan, haggard petitioner sought a ruling from Judge Richard B. Metcalf declaring that he was sound of mind and that his latest will was indeed valid, reflecting his true intentions.

Barely a month after his clumsy embezzlement attempt was foiled, Gene Hanson now had quietly returned to Columbus to obtain the court's imprimatur on his amended will.

Three months earlier, he had rewritten his will, disinheriting every one of his blood relatives. Instead he named John Barrett Hawkins as the sole beneficiary and executor of his estate. At the same time, Hanson also had signed an affidavit directing that should he die, his body was to be cremated and that none of the relatives were to be even notified.

Such a spiteful act of cutting off his family, even after death, did not come as a surprise to those who knew Hanson, even casually. For he never made a secret of the fact that he had not been in touch with his mother for more than a dozen years. Indeed, the last time that Katherine Lawley had seen her son was in 1976, when she visited him in Richmond, Virginia. That was when Hanson was a rising star in the fast-track world of merchandising—and when he was in the midst of a secret transformation from a dutiful Baptist son into an urbane, well-to-do gay hedonist. After that she never saw him again. Lawley heard from him two

years later, after her mother died, when he sent some
flowers. In the intervening years Hanson occasionally
telephoned his sister, Cecelia, but he stopped doing
even that by 1987. "He told my daughter he'd like to
come home, but he couldn't," Lawley recalled. "We
never had any fights or anything. I think he didn't want
to come around because of his life-style."

Just before calling the court to order, Judge Metcalf
scanned the legal documents before him. Quickly reviewing the scant facts in the case, and judging by
Hanson's sickly appearance, the judge wondered if
Hanson wasn't an AIDS patient in his last days.

The ensuing court session was as short and mundane as it was extraordinary. It was over in a matter
of minutes. Hanson was represented by Robert V.
Morris II, another attorney at the firm of Hamilton,
Kramer, Myers & Cheek. It was Morris who also had
handled the amendment of Hanson's will in November.

The attorney began by introducing the new will into
evidence and then called Hanson to the witness stand.
After Hanson identified himself by name and his position at Just Sweats, Morris asked him:

"At this point in time you are in the process of
selling your business to your partner, isn't that correct?"

HANSON: "Yes, we have a financial agreement."

MORRIS: "And you have ceased now working with
the day-to-day operations due to your illness?"

HANSON: "Right. I'm not active in the business
anymore."

MORRIS: "And this illness is a physical illness?"

HANSON: "Right."

MORRIS: "Gene, you are not under the care of a
psychiatrist?"

HANSON: "No."

MORRIS: "And you are not under the influence of
any drugs?"

HANSON: "No."

MORRIS: "Is there anybody influencing you to do
this?"

HANSON: "No. I had instituted this as far back as April, before I knew I was ill."

Morris posed eight more questions and then sat down.

Such a pre-probate proceeding was almost unheard of in Ohio jurisprudence. No more than a dozen had ever been held in the history of the state.

From the bench, Judge Metcalf also asked Hanson a few perfunctory questions, such as about his marital status and whether he had "any children that anybody claims are yours." Hanson said he did not.

"And this will was executed of your own free will?" the judge asked.

"Yes, sir. It was," Hanson replied.

That satisfied the judge. "The court finds Mr. Hanson competent and his will will be admitted to probate on a pre-probate basis," Metcalf declared.

Court was over. And just as quietly as he had come into town, Hanson slipped away virtually unnoticed. Soon afterward, John Hawkins began talking as if he expected Hanson to die. Soon. Real soon.

Nip and Tuck

In mid-February of 1988, a wealthy Miami plastic surgeon was paid a visit by an odd couple. One was a tired-looking man in his mid-forties with deep-set wrinkles and heavy bags under both eyes. The other was a tall, handsome young man with a deeply tanned and muscular body. It was the older man, wearing an expensive toupee, who did all the talking.

"I don't want to look sixty-five anymore, Doctor," said Wolfgang von Snowden. "Can you make me look as nice as my boyfriend?" he asked Dr. Daniel B. Friedsen, gesturing toward the younger man, Dell Bergen.

Gene Hanson, still going by the name of Wolfgang von Snowden, was shopping around for a face-lift. He wanted his face free of wrinkles and his eyes to appear larger. In short, he wanted Friedsen to take twenty years off his appearance. And he didn't want any scars.

$20,000? No problem. I'll pay by cash, Hanson replied.

The forty-four-year-old plastic surgeon was intrigued. "He didn't care about the expense and he wanted no one to see any incision lines," Friedsen recalled.

For what he wanted, the doctor told Hanson, it would take at least two surgical sessions. That was fine with Hanson. And so they scheduled the operations for May—after an important business trip that Hanson had to make in the middle of April to California.

In one session that took seven and a half hours and another that lasted three and a half hours, Friedsen removed the wrinkles from Hanson's eyes, nose, mouth, cheeks, and jaws. "I took thirty years off Hanson's face," the doctor would recall.

Later, long after Hanson had departed, the plastic surgeon and his secretary discovered that the patient had signed his last name in the various medical forms using different spellings. In one it was von Snowden: in another it was von Schnowden. Whoever the man was, Friedsen thought to himself, thank God that he paid in cash—all in $100 bills.

"I became very suspicious of him at the very end," Freidsen said years later. "But I didn't change his appearance. I just zero-wrinkled him."

Last Flight

In St. Petersburg, Florida, real estate agent Mike Rosenberg's ears perked up when a potential client strolled into his office one late-summer afternoon, announcing that he had "$100,000 in green to spend" on a piece of property.

Wolfgang von Snowden told Rosenberg that he was particularly interested in an area called Pass-a-Grille, a charming, 31-block long area of architectural hodge-podge that was on its way into the National Register of Historic Places. Full of stylish artists and upscale merchants, the area was teeming with open-air bars and restaurants behind low adobe walls twined about with bougainvillea and overhung by palms. But Pass-a-Grille also was full of quaint rental cottages, cute apartments in sprawling houses, and single-family residences, including many fixer-uppers. This, Hanson told Rosenberg, was where he wanted to make an investment.

By the middle of October, Rosenberg found him a white frame house just a block from the beach. The only problem was that it had a serious termite problem. But the house could be had for only $58,000—a steal if Hanson was willing to remodel the three-bedroom, eighty-year-old house.

Hanson decided on the spot to take the house, plunking down $25,000 by peeling off $50 and $100 bills. The delighted seller, George R. Pomponio, a resident of Seaside, New Jersey, took back a $33,000 second trust deed on the house.

Hanson immediately hired a local carpenter to begin renovating the house. But soon city housing inspectors came by and found that the termite infestation was almost twice as bad as initially thought. They condemned the house. It had to be torn down.

In New Jersey, Pomponio received the first monthly payment of $354 from Wolfgang von Snowden. But that was the end of the payments: Hanson felt cheated and no way was he going to keep paying. One day Pomponio got a frantic call from his hysterical sister-in-law in St. Petersburg. "Your house is gone!" she shouted. Hanson had had the house razed and had decided to sell the property to a commercial developer. He never slept a night in the house.

Instead, for most of the time that he was in St. Petersburg that autumn, Hanson lived at the Island's End Resort, a swanky hotel at One Pass-a-Grille Way. When he first pulled up there in a gray four-door Volvo, again as Wolfgang von Snowden, Millard and Joan Gamble had no rooms available. So Hanson put down a $100 deposit for the next available single unit. In a few days he moved in. The Gambles too remembered Hanson as a man who seemed to have an endless supply of ready cash. When Hanson sold the Volvo, he paid cash for a red Sebring Austin Healy convertible.

In St. Petersburg, Hanson was friendly but for the most part kept to himself, going to the Body Dynamics health club for daily workouts, having breakfast at the Sea Horse restaurant, eating steak lunches at the Pasta Bar, and having a few drinks every night at the Lighted Tree or some other gay bar in Pass-a-Grille.

During the fall, Hanson also kept up a busy travel schedule, going to the Cayman Islands, where he opened a bank account, and to Acapulco, where he explored the possibilities of purchasing a bathhouse or a nightclub.

When Hanson left Miami in late July, he had done so in a big hurry, his idyllic bayside splendor shattered by the news that his life insurance companies had begun questioning his "death." Even John Hawkins was on the run.

In a panic Hanson fled to Key West, where he rented

a cottage—using the name of Ellis Greene. The same day he also opened a bank account using Greene's name. But Key West proved too cozy for a man with a past. And so Hanson gradually worked his way up the Gulf Coast until he reached St. Petersburg, the largest city on Florida's west coast.

One evening shortly before Hanson moved out of the End Resort, during a chat over drinks with the Gambles, Millard casually mentioned that he also was a group-health insurance consultant. That made Wolfgang von Snowden perk up noticeably.

"Did you hear the story about the guy in Ohio who owned a bunch of stores and faked his own death?" Hanson asked the Gambles.

No, they had not.

Had they ever heard of anyone faking his own death and then getting away with it?

Yes, Millard Gamble had, and he recounted the case of a Florida entrepreneur who "drowned" in an attempt, ultimately unsuccessful, to collect $16 million in life insurance.

Wolfgang von Snowden, Millard Gamble recalled, "got a big kick out of the story."

Shortly after Christmas, Hanson told his real estate agent, Rosenberg, that he was going to California for some medical treatments. But he said he would stay in touch, since he hoped shortly to arrange a sale of his Pass-a-Grille property.

Rosenberg heard nothing for several weeks. Then one afternoon in late January, Hanson called to say that he had found a buyer for his land and that he would be back in town soon to close the deal.

But Hanson would never set foot in Florida again. Authorities were closing in on him.

California, Here I Come

It was one of those tiny, out-of-the-way newspaper ads so clearly aimed at unsophisticated people who were down on their luck: "Call if you have bad credit! We'll straighten things out!" the classified ad promised.

Within hours after the newspaper's morning editions had hit the streets, people from all over Southern California began calling. In fact, the phone rang almost nonstop for several hours in John Hawkins's cheap motel room near the Los Angeles International Airport. And by the time he checked out the next day, more than fifty people had responded to his ad. This latest scam was going to be a snap.

The callers were not only desperate but also gullible. And it was a cinch coaxing vital information out of them. Date and place of birth, Social Security number, credit history—anything Hawkins asked they provided. But instead of helping the callers untangle their financial affairs, Hawkins quickly sent away for their birth certificates. To be able to keep one step ahead of the law, it was vital to have phony IDs. And as he set about flitting across the country, the name that Hawkins liked best of all was Jerry Anthony Greene.

From Columbus, he had fled first to his mama's embrace. Immediately, Jackie Cerian realized that her son was exhausted—and deeply troubled. Together they took excursions into the Nevada desert and went for long, meandering walks in the mountains. But she could not get him to open up about his current woes. She only knew that Johnny was still stressed out from his business and that he wanted to sell it and then retire, preferably to some tropical isle. "He was tired and burned out. He wanted a break," she recalled.

"This is just something I have to work out, Mom," Hawkins told her.

Cerian was certain that her son would quickly bounce back. "Johnny has this built-in ability—probably because I moved him around so much as a young boy—to pick up and go, and not look back," she said.

On the very first day that he arrived in Las Vegas, Hawkins had called Erik De Sando, asking his roommate to pick up some of his clothes that were still at the dry cleaners and to send them, along with some other personal belongings, to him in Las Vegas. Then Hawkins made a more unusual request.

"Look," he told De Sando, "I need to borrow your birth certificate. I want to open an account and put some money in it for my mother. I'm worried about her not having any money if something happens to me."

Hawkins sounded unusually concerned. And De Sando, ever the loyal friend, promptly put his own birth certificate, along with Hawkins's clothes, in a Just Sweats shipping box and sent it off to a designated United Parcel Service depot in Las Vegas.

But De Sando was the only friend who complied with Hawkins's odd request. All the others, even Tim Browne, his childhood pal who had returned to St. Louis a year earlier, spurned the request for his driver's license, Social Security number, and credit cards.

"There's a possibility that I might be in a lot of trouble," Hawkins told Browne, pleading.

"I'm sorry, but you're getting a little out of my league," Browne replied. "I don't know what kind of trouble you're in, but I can't get involved. I'm not sending you my IDs." Browne was scared.

To Greg Gunsch, a former Studio 54 bartender, Hawkins proposed that they collaborate on a credit card scam. The idea was to create a phony company and obtain credit cards for the business. Next they would use the cards "to the max," buying tens of thousands of dollars worth of consumer goods that they would then sell or pawn. When Gunsch also turned him down, Hawkins sulked. Finally he said, "It's going to be a long time before you ever hear from me again."

Hawkins didn't like to scam alone, but he had little choice.

In Denver, while visiting Wanda Livingston, a pretty, petite airline stewardess, Hawkins got himself a Colorado driver's license, posing as Jerry Anthony Greene. He even showed her the phony ID, saying that with his business in Ohio, he didn't want people in Colorado to know who he really was. But that didn't make sense to Livingston, and she concluded that Greene was his real name and that he used John Hawkins for business purposes.

Livingston was not thrilled in the first place when Hawkins showed up at her doorstep, driving a battered-up rental car, for she now had a steady beau. And she was surprised to see him because on several earlier occasions when Hawkins had called her collect, Livingston refused to accept.

Still, she saw him off and on during the next four days. But for the most part, Hawkins spent his time working out at a gym near Denver's Stapleton Airport. A few days later, as he was leaving for California, he asked her to accompany him to Hawaii. When she refused, she figured that she would never hear from him again.

In Columbus, De Sando next heard from Hawkins in late August. And he was delighted to learn that Hawkins was calling from Las Vegas, for De Sando by chance was about to visit the Nevada gambling mecca with some friends that very next weekend. Maybe they could meet up and party. But Hawkins was surprisingly noncommittal.

"Where are you gonna be staying?" Hawkins asked.

"The Riviera Hotel," De Sando replied.

"I'll call you there Friday night," Hawkins said.

At the Riviera, De Sando knew when his phone rang Friday evening that it was Hawkins calling. But it didn't take him long to realize that Hawkins was not in Las Vegas, for within minutes he had to deposit coins into the pay phone he was using. Finally, Hawkins disclosed that he was calling from a stress clinic in California.

"I've got sixty days in this place—until they feel I'm going to be properly suited to re-enter the world," he told De Sando. "After that I'm gonna have to figure out what to do 'cuz I don't have the money. That's gonna be a major problem since I got this burning desire to travel."

De Sando was surprised by Hawkins's plea of poverty, for several days earlier he had read with great interest the first of the *Columbus Dispatch* articles about the million-dollar insurance scam involving Hawkins and Hanson.

"What about all this money you got?" he asked Hawkins.

"What money?" Hawkins asked.

"Well, the money. Everybody says you got all this money," De Sando said.

Then he pulled out the August 25 *Dispatch* story, which was based on the civil lawsuit filed by Mel Weinstein on behalf of Farmers New World Life, and read it to Hawkins word for word.

Hawkins was startled. This was the first that he realized the scandal had gone public. When De Sando was through reading, Hawkins told him, "That's not true, Erik."

Still, Hawkins did not seem to comprehend the severity of the situation, for he quickly changed the subject and the two old friends spent the next half hour chatting about life's more important matters—girls and sports. De Sando could tell his friend sounded tired and lonely, and he wished Hawkins well as they hung up.

Next, Hawkins again placed a call to his best girl, Margaret Moulson, hoping that she was no longer mad at him. Shortly after they had last spent the night together—in mid-July, just before Hawkins fled from Columbus—Moulson had resolved never to have anything to do with him again. He had once more been unfaithful. And so when he had called her from out West less than two weeks after splitting town and asked her to join him in California, she refused, telling him cooly that she could not get away from her job on such short notice. "I didn't want to go out with him any longer," she recalled. "He cheated on me a couple of times, and I didn't trust him that well."

But a few days later, Moulson regretted her decision. During a heart-to-heart chat, Pamela Johnston, De Sando's girlfriend, convinced Moulson that Hawkins had only "dated" other girls two or three times and that she was the only one that Johnny truly cared for.

And now, finally, Hawkins was on the line again. Please come to California, he said.

Yes, Johnny. Oh, yes, I'll be there, she told him.

Good-bye, John

San Francisco never failed to surprise her summertime visitors. Socked in by dense fog that rolls in daily from the Pacific, all but enveloping the Golden Gate Bridge, August often is the city's coldest month—with daytime highs rarely reaching the mid-fifties.

And it was on such a gray, bone-chilling day that a late-afternoon sightseeing ferry slowly pulled away from Alcatraz Island with barely a dozen tourists aboard. Among them were John Hawkins and Margaret Moulson. As the one-time prison, where so many of America's infamous criminals had spent their last years, slowly faded from view, Hawkins and Moulson gazed silently at the Rock, each nursing a steaming cup of hot chocolate, lost in thought. Then Hawkins broke the spell.

"I could never go to prison," he said. "I'd kill myself before I'd ever spend so many years in a prison."

For Moulson, that bizarre comment was the last straw. Take me to the airport, she demanded. I want to go home.

Her visit to California had started off well enough, with Johnny meeting her at the airport—with a pair of diamond earrings. But then things immediately began to get weirder and weirder by the hour.

As soon as she saw him, she knew that he was depressed and very lonely. Even before they had pulled out of the airport parking lot, Hawkins asked her to move out to California. The invitation might have been heartfelt, but it was hardly a serious proposal and it required no direct answer.

They didn't have far to go. Within minutes Hawkins

pulled the clunker of a rental car into the potholed
parking lot of a cheap hotel near the airport. Halfway
down the block, several winos or homeless people
milled about. Surprised, Moulson shot Hawkins a look
that demanded an immediate explanation.

"I don't have as much money as I used to in Columbus," he said sheepishly. "And you'll have to help
me out." As he shut the car engine off, he asked her
to go in and register. He would wait in the car.

The next morning, he paid for the room but she paid
for breakfast.

Setting out to do some sightseeing, they strolled
hand in hand out on the Santa Monica Pier, visited
Venice's famous Muscle Beach, and then drove to Hollywood. But within minutes after arriving, their car
got side-swiped by a tour bus. No one was injured.
But when somebody called the police, Hawkins
quickly disappeared, forcing Moulson to cope with the
situation. Only after the cops had gone did Hawkins
reappear, as mysteriously as he had vanished. "By the
way," he told her, "if anyone asks, my name's Jerry
Greene."

Then they left Los Angeles and drove north on
Highway One, heading up California's breathtakingly
beautiful coast, stopping along the way in Santa Barbara and Carmel. Perhaps inspired by the rugged, sce-
nic coastline, Hawkins once more talked dreamily of
moving to Hawaii, buying a boat, and starting a business he would call the Booze Cruise.

"Hawaii," Moulson recalled, "was the only place
that he wanted to live. He talked about it on the first
and last day I saw him."

Hawkins clearly was on the run, but from what
Moulson wasn't sure. As they drove from Carmel toward San Francisco, she began gently coaxing him to
talk of his troubles, hoping to understand the deep
funk he was in.

By the time they were negotiating their way down
into Carmel on the narrow roads just outside of town,
Hawkins had explained how he came to possess a Colorado driver's license under the name of Jerry Anthony

Greene. And he had so many other IDs that Moulson couldn't count them all. He had also talked, almost boastfully, about the furniture-insurance scam in New York that netted him and Hanson $109,000.

And now, Hawkins told her, he was thinking about faking his own death to collect on his life insurance policies.

How?

His plan was to go up in a helicopter out over the Pacific Ocean, parachute out, and then have the helicopter blown up out of the sky. His body naturally would be presumed lost at sea. Seeing a side of Hawkins that she did not know existed, Moulson was appalled—and didn't know if he was serious or pulling her leg.

What of his current troubles back in Ohio? she finally asked. At that moment she knew nothing about the emerging scandal, for she had left Columbus the day before the first of many page one *Dispatch* stories appeared about Hawkins and Hanson.

Hawkins told her that he was on the run because he had been set up as the fall guy after helping launder $200,000 in drug money through Just Sweats. Alluding to the newspaper articles, Hawkins told her, "You'll find out soon enough."

Once in San Francisco, he suggested that she call Columbus to assure whoever knew that she was with him out in California that she was safe and well.

Puzzled, Moulson called her roommate, who promptly filled her in on all the juicy details being chronicled almost daily by the *Columbus Dispatch*. Shocked, an enraged Moulson confronted Hawkins. But he parried her accusations, saying the articles were simply not true. "They're trying to set me up," he told her repeatedly.

Moulson had planned to stay in California for ten days. But now, less than halfway through her visit, she was ready to get on the next plane home—just as soon as the Alcatraz ferry reached shore. "Something was weird. He was acting funny, acting different," she said. "It kind of scared me."

As they parted at the airport, Hawkins told her, "It's been nice knowing you." At that point Moulson didn't really care if she ever saw him again. As soon as she got home, she read all the *Dispatch* articles on Hawkins and Hanson, which her roommate had saved. Most shocking of all were the reports that Hawkins was a bisexual and a gay gigolo. Moulson suffered a nervous breakdown.

From California, Hawkins headed for the East Coast, visiting a string of female admirers in Camden, New Jersey, New York City, and Boston. Some of the women didn't recognize him at first because he had grown a beard and allowed his hair to grow long enough to sport a ponytail. But he eventually shaved off the beard and cut his hair because he became convinced that they were cramping his style in the singles bars.

As autumn faded in the Northeast, Hawkins finally made his way to Hawaii. From there he once more called Wanda Livingston, the stewardess in Denver, asking her to join him for some skiing in Vail. No thanks, she said. She was now living with a new boyfriend.

Still Hawkins persisted. Then what about St. Croix in mid-January? He was about to go to the Caribbean to buy a boat and then sail it around the world. Would she like to come along?

Good-bye, John, she said.

Through the early winter months, from Honolulu to Boston, from Seattle to the Caribbean, John Hawkins flitted about from one girlfriend to another, oblivious to the authorities who were hot on his trail and on several occasions came tantalizingly close to finding him.

Second Opinion

By November 1988, with the murder victim's identity well established and with a full-scale homicide investigation underway, Kurt Stoutsenberger knew his role in the case was quickly coming to an end. But the coroner's investigator had one last mission to perform, and he had to succeed in it if there was going to be a murder prosecution at all.

Hence he was immensely relieved when Dr. Evancia Sy readily agreed to meet with him and several other investigators about the case.

When Sy had performed the autopsy on a man she thought was Gene Hanson back in April, the Philippines native was nearly halfway through a two-year fellowship in forensic pathology at the L.A. County coroner's office. Shortly afterward, as a part of her continuing training, she had spent the following July through November on "outside rotation," working at UCLA-Harbor General Hospital. It was shortly after she returned to the coroner's office that Stoutsenberger called, quickly bringing her up to date on the case.

After talking to Stoutsenberger, without even waiting for the meeting to convene, Sy went to her supervisor, Joan Shipley. Together with the office's chief forensic pathologist, they painstakingly reviewed the case. They looked closely at the old slides. They prepared new ones. They methodically reviewed every circumstance of Ellis Greene's death and his misidentification. Clearly there was no doubt that the case had to be formally reopened.

Shortly thereafter, Sy met with Stoutsenberger, Jerry Treadway, head of the state insurance department's fraud bureau in Los Angeles, Al MacKenzie, the Los Angeles County deputy district attorney, and several other investigators, including a homicide detective from the Glendale police department newly assigned to the case, Jon Perkins.

By prior consensus the investigators had decided not to pressure Sy to change her mind about how Greene had died. "Our ultimate goal was just to see if there was something else she didn't check for, to find a cause of death," Stoutsenberger recalled. But then, there was no need for them to have pressed in the least. Sy and Shipley knew what had to be done. And on January 4, 1989, Sy formally amended Ellis Greene's death certificate, changing the official cause of death from nonspecific focal myocarditis to "undetermined."

The medical authorities could not say flatly that Greene was murdered. Still, the amended death certificate spelled bad news for the three co-conspirators, for it now allowed an unimpeded, full-speed-ahead homicide investigation. In the end, the question of just how Ellis Greene had met his demise—and whether it was at the hands of another—would be left for a jury to decide.

"We don't know why he died," Sy candidly admitted. But owing to the bizarre circumstances surrounding Greene's death and his deliberate mis-identification, the coroner's office arrived at its new conclusion through a process of elimination. "We ruled out accident. We ruled out suicide. We ruled out natural death. We ended up with homicide," Sy explained. "We didn't guess. We went through a process of elimination."

During their formal review Sy and her supervisors also had gone back and reviewed a number of scholarly articles on myocarditis in various medical journals. Among them was a 1980 report in the *British Heart Journal* entitled "Acute Myocarditis: A Diagnostic Dilemma." In order for a physician to reach a finding of myocarditis, it said, there should be many inflammatory cells, as well as death and decay of the myocardium, the muscular substance of the heart. But in the case of Ellis Greene, there was no such evidence. "We know that he didn't die of nonspecific myocarditis," a chastened Sy concluded.

With Stoutsenberger gone from the scene as an active investigator, the case now fell squarely in the hands of Mike Jones, the insurance-fraud investigator, and Al MacKenzie, the deputy D.A. who would prosecute Boggs for first-degree murder. Or did it?

As the pair soon discovered, much to their chagrin, a private eye in Ohio hired by the swindled Farmers New World Life Insurance Company was already way ahead of them.

Talking Trash

At first the two undercover operatives didn't think any-one had spotted them. All morning long, they had sat in their van, waiting for Erik De Sando to leave his Ellerdale Drive town house. And now their patience was finally paying off as De Sando emerged and drove off in his well-polished silver Isuzu Impulse. The two agents even followed De Sando all the way to I-270 just to be sure that he had left the area. Then they quickly doubled back to the town house.

Pulling up at the curb, they were relieved to see that they had arrived ahead of the garbage trucks. Quickly they tossed into the van the two bags of trash De Sando had put out earlier in the morning.

But as the two men sped away, they saw a stocky, sharp-eyed woman looking out her window. It was De Sando's next-door neighbor, and she was looking straight at them.

Damn! they thought. Only two days into their covert surveillance of De Sando and already their cover might be blown. Chagrined, the agents raced back to their office in downtown Columbus to report to the boss. The Just Sweats investigation was not off to an auspi-cious start.

But as it turned out, Vincent Volpi was not too con-cerned. The important thing, the private eye reminded his men, is we've got the trash. Now let's see what's in the bags. Besides, Volpi added, a twinkle in his eyes, I already have an idea about keeping De Sando from getting suspicious.

Volpi had become intrigued by the case even before Farmers New World Life Insurance Company hired

him to track down John Hawkins and Gene Hanson—
and to get the company's $1 million back. It had been
nearly two weeks since Robin Yocum and Catherine
Candisky, two energetic reporters for the *Columbus
Dispatch*, had begun peeling away the mystery, reporting their findings layer by layer as they proceeded.
And Volpi had followed each new development with
fascination as the stories—including some from Glendale—raised numerous serious questions about the
lackadaisical manner in which authorities in California
had handled the investigation.

And so when he and Weinstein talked on September
7, the thirty-three-year-old Volpi was already well
versed on the public aspects of the case, and the detective was elated to be hired to look further into the
matter.

Weinstein badly needed help. It was one thing to
have obtained a restraining order barring John Hawkins from spending the $1 million of his client's
money. But the court order was next to meaningless if
Hawkins couldn't be found for the papers to be served
on him. And by then Hawkins had been gone for six
weeks. Indeed, official notice of the action against
Hawkins by the Franklin County Court of Common
Pleas had to be served on De Sando. To be doubly
sure, Weinstein also had copies of the legal documents
delivered to Hawkins's mother as well as to her attorney in Las Vegas.

Right after that, Weinstein flew to California and
began taking depositions, or sworn statements, of authorities in Los Angeles who had been involved in the
case, including Glendale police detective Jim Peterson. Weinstein needed to learn as much as he could
about the scam, and fast.

Once back in Columbus, he took further depositions
of people who were familiar with Hawkins and
Hanson, especially Just Sweats officials and its two
primary attorneys, Dick Curtin and Austin Wildman.

Through those and other pre-trial discovery proceedings, Weinstein quickly began to sense the enor-
mity of the daring plot: Hanson's embezzlement in

January, his unusual pre-probate court hearing in February, the April murder of an innocent person and his deliberate mis-identification as Hanson, Hawkins's mad dash as he looted the company's bank accounts in July—it all began to come into sharp focus.

"At first nobody knew the magnitude of this thing," Weinstein recalled. That Just Sweats was on the brink of ruin also came as a surprise. "The company was well-known. It was a growing business," he said. "I don't think it was realized by the general public that it was in financial trouble."

And now, as Ed Laramee, Melissa Mantz, and Wildman struggled valiantly to resuscitate the bankrupt company, the challenge facing Weinstein was as clear as it was daunting. To have any chance of recovering his client's $1 million, he had to first find Hawkins and Hanson.

At the sixty-lawyer firm of Emens, Hurd, Kegler & Ritter, Kevin Kerns, one of Weinstein's colleagues, introduced him to Volpi, a talented sleuth who had once worked as an investigator for the Franklin County district attorney's office.

Volpi went to work on the case immediately after talking with Weinstein. One of the first things he did, as a matter of courtesy, was to notify every jurisdiction that had any involvement whatsoever with the case of his entry into the investigation, from the FBI to the Glendale police department. Volpi even telephoned the tiny police department of Whitehall, a Columbus suburb where Mike Guglielmelli had gone in mid-July to report that Hawkins had fled with Just Sweats funds. The U.S. attorney's office pledged its cooperation and assistance. At the Columbus police department, a detective in the organized-crime bureau was less encouraging, saying the agency would not yet be able to cooperate, since this was still only a civil matter. At the Columbus office of the FBI, the agent already looking into the case was downright obstreperous, telling Volpi bluntly, "Stay out of my way. Don't step on my toes."

Volpi was hardly surprised to find that no single

agency was interested in taking on the case in its en-
tirety. "We were beating the drums to get the law enforcement agencies involved," he said, shaking his
head as he recalled his frustration. "But everybody
was waiting for somebody else to act." Cases such as
this, involving so many different jurisdictions, especially across state lines, often expose one of the major
weaknesses in America's criminal justice system: an
utter lack of coordination.

Volpi quickly realized that he couldn't count on the
public agencies for assistance, much less cooperation.
Still, this was a job for which the wily private eye
seemed particularly suited. A handsome, outgoing
man, Volpi also has a quick smile and long dark curls
that tumble down over his shirt collar. But his gregar-
ious nature belies the wile that it takes to make a living
as a successful private detective.

Volpi had begun studying criminal justice in college, but it took him a decade to get his degree because of a variety of part-time and full-time jobs,
mostly in law enforcement, that he took during his
college "career." He had been first steered into such
work by a college roommate who had been a military
policeman in Vietnam. And as soon as Volpi turned
eighteen, he too got a job as a private security guard,
working alongside his roommate. Off and on, Volpi
worked at a number of such jobs, as far away as Colorado, before he finally returned to Columbus and became an investigator with the Franklin County district
attorney's office.

Tired of the bureaucracy, he set out on his own in
1982. And by the time Weinstein came calling in early
September 1988, Volpi had developed a large network
of employees and collaborators around the country,
including his brother, Vaughn, in Tampa, Florida. In
Columbus, Volpi had about twenty-five investigators,
nearly half of whom he would assign to the Just Sweats
case before it was over.

To find Hawkins, the most logical starting point was
Erik De Sando, the missing businessman's roommate.
And as soon as Volpi returned from his meeting with

Weinstein, he called a staff meeting to give everyone a full, up-to-date briefing on the case as he and Weinstein understood it. While some investigators were assigned to gather information on Hawkins's parents and friends, possibly for surveillance, Volpi instructed two of his top operatives to begin an immediate surveillance of De Sando.

At 9:45 that night, De Sando emerged from his town house and drove away at speeds up to eight-five miles per hour, quickly losing the two investigators.

In the meantime, another investigator was assigned to approach De Sando directly, posing questions under the guise of being a free-lance magazine writer from Chicago. With pen and a reporter's notebook in hand, the investigator walked up to De Sando's condominium on Friday morning, September 9.

But De Sando was already gone. His next-door neighbor quickly came out and engaged the investigator in conversation. The chunky woman was clearly a gossip and knew all about the case. "I even fed Erik's cat while he was in Las Vegas," she told the investigator, as if proud of her little role in the unfolding scandal. She suggested that he come back a little later, for De Sando came and went frequently throughout the day. "He's a real nice guy," she added.

The investigator left to get some coffee and, sure enough, when he got back a half hour later, De Sando was there. The investigator introduced himself as a Chicago writer who was visiting relatives in Columbus and, while in town, had decided to look into the story a bit as a possible future magazine piece.

De Sando was not uncooperative, but he said he had only a half hour to spare, and that in any case he had a contractual obligation with a local television station that limited the amount of information about the case that he could discuss with other news media. A short time later, De Sando ended the conversation, saying he had to run.

It was after De Sando left that the two Volpi agents maintaining surveillance outside picked up De Sando's trash—under the watchful eye of his vigilant neighbor.

In hopes of preventing suspicion from falling on the investigator posing as the free-lancer, Volpi told him to seize the initiative by calling De Sando to tell him that he had seen two men in a van "messing" with De Sando's trash. Not a problem, De Sando said, there's nothing of value in my garbage.

Ten days later, the investigator again met with De Sando, still posing as a free-lancer. This time De Sando was inexplicably expansive, offering detailed background on Hawkins, Hanson, and the origin of Just Sweats—including the furniture scam in New York that had earned the two men their seed money for Just Sweats. De Sando also talked about Dr. Richard Boggs, saying he had provided Hawkins and Hanson not only Quaaludes but also spurious medical documentation with which to defraud insurance companies.

Back at Volpi's shop, as they picked their way through De Sando's trash, the investigators uncovered a treasure trove of leads on Hanson and Hawkins. "It's a procedure that we use a lot more than I'd like to think about. But it's very successful," Volpi recalled, grinning broadly. "People throw out a lot of evidence with their trash."

Among the two garbage bags' contents were telephone bills going back to the beginning of July—when Hawkins was still in Columbus. Like most telephone bills, they listed every long-distance call.

Painstakingly, Volpi and his staff set out to account for all the long-distance calls. And with the help of various telephone company sources, Volpi also obtained the names of all recipients of the long-distance calls made from the town house. And then one name stood out. The number had a 315 area code—Miami, Florida. And it belonged to someone with the unlikely name of Wolfgang von Snowden.

Reaching Out

In Key West they had known him as Ellis Greene. But nobody knew where he had gone. Or at least that's what they told Mike Jones, who showed up there in early October, looking for Gene Hanson.

Initially, Jones was skeptical, for two reasons. One, was Hanson really so stupid to have assumed the identity of the man he had killed? Or was the gay community in Key West merely protecting one of its own from the prying eyes of the law? "Gay communities usually don't like outsiders. And here we were, inquiring about Gene Hanson and a gay doctor," Jones recalled.

But he doggedly pursued his inquiry, visiting bars, restaurants, and other public places, showing a picture of Hanson to anyone willing to take a look. And when those who heard him out finally realized why Jones was there, some stepped forward. Yes, they said, pointing to Hanson's photograph, that's Ellis. But nobody had seen him since late summer. Some of the men Jones talked to actually became outraged that another gay person had been so cold-bloodedly murdered—and by a gay cabal. It's come to *this*, several fumed.

And they led Jones to the·local realty agent who had rented Hanson the bungalow, which was still in his name. Accompanied by the agent, Jones went to the bungalow with a search warrant, and the complex's manager readily opened up the cottage for Jones, now accompanied by a Glendale homicide detective newly assigned to the case. Soon a Miami-based FBI agent joined them with a fingerprint kit.

On the glass-topped coffee table was a pile of mail—all addressed to Ellis Greene. Some of it was no more than a month old. One letter was addressed to Wolfgang von Snowden in care of Ellis Greene. Old phone bills showed numerous long-distance calls from the bungalow to Boggs and Hawkins. And back at the lab, criminalists later confirmed that fingerprints lifted from inside the˙ house indeed were Gene Hanson's.

The investigators were deeply disappointed when they realized how close they had come to nabbing Hanson, for the fugitive clearly had left in a hurry, with no intention of returning. But Jones reminded his companions: "We're now only a month behind him."

Though Jones flew back to California empty-handed, he was encouraged. He knew now that it was only a matter of time before he would meet face to face with Hanson. The weeks of quiet, dogged spadework seemed about to pay off.

From the very beginning Jones had tried to conduct a low-key investigation. True, there had been no choice but to question Boggs immediately. But otherwise Jones had tried assiduously not to do anything that might spook the doctor lest he flee. "I was trying to keep a low profile because I didn't want to set off the red lights yet," Jones recalled.

Still, the floodgates opened as many who knew Boggs came forward with firsthand accounts of the doctor's deteriorating personal life, his string of business failures, and his many professional setbacks, including the loss of staff privileges at three Glendale hospitals.

And when Jones first learned about Hans Jonasson, he immediately suspected that the doctor's young Swedish lover also was involved in the murder, perhaps serving as "bait" to lure a victim to Boggs's office. Only near the end of his investigation did Jones conclude that Jonasson had known nothing about the killing. Boggs simply kept him around as "the little bitch," Jones said.

Other investigators in the meantime also uncovered many tracks left previously by John Hawkins. They learned, for instance, that when he had first arrived in L.A. years earlier, he lived in a seedy Hollywood apartment building known as a thriving location for the filming of porno movies. Later, after Hawkins became a bicoastal male escort, investigators linked him to some of the biggest producers in Hollywood and wealthiest men in Beverly Hills.

Jones also ordered a meticulous audit of Glendale's 911 operation for the morning of April 16, 1988—the day Boggs said he was initially unable to get through after Gene Hanson collapsed in his office shortly after 6:00 A.M. And from that a crucial piece of incriminating evidence emerged. Just to give the doctor the benefit of doubt, Jones made sure that the audit went as far back as to two-thirty that morning. "We found that there were always at least a half-dozen lines open and operational," Jones said.

Telephone records had also led Jones to South Florida, hot on Hanson's trail. His boss, Jerry Treadway, had a keenly analytical mind, perhaps owing to his training and service in military intelligence. And he was one of the early believers in the power of computer. And so after Jones returned from his searches of Boggs's home and office, carting boxes full of telephone records, it was Treadway who suggested that they work out a program to analyze the hundreds upon hundreds of long-distance calls. And even though Treadway had many supervisory responsibilities, he willingly offered to help out. Above all, he thoroughly enjoyed doing investigative work. And such infectious enthusiasm started right at the top. Even Ron Warthen, the bureau's chief, often would pitch in. One day, for instance, when the investigators needed to verify that a certain pay phone was near Boggs's apartment, Warthen readily volunteered for that duty—he would check it out on the way home, he said.

It took Treadway and Jones several days at the computer terminal to develop a method to analyze and cross-check all the telephone calls quickly. But once it was up and running, the program yielded results almost instantaneously. "This was when the pattern clarified," Jones recalled.

Starting around the beginning of 1988—about the time of Hanson's embezzlement of Just Sweats funds—he and Hawkins had been on the phone with Boggs with growing frequency. But the long-distance calls became spectacularly bunched around two notable events that spring. One was April 1—the night that Barry Pomeroy was attacked by Boggs with a stun gun. The other was April 16—the morning that Ellis Greene was murdered and found in Boggs's office.

The rash of calls was strong circumstantial evidence that the three men were engaged in a murder-for-insurance plot.

On the day after Boggs had met Pomeroy—the original intended murder victim—the doctor and Hanson called each other a half-dozen times. Throughout the week the calls continued, soon involving Hawkins as well—right up to the wee hours after Boggs had bungled the murder attempt. That night alone there were nearly a half-dozen calls between the conspirators.

Shortly afterward, the number of calls diminished a bit, but not for long. They picked up again in intensity as the fateful night of April 15 approached.

In addition to these telephone records, an analysis of motel and airline records further revealed to Jones that Hanson had arrived in L.A., from Miami, on April 15, and then checked into the Glendale Holiday Inn—as Wolfgang von Snowden—around six the next morning. Less than an hour later, Boggs called 911 to summon paramedics, reporting that a patient named Gene Hanson had died in his office.

Later that same morning, still from his motel room, Hanson spoke twice to Hawkins, who was still in Columbus, and then quickly finalized his flight plans back to Miami—as Wolfgang von Snowden. That night, back in Florida, at 10:25 Eastern time, he had a twenty-five-minute telephone conversation with Boggs.

There wasn't much doubt, at least in Jones's mind, what the topic of conversation was in all these calls.

In the beginning, it was easy to identify Hawkins's

number in Columbus. But who, Jones wondered, owned the number in the 315 area code, and why did he have so many conversations with Boggs? From Florida soon came word that the number belonged to a Wolfgang von Snowden.

The name instantly rang a bell.

Jones had first come across that unusual name on a telephone message seized earlier from Boggs's office. The name showed up again on a scribbled note in Hawkins's handwriting that Melissa Mantz at Just Sweats had found over the summer. "Get the money. Get the birth certificate," Hawkins had written. "Distance myself from Wolfgang."

Jones knew that von Snowden was either a previously unknown co-conspirator or, more likely, a pseudonym for Gene Hanson. It was time to head for Florida.

But in Ohio, Vince Volpi also had figured out that von Snowden was Hanson's alias—and his people were already snooping around in Miami well ahead of Jones.

Miami Vice

They clashed almost from the moment that Rick Aeschbacher stepped foot into the Brickell Point Hotel to meet with Mike Jones and Jon Perkins, a self-important Glendale homicide cop newly assigned to help out in the case. Perhaps it was inevitable.

Aeschbacher was one of Volpi's investigators, based in Tampa, and he was a major reason why the private investigation was miles ahead of Jones and Perkins. But then, that had been partly by design. Earlier in the fall, as the pace of the investigation quickened, authorities in California and Ohio had agreed to split up the formidable work load. California would concentrate its resources on developing the case against Boggs; Ohio would focus on finding Hanson and Hawkins.

But by early October, after the identification of Ellis Greene as the murder victim, Jones felt his investigation had reached a point that by turning to Hanson and Hawkins, more information on Boggs might turn up. And so when telephone records uncovered Hanson's trail in Miami, Jones rushed down for a personal evaluation, taking Perkins along for the ride.

At the hotel, Aeschbacher wasted little time letting Jones and Perkins know, perhaps a bit too smugly, all that he had learned. Hanson had recently obtained a Florida driver's license using the name of Wolfgang von Snowden. Hanson also had a New York driver's license under the name of Melvin E. Hanog. And until he vanished over the summer, he had lived in a luxury high-rise called the Brickell Shores, occupying a penthouse overlooking Miami's Biscayne Bay. Some referred to that portion of Bayshore Drive as the "Park Avenue of the South." But others knew it also as a haven that attracted drug kingpins, with their bundles of cash. Hanson had signed a one-year lease on February 1, but quickly left at about the time that Farmers New World Life began questioning the identity of the dead man in Boggs's office. Hanson's rental application was accompanied by a glowing letter of recommendation—from Boggs.

When Aeschbacher was done reciting the information, he also liberally dispensed unsolicited advice. Go find Dell Bergen, and quickly, he told Jones and Perkins. Bergen was bound to have more information about his fugitive lover. And by the way, don't bother with Dr. Friedsen; you'd be wasting your time with the plastic surgeon. Besides, Aeschbacher added, I'll soon be getting from him the before-and-after pictures of Hanson.

Jones and Perkins were extremely wary of Aeschbacher and Volpi, wanting as little to do with them as possible—but anxious to learn what they knew. Jones, for one, suspected—accurately, as it turned out—that Volpi was leaking information to the Columbus news media, especially the *Dispatch*. "We didn't want Aeschbacher with us—or even to learn all that we were doing," Jones said. "What could Aeschbacher do even if he found Gene Hanson? At least Jon and I could 'cuff him."

Moreover, Jones was worried that Aeschbacher and his associates might somehow screw up their homicide investigation. And so Jones and Perkins persuaded the FBI office in Miami to tell Aeschbacher in no uncertain terms to back off—much to the outrage of Volpi. If not for him and his private investigators, Volpi felt, authorities in California would have been hopelessly behind Hanson instead of closing in on the man.

With the private detectives out of their way, Jones and Perkins drove to Dr. Friedsen's multimillion-dollar, gated mansion. Behind the house was a tennis court presided over by a tall statue of a nude man, his loins concealed by the looping tail of a dragon. Just beyond that were two yachts sitting on the pristine bay. The plastic surgeon was initially cool, but his demeanor changed abruptly when Jones casually mentioned that he had a subpoena for Hanson's records. "Then you could hardly shut him up," Jones recalled, for Friedsen chattered endlessly—mostly raving about Dell Bergen being "such a pretty boy." Eventually, Jones and Perkins managed to coax out of Friedsen details about Hanson, including the fact that he had paid for the expensive procedures in cash.

To kill a subsequent afternoon before heading to Key West, Jones and Perkins tagged along with FBI agents on a drug raid, which the Glendale detective found extremely exciting.

In many ways Perkins did not look like a cop. A short, compact man around forty, the balding Perkins often showed up in court wearing expensive double-breasted suits and Italian shoes, looking more like a well-heeled defense lawyer than a streetwise cop. And he was as full of himself as many lawyers—arrogant, moody, thin-skinned, and abrasive.

"That Perkins," one courthouse observer snorted, "he can't make up his mind whether he wants to be Kojak or Clarence Darrow." But in other ways Perkins was a wily cop through and through. And he could tell war stories with the best of them—and the racier, the better.

Off the job, he had a penchant for dressing as if he had just walked off the set of *Miami Vice*—lots of gold jewelry, spanking white L.A. Gear sneakers, black casual wear, topped by an expensive, foreign-cut sports jacket. Perkins indeed had a fascination with Hollywood and already had sold one movie script.

He had been ecstatic when he was assigned the case a few weeks earlier. All summer long, he had been one dejected cop. After serving in the Glendale police department for fifteen years—the last few as a homicide detective, which was all he ever wanted to be—he had been forced to make a Hobson's choice. Either go back out on the street as a uniformed cop on the beat or take an inside job as the department's new human relations officer. Perkins believed that he was being demoted in retaliation for having served too vigorously as president of the police association, which regularly brought him into close contact with the department's brass over workplace issues.

Humiliated, he chose the desk job, and soon set up shop in a tiny, windowless room in the back of the detective bureau. "It was kind of shitty, and it rubbed me the wrong way," Perkins recalled.

But he didn't have long to stew. Less than two months later, a captain dropped by Perkins's dreary little office for a private chat. Ellis Greene had just been identified as the dead man that Dr. Boggs insisted was Gene Hanson. And the department was coming under increasing heat for the way it had botched the investigation. It was time to reopen the case, and the department might be able to salvage its reputation if it could help unravel the mystery and then bring the murderers to justice.

The captain wanted Perkins to take the job. Much as they might have found Perkins personally unlikable, the powers-that-be knew that if anyone could help the department recoup from a severe embarrassment, it was Perkins. "Jon has just the right degree of obsession, and he's aggressive and intelligent," Charles L. Lindner, a prominent Los Angeles County defense lawyer, said with grudging admiration. Earlier in 1988, for instance, Perkins had been the lead investigator in a case in which a Domino's Pizza delivery boy was murdered in Glendale. During the ensuing trial of the two accused murderers, when Los Angeles County refused to buy two dummies that Perkins and the prosecutor wanted to use in court for demonstration, Perkins and the deputy D.A. went out and bought the dummies with their own money.

Perkins was elated by the offer to take on such a high-profile assignment, one that also had the entire department's reputation on the line. It was an immensely ego-boosting turn of events—and a dramatic comeback after his demotion just two months earlier.

The discovery of Ellis Greene's true identity came

at a propitious time for a bureaucratic reason as well. At the time detective Jim Peterson was on summer vacation. But given the urgency to reopen the investigation, someone had to be found immediately to take over the case. The Pomeroy case file was still sitting on Peterson's desk.

Happy as Perkins was, however, he nevertheless had some misgivings about taking on the assignment. He had little understanding of insurance-fraud cases. "I hated insurance," Perkins recalled. What he liked were old-fashioned homicides. For instance, three years after he had investigated a savage double murder committed by a serial killer known as the Night Stalker, Perkins often still spoke animatedly about the gory details.

Sensing Perkins's ambivalence, the captain knew just what to say. He assured Perkins that he would have a totally free rein. Perkins accepted. "I feel very protective of what I do," he explained later. "Nobody's gonna tell me what to do."

It didn't take him long to spot the early shortcomings of the investigation—or to tell anyone who would listen all about it. "There were a lot of things that were missing. These people have never investigated a homicide," Perkins said, referring to Mike Jones, Jerry Treadway, and Al MacKenzie. "Everything was missing," Perkins fumed haughtily. "This was not only a case of whodunit, but who didn't do what. I was an outsider fighting my way in."

As the newest comer to the burgeoning investigation, Perkins indeed had to work his way in. But he didn't make it easy for himself.

Before stepping up the probe, MacKenzie and Jones realized that it would be useful to hold a meeting to coordinate efforts among the growing number of agencies getting involved. And in early October, the meeting was scheduled at the insurance department's fraud bureau in downtown Los Angeles. "You're welcome to attend and to be a part of the task force," MacKenzie told a senior Glendale police official. "But it's not your investigation. This task force is now being run by the L.A. district attorney's office and led by Mike Jones.''

When Perkins showed up at the meeting with a chip on his shoulder, Jones was not surprised, for he had been warned by Kurt Stoutsenberger, who had already dealt with Perkins. While Jones was reviewing the police searches of Boggs's office and home, Perkins began moaning and shaking his head, contemptuously criticizing the investigators for not having seized certain evidence, such as the ''sex toys'' in Boggs's apartment.

Finally, to the shock of the dozen or so officials gathered around the conference table, Al MacKenzie erupted. It was so unlike the usually soft-spoken deputy district attorney to lose his cool. But MacKenzie, who had had a distinguished career prosecuting complex fraud cases that required a special analytical knack, yelled at Perkins to ''put up or shut up,'' pointedly challenging him—as the Glendale police representative—to come up with something useful.

''Fuck you,'' Perkins said.

''Fuck you,'' MacKenzie replied before others quickly intervened to cool tempers.

Eventually the two men patched things up, although Perkins continued to confide in others his unhappiness over having to work with fraud investigators and especially a fraud prosecutor on a murder case.

After the meeting broke up, Perkins set out pretty much as a lone ranger, rarely bothering to coordinate his efforts with others, rarely bothering to tell Jones of interviews that he had conducted until long afterward. But as far as Jones and MacKenzie were concerned, while Perkins certainly performed a useful role in the investigation, such as uncovering Hawkins's past in Southern California, the detective was hardly making himself indispensable.

The California authorities did not invite Volpi to the October meeting because they felt that as an investigator for the insurance company, Volpi was looking into the matter as a civil case. But there was another reason as well. Jones and MacKenzie wanted to conduct their investigation away from the prying news media. They were increasingly convinced that Volpi was leaking material to the press—including information that Jones and MacKenzie had passed on to him. Volpi in fact had given information to Catherine Candisky and Robin Yocum, the two *Columbus Dispatch* reporters. But in return they had given him useful information as well.

Despite being excluded by authorities in California, Volpi continued to uncover important new evidence. For instance, by the end of September, after nearly a month of covert surveillance on Erik De Sando, Volpi decided it was time to confront Hawkins's former roommate. He persuaded a Columbus police detective to join him for the De Sando interview, which they secretly taped. Bluffing, the two men feigned a degree of familiarity with the case that far exceeded their true knowledge. To Volpi's delight, a nervous De Sando not only confirmed virtually everything that they already knew but also provided vital new information— such as Hawkins's payment of $6,500 to Boggs right after the Memorial Day weekend.

As the leads on Hanson increasingly pointed toward Florida, Volpi realized that despite the growing evidence of Hanson's criminal activities, there were still no criminal charges filed anywhere against him. Even if authorities found Hanson, they had no legal right to detain him.

On October 14, Volpi and attorney Mel Weinstein paid a visit to Bob Smith, a Franklin County assistant district attorney with whom Volpi had once worked. They quickly brought Smith up to date on the case. Smith was fascinated, but he said that with authorities in California still struggling to figure out just what kind of criminal case they had on their hands, he was reluctant at the moment to file criminal charges. At least not yet, Smith said.

He did take the unusual step of authorizing Volpi to go to the Franklin County Municipal Court and file the charges himself—on behalf of Farmers New World. Volpi then went directly across the street to the Franklin County Municipal Court to swear out two warrants for the arrest of Hanson and Hawkins, charging them with "theft by deception in excess of $100,000"—a second-degree felony under Ohio law.

It was already late Friday afternoon by the time Volpi got to the courthouse. And to his dismay, the legal forms required were bewilderingly voluminous and they had to be typed. Volpi didn't know how to type. And the office was about to close for the weekend.

Much to Volpi's relief, a dedicated FBI agent, Mark Chidichimo, offered to stay late and wait for Volpi to finish. Chidichimo also wanted to see justice done.

Grateful, Volpi sat down before an old manual typewriter and began pecking away. It took him three hours to finish the forms. Chidichimo was still there. Then the two men drove to the home of a local magistrate to have the papers signed.

It was now ten. But at last there were now warrants for the arrests of Hanson and Hawkins, based on state charges for unlawful flight to avoid prosecution, or "U-FAP," in the parlance of law enforcement. The warrants then were quickly teletyped to FBI offices across the nation. Any murder charges, however, had to await the fruits of the investigation in California.

Volpi also took one other measure that proved vitally important in the apprehension of Gene Hanson. He called Michael Goldsmith, a one-time employee who now worked as a U.S. Customs agent, and persuaded him to enter the names of Melvin Eugene Hanson and Wolfgang von Snowden into the U.S. Treasury Department's Enforcement Communications System. Volpi knew that Customs officials routinely check the computer listings of fugitives whenever they come across a suspicious traveler seeking to enter the United States.

That done, and with Hanson's trail now cold, neither Volpi nor the investigators in California had much else to go on. Their best hope was for Hanson to slip up.

Grounded

American Airlines Flight 150 landed on time at Dallas–Fort Worth Airport, carrying about 160 passengers, nearly all U.S. tourists returning from Acapulco. It was Sunday evening, January 29, 1988, and most of the casually dressed, slightly sunburned passengers seemed eager to retrieve their luggage and head home to get ready for work the next morning.

Dave Berry, a U.S. Customs inspector, also was thinking about going home. It was seven-twenty and he was tired. Berry, twenty-eight, had been on the job since eleven-thirty that morning, searching arriving aircraft and inspecting passengers and their baggage. It had been a typically busy Sunday. No fewer than 1.5 million international travelers pass through customs at Dallas–Fort Worth every year. Of those, less than five percent are ever detained for questioning or special baggage inspection; on flights from a tourist mecca like Acapulco, only one out of every one hundred passengers is stopped for questioning, usually on suspicion of drug smuggling.

Berry was grateful that his shift was ending, for American's flight 150 was only one of three arriving international flights now disgorging hundreds of passengers into the crowded terminal. He left his inspection station and headed for the employees restroom to get cleaned up. To reach the washroom, Berry had to walk past a luggage carousel area where disembarking passengers on Flight 150 had begun to congregate, awaiting their bags.

But something about one of the passengers caught Berry's well-trained eyes. It was a man in red gym shorts and sneakers. "He's dressed the part, but he just doesn't look like a regular tourist," Berry said to himself. The traveler seemed quite nervous, even jittery, and clearly was in a big hurry.

Berry stopped in his tracks, and from a discreet distance he continued watching the man, who was chain-smoking, as the luggage carousel's conveyor belt lurched into action, soon disgorging suitcases of every color and shape. The traveler, Berry thought, seemed to have a slight edginess that so often betrays the inexperienced drug smuggler.

Berry waited until after the traveler had reclaimed his suitcase before approaching.

"Coming in from Acapulco, sir?" Berry asked.

"Yes."

"Are you a United States citizen?"

"Yes." Then the man produced a birth certificate and a Massachusetts driver's license that identified himself as George Soule. The photograph on the license certainly was that of its owner.

Was he in Mexico for business or pleasure?

Vacationing, Soule said, his voice nearly cracking. Uh, he added quickly, clearing his throat, I was renting a condominium. Soule said he was en route to St. Petersburg, Florida, to close out a real estate deal.

Something didn't add up.

Berry looked at the Customs Baggage Declaration form that Soule had filled out.

"Is this declaration correct?" Berry asked politely.

"Yes, I have nothing to declare," Soule replied warily.

Berry asked to inspect Soule's leather knapsack.

Soule's hands quivered ever so slightly as he surrendered it to the young inspector.

As soon as he opened the bag, Berry saw bundles of $50 bills inside, wrapped in cellophane.

"If this is over $10,000," he told Soule, "you've got a problem."

The money, it's to buy an antique car with, Soule said. No, it was for the condominium in Acapulco, he corrected himself.

It was time for a more thorough search. Berry radioed Jim Starnes, a fellow inspector, asking him to come to the search room.

Once the three men were inside, Berry performed a quick search of Soule's person and, finding nothing, removed the cash from Soule's bag and began counting. It took awhile. The amount came to $14,000, or $4,000 over the legal limit. Soule had broken a federal law. Berry told Soule to have a seat on the bench. Berry now had some major paperwork to do. Dinner at home would have to wait.

Starnes, forty-two, continued watching Soule and soon he realized that something else was wrong. Soule was still nervous, and that's unusual because most smugglers once detected no longer are nervous. If all that Soule was guilty of was not declaring the cash, the man should no longer be so edgy. "There has to be something more," Starnes said to himself.

As Berry continued with the paperwork, Starnes performed a more thorough search of Soule's belongings. He immediately came across several checkbooks and receipts bearing names other than George Soule. One checkbook belonged to Ellis Greene; it was a bank account that Gene Hanson had audaciously opened in Key West.

Also in Hanson's possession was a book entitled *How to Create a New Identity*. It had been checked out of a Miami public library eight months earlier.

And inside the traveler's eyeglass case, Starnes found a Florida driver's license bearing the name Wolfgang von Snowden but containing a mug shot of Soule. "That's my partner's," Hanson explained unconvincingly.

The traveler asked for some coffee. But the snack bars were now closed. The inspectors got him a can of soda. They also called in Customs special agents to continue the investigation.

In the meantime, Berry and Starnes ran a check on every name that showed up on the various documents in Soule's possession. Nobody believed Soule when he said that he was carrying the various IDs and documents home for business associates and that he himself was using a phony ID to avoid people to whom he owed money.

It took only minutes for the Treasury Department's Enforcement Communications System to supply the real answer:

Wolfgang von Snowden was an alias for Melvin Eugene Hanson. There was a warrant out for his arrest for unlawful flight to avoid prosecution.

The agents took Hanson straight to the airport's drab two-cell holding facility, where he spent the night.

Prisoner with No Name

It looked hopeless. There seemed no way that Mike Jones and Jon Perkins could reach the airport in time to catch their flight to Dallas–Fort Worth. It was already 4:00 P.M., and their flight was due to depart Los Angeles International at 5:05, barely an hour away.

The rush hour was already in full swing, and Jones and Perkins were still in Pasadena. By car, they were a solid hour, probably more, from LAX.

Word of Gene Hanson's arrest had reached Jones via his car radio. He had been out in the field conducting interviews involving physicians bilking Medicaid in a case unrelated to the Boggs investigation. There was no question that Jones needed to get down to the Tarrant County Jail immediately—hopefully ahead of the Ohio authorities.

Perkins had gotten the news while sitting in a courtroom in Pasadena, where he was assisting in the prosecution of a case in which he had been the lead investigator.

Their plan was this: Jones's office would book him and Perkins on the next available flight to Dallas–Fort Worth. Jones meanwhile raced home to pack. Then on the way to Pasadena to pick up Perkins at the courthouse, he swung by the detective's house to pick up his things, which his wife had hastily thrown together.

From Pasadena they drove quickly to the Glendale police headquarters, just west of Pasadena. There a helicopter was waiting to fly them to LAX. It was well after four by the time Jones and Perkins screeched to a halt at the Glendale P.D. headquarters.

But there was a hitch: The chopper had developed a

malfunction. Next they jumped back into the car and
raced to a heliport in Burbank, the next adjacent town.
Burbank police had agreed to fly them in their helicopter.

It was four-forty by the time they finally lifted off.
No problem, the pilot assured the two, glancing at his
watch. There was still time.

They made it with less than five minutes to spare.
Grateful that it was a nonstop flight, Jones collapsed
into his seat.

He was in such a hurry to get to Hanson not only
because he simply wanted the satisfaction of beating
the Ohio authorities there; he also hoped to obtain from
Hanson information on Hawkins's whereabouts before
news of the arrest became widely publicized, thus giving Hawkins time to flee.

The arrest had come too late Sunday evening to
make the Monday papers. But authorities knew that
the *Columbus Dispatch* would play up the news in a
big way in its Tuesday morning editions. Of that there
was no doubt, for reporter Robin Yocum by Monday
evening was already in Texas, having been tipped off
late Sunday night by Vince Volpi. The private investigator, in turn, had gotten the news from Mike Goldsmith, the customs agent.

From the Dallas–Fort Worth airport, Jones and
Perkins rented a car and drove straight to the Tarrant
County Jail. Much to their chagrin, they encountered
not only Volpi but also Dan Abraham, an assistant
Franklin County prosecutor now handling the
insurance-fraud case, and Yocum.

It was the first face-to-face meeting between the
California and Ohio investigators, and there was instant friction. Perkins was enraged that Abraham and
Volpi already had interviewed Hanson—and searched
his belongings. Jones was equally astounded, for the
Ohio investigators had booked Hanson's belongings as
personal property instead of as potential evidence.

When Volpi and Abraham first saw Hanson, he
looked extremely unhappy in his jail-issued plastic
thongs and a baggy, dark green V-neck jumpsuit. He

looked beaten, worn, and uncharacteristically shaggy with a circular fringe of long, wispy strands of dirty blond hair.

Hanson waived his right to an attorney and agreed to listen to what Volpi and Abraham had to say. Volpi did most of the talking. And Hanson sat stone-faced, smoking one cigarette after another, as Volpi outlined everything that he knew about the events leading up to and including Ellis Greene's murder. Volpi concluded by urging Hanson to make amends by cooperating with authorities. He might, Volpi said, earn himself a lighter sentence. Hanson was in no mood to cooperate. Initially he even refused to confirm his true identity. It was only after being told that authorities were at that very moment running a fingerprint check on him that Hanson sagged. Then he admitted who he was.

"Our focus with Hanson in that first meeting was twofold: to find out where John Hawkins was and to get Gene Hanson to admit to the insurance fraud and the embezzlement," Abraham said. "But he was evasive."

The one thing that Hanson volunteered was that neither Dick Curtin nor Austin Wildman, the Just Sweats attorneys, had anything whatsoever to do with the matter. "He was adamant in this regard and repeatedly reiterated their lack of culpability," Volpi recalled.

From jail Hanson had called his mother, the first contact between mother and son in years. "You know, Mother, I'm gay," Hanson had begun.

To Volpi and Abraham, Hanson made clear that he badly wanted out of Tarrant County Jail, saying he would happily waive extradition and return voluntarily to Columbus.

In all, Volpi and Abraham spent nearly two hours with Hanson. Then, as they were about to leave to find lodging for the night, Jones and Perkins arrived.

Initially, Jones was more interested in the evidence—that is, Hanson's belongings—than in talking to Hanson. And the next morning, he returned with a properly executed search warrant. Later, by the time

Jones and Perkins were ready to interview Hanson, he was represented by a local defense attorney.

Like Volpi, Jones wasted little time letting Hanson know how much the authorities had on him, including a detailed record of his itinerary between Miami and California on April 15 and 16—the hours just before and after Ellis Greene's murder.

Told that Hawkins had confided in various girl-friends and in Erik De Sando about some of their scams, Hanson snapped, waving his hand dismissively and shaking his head: "I can't believe that. That's absolute fabrication."

Hanson spoke glowingly about Hawkins. "He was my friend then and he's my friend now. I'll always care for him." Hawkins, he went on, always "simply wanted to be rich. He wanted to be in the Fortune 500 by the time he was thirty." Hawkins, he added, was plain impatient. "John was a smart boy. But he came from a family with no polish, no education. But he learned very fast, very quickly. If he had had an education, he would have been a genius."

Jones pressed on, sparing few details of what he knew about the case. And when he finished, Hanson said with a begrudging smile, "Damn, you guys know a lot of shit, don't you?"

Unflattered, Jones asked Hanson about Boggs. "No comment," Hanson replied.

"You boys have the death penalty in California?" Hanson's attorney chimed in.

Yes, Jones said, most definitely.

Hanson looked aghast.

Still he refused to cooperate. But Jones left town convinced that Hanson knew where Hawkins was.

A few days later, Hanson was voluntarily flown back to Columbus. Behind bars, he was a model prisoner, devouring one biography after another—preferably of "forceful men . . . who started from nowhere and ended up somewhere."

But if authorities thought Hanson was going to be a pushover, they were quickly in for a surprise. As soon as he took up residence at the Franklin County Correctional Center, a square, depressing building in downtown Columbus, he adopted a new tack that would bedevil the criminal justice systems of both California and Ohio for more than a year to come. He decided to become a prisoner with no name.

Two Down

Richard Boggs emerged from his Glendale office building through the back exit, lugging a bulky cardboard box. Right behind him was Hans Jonasson, also carrying a large box. They appeared to be moving. Or was the doctor finally about to flee now that one of his accomplices had been nabbed?

Watching from various unmarked police vehicles strategically deployed around the parking lot in order to choke off any escape, authorities weren't about to take a chance. They quickly swooped in and slapped handcuffs on Boggs and Jonasson.

The young Swede at first thought they were being busted on a drug rap, but the doctor knew better. As he was put into a police car for the short ride to the Glendale police headquarters, he haughtily demanded to know why he was under arrest.

"For the murder of Ellis Henry Greene," said Mike Jones.

"I find that amusing in light of the autopsy report," Boggs replied combatively.

"Doc, you're going to be happy to know what we've learned about this case," Jones said as the car pulled away. Boggs said nothing more.

As soon as authorities in California learned of Gene Hanson's arrest in Texas on Sunday night, they had placed Boggs under twenty-four-hour surveillance, sure that he now would flee—penniless perhaps, but driven by sheer desperation. The order went out that if Boggs drove to the airport, stop him and put him under arrest immediately. But the doctor made no attempt to flee. Instead he continued going about his business as usual, bar-hopping mostly. And for that authorities were lucky. During the five-day surveillance, an Insurance Department fraud investigator fell asleep on the job. He was snoring blissfully in his unmarked vehicle, parked outside Boggs's apartment building, when a Glendale cop showed up to relieve him. But the Glendale P.D.'s glee was short-lived. The very next night, another Glendale cop assigned to the surveillance lost Boggs on the freeway. But the doctor had merely gone out partying and returned later that night.

When Boggs was arrested on Friday morning, February 3, he in fact was not trying to flee. Rather, he and Jonasson were simply vacating his office, for he had been evicted by his landlords for falling $20,000 behind in rent. After several hours of questioning, police released Jonasson.

The doctor's arrest came as a surprise to few people. In anticipation of just that, the local news media had virtually camped out at the office building every day since Hanson's arrest. Indeed, ever since September, when the dead man was identified as Ellis Greene, increasingly skeptical reporters regularly came around seeking interviews with Boggs.

The doctor remained invariably arrogant. He told a *Glendale News-Press* reporter that he was making between $200,000 and $300,000 a year and therefore would have to be insane to have gotten involved in some cheap insurance scam. "Something like this, I don't need it. I'm making a comfortable living," Boggs lied.

And if he *had* been involved, the doctor said, why in the world would he still be here, practicing medicine, taking care of sick people? "If I were involved, I'd be in Rio. But I'm still in town. I haven't run. All I can do is continue to practice and hope they find Mr. Hawkins and find some answers to what happened to the money and who it was who was in my office," Boggs said.

"If it wasn't Hanson, I was set up," he told another reporter. "My job is to treat medical ailments, not to

check into people's backgrounds. If he wasn't who he
said he was, I don't know who he is. I'm not in the
business of ascertaining identifications. If Joe Schmoe
comes in here, I don't take fingerprints. I thought I
was treating Mr. Hanson.''

Boggs said he was "shocked, dumbfounded" when
police discovered that it wasn't Hanson who had died.
''Frankly, I'd like to wring Mr. Hawkins's neck. I feel
like a sitting duck. I don't need to be taking any heat
for Hawkins and Hanson.''

To a TV news reporter, Boggs added, "All I know
is that someone passed away in my office I thought
was Mr. Hanson. I haven't received anything out of
this except unneeded and unwanted publicity.''

And perhaps with unintended irony, the doctor said
poignantly, "I keep thinking I'll wake up from a bad
dream." Whatever bright dreams Richard Pryde Boggs
had once nurtured during his troubled fifty-seven years
had gone tragically sour.

Even his son Dana, who had spent more time working in his office than any of the other children, finally
walked out on him.

Several years earlier, his father had come to him
with a promising money-making idea. The doctor had
a friend in Canada with a $30-million-a-year business
selling gourmet-food gift baskets. And the friend was
willing to sell Boggs the exclusive rights to use the
name, Epicurean Gourmet Gift Foods, in the United
States. It seemed like a can't-miss proposition, and
Dana jumped into the project with total enthusiasm,
happy also to be involved with his dad in such a venture.

They would sell the food baskets to businesses such
as car dealerships and real estate companies, whose
sales staffs then would give such baskets—instead of,
say, flowers—to clients. If the business really took off,
Dana thought, they could sell distributorships throughout the country, and maybe even retail directly to the
public.

Over the course of the next year or so, Boggs sank
more than $20,000 into the venture, even attending

some international gourmet foods conventions. Father and son also drew up a contract and designed some color brochures that they had printed up. But that was about as far as things ever got. "We had plans and goals, but nothing materialized," Dana said ruefully years later. "Things just kept getting put off."

With fewer and fewer patients coming to the doctor's office, coupled with the increasingly bad publicity over the Ellis Greene death, Dana came to the realization that it was time for him to get on with his own life. "I had to get on with my goals," he said. By the end of 1988, about a month before his father was arrested, the personable young man got married and moved to Sacramento.

Shortly after that Jean Walker, the doctor's faithful employee for fifteen years, also quit.

In the end, all Boggs had left was Hans Jonasson, a beat-up pickup truck, and a small, barely furnished apartment whose rent he could not pay.

Moving On

With Richard Boggs now behind bars, facing first-degree murder charges, Mike Jones knew it was time for him to move on. Several months earlier, he had received the good news that he had passed the California Bar examination.

Jones was now a lawyer, but he had postponed taking a job as an attorney until the Boggs investigation was complete. And now, with Al MacKenzie taking over the case as the prosecutor, Jones resigned from the state Insurance Department. Jerry Treadway and Ron Warthen were sorry to see him go, but they had known when they hired him that this day would come.

Jones had nourished the hope of becoming, like MacKenzie, a deputy Los Angeles district attorney. But the office had a hiring freeze. And so Jones went to work for a private law firm in Los Angeles that specialized in medical malpractice cases. But even then he often got calls from MacKenzie, Perkins, and the others with questions about the case.

Jones had been on the job barely a month when he got another call one afternoon from the D.A.'s office. But this one was from Curt Livesay, a slow-talking Oklahoman who was the number two man at the D.A.'s office. Livesay offered Jones a job as a deputy district attorney.

At first Jones was torn. It was a solid law firm where he was working and the job paid handsomely. But Jones also knew that it would be as many as seven years before he got the chance to do actual trial work because the firm was so large and he was so junior. As he and Livesay chatted, Jones began to realize what his answer would be. Still, he wanted to sleep on it and talk to Kim about making the change. That night Jones faced up to the truth. He had not been entirely happy practicing civil law. It was the hurly-burly of criminal law that he loved. "I want to be a trial lawyer and to prosecute cases," he told Kim.

The next morning he accepted Livesay's offer.

It went unsaid, but Jones suspected right along that he might be groomed as the co-prosecutor for the Boggs and Hanson trials. MacKenzie was delighted— but not surprised—to have Jones as a colleague. And he advised Jones to get as much trial experience as possible. "Volunteer for everything," he told Jones.

Jones did, but he became upset when he was assigned to prosecute misdemeanor jury trials. These were petty cases that no one really cared about, Jones complained to MacKenzie one evening. Most of the other newcomers, he said, were being assigned to felony preliminary hearings. In California, before a criminal suspect can be tried, a prosecutor must persuade a judge during what is called a preliminary hearing that sufficient evidence exists. But when MacKenzie heard the news, he was ecstatic. "Great!" he told Jones. "You don't need to do prelims. I want you to get actual trial experience."

Jones realized that MacKenzie was right—and he had no more doubt that he was being prepared to help MacKenzie prosecute Boggs and Hanson.

In the next few weeks, Jones volunteered for every jury trial that came along. Never mind that most cases involved drunk driving or assault and battery stemming from domestic squabbles. The opportunity to perform before a jury—presenting evidence, arguing, thinking on his feet—was invaluable experience. Altogether, Jones had six jury trials and one bench trial, and he won them all—including one in which the judge and the defense lawyer had been law school classmates while one of their professors ended up as the jury foreman!

By early summer, Jones was transferred to the Criminal Courts Building, a grimy nineteen-story building across from City Hall that houses virtually nothing but courtrooms and offices for judges, D.A.'s, and public defenders. This was where Ira Reiner, the Los Angeles County district attorney, had his office. Jones, in other words, had arrived.

Assigned to central trials, Jones continued following MacKenzie's advice, volunteering for everything that came around, taking as many felony preliminary hearings as anyone. Within six months, he was promoted again—this time to the major frauds division. That was where MacKenzie worked. Jones didn't know it at the time, but when his promotion to major frauds was being considered by the brass, some expressed deep reservations, noting that he had been a deputy D.A. for less than a year. Yeah, but Jones has over twenty trials under his belt already, someone pointed out. MacKenzie's advice had paid off. Jones got the promotion.

It was now the spring of 1990. More than a year had passed since Boggs and Hanson had been arrested—and two since Ellis Green had been murdered. Hanson was still in Ohio fighting extradition to California. But Boggs already had had his preliminary hearing, after which a municipal judge had ordered him bound over to Superior Court for trial.

All along, MacKenzie had diligently stayed in touch with Jones, keeping him more or less up to speed on the case. And now, working alongside MacKenzie, Jones began really studying up on the case—reading, for instance, line by line the transcripts of Boggs's preliminary hearing, held the previous autumn. As a precaution Jones had stayed away from that proceeding because, having been the primary investigator in the case, he was a potential witness.

Jones and MacKenzie, a forty-four-year-old native Californian who specialized in prosecuting complex fraud cases, were faced with a murder case in which there was not a scintilla of hard evidence that a homicide had taken place. Certainly there was a wealth of circumstantial evidence linking Boggs and Hanson to Greene's death. But any jury trial was a crapshoot, and relying solely on circumstantial evidence was even more so. But there was no choice. The two simply resolved to do the best they could, often staying up until ten or eleven at night, talking tactics, exploring theories. "We took it step by step. It was going to be like telling a story chapter by chapter. And we had to make the jury understand," Jones said.

They knew the defense lawyers would have a field day posturing before a jury over the coroner's initial finding that Ellis Greene had died a natural death. Even now, no one could say for sure just how Greene had died. "Without doubt, the defense would argue that the murder hadn't happened," Jones said. "But we knew our strength was fraud—there was no question that Boggs knew who the real Gene Hanson was."

Since the evidence against Hanson and Boggs was largely the same, Jones and MacKenzie had hoped to try both men at once—in the same courtroom, before the same judge, but before two different juries. That would reduce by more than half the enormous time and energy required to marshal witnesses and evidence. And if Hanson could be persuaded to testify against the doctor, perhaps in exchange for a prosecution vow not to seek the death penalty against Hanson, the case against Boggs would be vastly strengthened.

But Hanson, still biding his time in the Franklin County Correctional Center in Columbus, would have no part of such a plea bargain. In fighting extradition to California, Hanson evoked an unusual, even comical tactic. He simply stopped admitting to who he was. Judges and prosecutors alike had no choice but to refer to him in court and in legal documents as "the individual being held under the name Melvin Eugene Hanson."

The job of extraditing Hanson to California fell to Dan Abraham, the assistant Franklin County district attorney who had accompanied Vince Volpi to Dallas to interview Hanson right after his arrest. A Columbus native, Abraham had gone straight from law school to the prosecutor's office, where he had been assigned to the white-collar crime unit, which he now headed. The personable thirty-two-year-old prosecutor had initially become involved in the case in the autumn of 1988, after Bob Smith left the D.A.'s office to go to work for the state attorney general. And having subpoenaed numerous Just Sweats documents and bank accounts while investigating the insurance-fraud and embezzlement cases, Abraham was intimately familiar with the landscape.

But trying to extradite a prisoner who would not admit to his identity was a novel challenge for Abraham. In court, the prosecutor steadfastly argued that the issue was not guilt or innocence, but rather simply whether there was probable cause that the suspect should be returned to California to face charges there. Abraham certainly could have ordered comparisons of Hanson's dental charts or fingerprints, but he didn't want to set a precedent by having to obtain "excessive proof" for what he strongly felt should be a routine procedure. He also could have called Volpi to testify to the fact that "the man being held in Franklin County jail" had identified himself to Volpi as Melvin Eugene Hanson during an interview at the Tarrant County Jail in Fort Worth, Texas.

In due time, the lower courts ordered Hanson extradited. But Hanson's defense lawyers quickly appealed, and then they refused to agree that the case be put on a fast track at the Court of Appeals. That meant a delay of many months, Abraham informed MacKenzie and Jones. Thus the Los Angeles prosecutors abandoned any hope of trying both Hanson and Boggs at once.

In the meantime, Abraham assigned an intern in the D.A.'s office to go from their fifth-floor offices down to the fourth floor at noon every Tuesday and Thursday to check for any Court of Appeals decision on the Hanson extradition matter. Abraham knew that Hanson's defense lawyers would appeal an unfavorable ruling to the state Supreme Court, which could delay Hanson's extradition by perhaps another year. But if, with a favorable appellate court ruling, authorities could quickly hustle Hanson out of Ohio en route to California, that would be a fait accompli. No amount of defense squawking would do any good at that point.

This twice weekly ritual went on for more than a year. "I went through two or three interns," Abraham recalled. But in the spring of 1990, the effort finally paid off. It had been worth the wait. The Court of Appeals upheld Hanson's extradition.

Hastily, Abraham made arrangements for Hanson to be taken from jail to the airport for the long flight to California. In the meantime, however, Hanson's public-defender attorneys rushed over in person to consult with Abraham and his boss, Mike Miller. Together they went to discuss the matter with the Court of Appeals judge who had upheld Hanson's extradition. Hanson's attorneys pleaded with the jurist for a stay of execution. "You really don't have anything here," the judge finally told them.

All this time Franklin County sheriff's deputies were at the airport, with Hanson in custody, awaiting further instructions.

Still, Miller agreed to give Hanson's lawyers one final crack. It was already after four in the afternoon, but the public defenders rushed to the Ohio Supreme Court and quickly got in to see Thomas Moyer, the chief justice. But Moyer also turned them down.

At long last, after more than fourteen months, the Franklin County jail inmate with no name was en route to California to face first-degree murder charges.

"You guys might as well have the first shot at him," Abraham told MacKenzie and Jones.

We the Jury

Opening statements in Richard Boggs's first-degree murder trial began on an overcast, miserably damp morning, the first day of business after a very rainy Memorial Day weekend. It was Tuesday, May 29, 1990—more than two years after Ellis Greene had turned up dead in the doctor's office. Mike Jones and Al MacKenzie were seeking the death penalty.

In Columbus, the delaying tactics by Gene Hanson's attorneys had ensured that Boggs would go on trial alone. And that was just fine with Dale Rubin and Charles Lindner, the doctor's two court-appointed lawyers. The farther away Hanson was, the less likely he was to cop a plea and testify against Boggs.

Thus, all along Rubin and Lindner were eager to get Boggs's trial underway—and get it over with before Hanson was extradited to California. His return, they knew, was only a matter of time. But without Hanson's testimony for the prosecution, Jones and MacKenzie had nothing but circumstantial evidence.

The defense attorneys' eagerness to go to trial was highly atypical because the overriding strategy among defense lawyers is to stall. The longer a suspect's trial is delayed, the more it works in the defense's favor. Memories fade. Evidence gets lost. Witnesses die.

On the other hand, Jones and MacKenzie were in no special hurry, much as prosecutors usually grouse about justice delayed. To some extent they were willing to wait for Hanson to be extradited to California—and hoping at the same time to nab Hawkins as well. With all three defendants in L.A., each looking out for his own interest, the odds would be far higher of working out a plea bargain with either Hanson or Hawkins in exchange for their testimony against Boggs. The prosecutors wanted most of all to nail the doctor. Jones in particular was outraged that Boggs, in committing murder, had betrayed a special public trust that society bestows upon physicians to heal and comfort.

But Jones and MacKenzie also knew they could not delay the proceedings merely on the slim hope of negotiating plea bargains with the other co-conspirators, especially with one of them still on the lam. And so they forged on, day by day marshaling the web of evidence with which to entangle the doctor.

The two prosecutors worked well together, and Jones had immense respect for MacKenzie. "Al's a true trial lawyer—the most ethical I've ever met," Jones said. And that was a widely held opinion among the eight hundred-plus prosecutors in the Los Angeles County district attorney's office.

MacKenzie had not attended one of the more prestigious law schools in California. Rather, he had been a 1970 graduate of the Glendale College of Law, a state-accredited school that was not on the list of schools approved by the American Bar Association. But MacKenzie, a bachelor who lived in a high-rise apartment downtown, proved to be a cool-headed, methodical trial lawyer with a keenly analytical mind. He had spent most of his career working in the D.A.'s major fraud division, prosecuting white-collar criminals in complex cases involving long and byzantine paper trails—cases that most ambitious young prosecutors shied away from because they were so complicated and mind-numbing. But not MacKenzie. Shortly before taking on the Boggs case, he had successfully prosecuted another attorney, a woman in private practice who had stolen from the estate of a client after he was murdered apparently as a result of a drug-related dispute.

Much to Jones's chagrin, he was barred from questioning witnesses during the trial. The trial judge, Florence-Marie Cooper, made this ruling after Rubin and Lindner pointed out that Jones, having been the chief investigator in the case, was a potential witness during the trial. Jones was especially disappointed by the ruling because he had anticipated such an issue even while investigating the case, and that was why he had almost always had another investigator with him. When time came for trial, Jones reasoned, the other investigator could serve as the witness to testify about the investigation. But Rubin and Lindner were adamant, and Cooper ultimately ruled in their favor.

And now Jones watched as MacKenzie rose to address the jury of seven women and five men, along with six alternate jurors. Cooper had insisted on having the backup jurors because Jones and MacKenzie predicted that the trial could take up to a year—an estimate based largely on the number of potential prosecution witnesses, which was more than one hundred. In all but the simplest criminal cases, the prospect of a long, drawn-out criminal trial looms with great regularity. It is as much an ingrained way of life in Los Angeles as driving. But Cooper was determined to keep things moving. If she had anything to do with it, no way was the trial going to take a year.

The fifty-year-old judge had a reputation for running a tight ship. Indeed, that was why she had been assigned to the Los Angeles County Superior Court's "long cause" program, handling nothing but long, complex trials five days a week. Other judges, even when they also were presiding over jury trials, still were saddled with "calendar" work for a good portion of the morning and afternoon. The tedious work of calling calendar—bail hearings, probation revocations, setting new court dates in a string of different cases—often ate up much of the day, leaving but two or three hours for actual trials.

Prosecutors and defense lawyers alike in the Criminal Courts Building were not surprised that Cooper was given the prestigious "long cause" assignment. "She knows the law and she doesn't put up with a lot of waste of time," said Sterling E. Norris, a senior deputy Los Angeles district attorney.

But Cooper also presided over her courtroom with

grace and charm. She had worked for seven years as a legal secretary and then decided to become a lawyer herself. At age thirty-five, she graduated from the Whittier College School of Law—first in her class. After working for a year as a deputy Los Angeles city attorney and five as a researcher at the state Court of Appeal, also in Los Angeles, she had been named to the bench in 1983 by Governor George Deukmejian.

Despite her determination to shorten the trial from its projected one-year duration, she took the precaution of issuing to each of the twelve jurors and six alternates notebooks and pencils. They certainly didn't have to take notes, Cooper told the somber-faced men and women after they had settled into their well-cushioned seats. "But I personally take notes during trial. I find that it helps me to remember testimony and to tie testimony in together at the conclusion of the trial, particularly in a trial of this duration," the judge said. Then she nodded crisply to MacKenzie, signaling for him to begin.

At the defense table, the nattily dressed Boggs, his face ghostly pale after more than fifteen months of incarceration, sat meekly between his defense lawyers. He had on tassled black loafers, a blue blazer, and gray slacks with cuffs. From an adjacent holding cell he had entered carrying a hardback edition of Robert Ludlum's *The Bourne Ultimatum.* He listened intently as MacKenzie began his opening statement, and as he would throughout his trial, he took copious notes on a legal pad and consulted frequently with Rubin and Lindner.

"The evidence," MacKenzie told the jurors, "will establish that a murder was committed as part of a scheme to commit insurance fraud and to collect money on several life insurance policies."

The doctor, he said, "was the necessary ingredient to kill a man and to do it in such a way that a murder would not be obvious." As he spoke, he turned away from the jury box to look at Boggs. As if on cue, the jurors and alternates also turned toward the defendant.

Boggs continued looking down, writing on his legal pad.

"Rather," MacKenzie then went on, "it would be done in a way that the dead man could be passed off as being a natural death as a result of a heart attack or heart disease so that they could collect on life insurance."

Without histrionics and in his characteristic monotone, MacKenzie then ran through the evidence that the jury would receive: the manufactured medical file for Gene Hanson, including the three EKG strips; the conflicting accounts that Boggs had given on the morning of April 16 as to how the dead man got to his office; the $6,500 payoff that John Hawkins sent Boggs by way of Erik De Sando in Columbus and Hans Jonasson in Glendale. Even after murdering Ellis Green, MacKenzie said, the doctor had committed yet another crime by submitting a bill to Gene Hanson's health insurance carrier, seeking payment for the emergency treatment that he had supposedly provided. If MacKenzie was outraged or even upset by what the doctor had done, he did not betray the least bit of emotion or contempt. But that was just MacKenzie's style, and he wasn't about to change it now.

Droning on, MacKenzie told the jury that they will see volumes of telephone records that, he said, would clearly establish that "these men were in constant communication during the events that were part of the scheme." Among these was a telephone call placed in the early morning hours of April 16—from a pay phone at the Rawhide bar, where Ellis Greene had been on the last afternoon of his life, to Boggs's office. It had been charged to a third telephone number—the one at Boggs's home.

Several jurors' eyebrows shot up when MacKenzie further promised that before the trial was over, they would get to see Gene Hanson in the flesh. "We wanted the jury to know and to see that there really is a Gene Hanson," Jones explained. The prosecutors also wanted jurors to be able to appreciate the close physical resemblance between Hanson and Barry Pomeroy—the original murder target.

But not once during his twenty-three-minute opening statement did MacKenzie provide the slightest hint of the prosecution's theory of just how Ellis Greene had been killed. When he was done, Judge Cooper declared a short recess. As many relieved jurors made a beeline for the snack bar to get coffee, it looked as if Jones and MacKenzie faced an uphill climb. And they were going up against two of the best criminal defense lawyers in town.

Rubin, thirty-nine, and Lindner, forty-three, had previously teamed up in three death-penalty trials, and they worked well together. So comfortable were they with each other that they took turns being the lead counsel. "We're like Batman and Robin," Lindner said, "except neither one of us looks good in tights."

Rubin had grown up in Burbank and never left Southern California. Like MacKenzie, he is a product of a state-accredited law school, the University of LaVerne. His first job out of law school had been with a personal injury firm, and he hated just about everything about the job. Representing people who had been badly maimed in accidents as a result of someone else's neglect, Rubin wanted to go to the mat each time for his client, taking the case as far as he could and that included going to trial if necessary. But he quickly learned that that was not the way to do business, at least at that law firm. He came under increasing pressure from the senior partners to obtain quick settlements instead. That way the firm could quickly take its cut—ranging anywhere from twenty-five to fifty percent or more—and then move on to the next case. Soon Rubin quit and struck out on his own. Following his own inclinations, he eventually found more and more of his work in criminal law.

In court, Rubin has an easygoing mien that resonates well with jurors—even if the facts are not always on his side. He is a man who enjoys a good laugh, even if it's at his own expense.

Lindner is a Chicago native, the son of German immigrants. His parents divorced while he was still young, and he moved with his mother to San Francisco. While attending the University of California at Davis as an undergraduate, Lindner developed osteosarcoma and had a leg amputated. After a year in the hospital, he completed his undergraduate studies and went on to law school at Davis, which is near Sacramento.

Growing up, Lindner knew early that he did not want to be an accountant—his father was a CPA. "The work just didn't look appealing," he said. That left him three career choices: doctor, rabbi, or lawyer. But a "D" in an undergraduate chemistry course ruled out the feasibility of staying in premed. And friends told him that he talked too much to be a rabbi.

In the Boggs trial, Rubin would act as the lead counsel, and so it was he who rose to address the jury after the morning break. Keep an open mind, he urged. "It isn't over until it's over. You are going to have to be very attentive because much of the defense case will be put on during our cross-examination."

At the prosecution table, Jones and MacKenzie exchanged knowing glances. Rubin had clearly telegraphed the major defense strategy. What he meant was that the defense would not be calling many significant witnesses on Boggs's behalf. Rather, Rubin and Lindner were going to concentrate on attacking the weaknesses in the prosecution's case. After all, Rubin and Lindner only had to create reasonable doubt—and in just one juror's mind.

Then Rubin ran through the defense theory of the case, citing Dr. Evancia Sy's initial autopsy findings and Ellis Greene's poor health, including his diseased liver and heart infection. Rubin even disclosed that blood tests had revealed that Greene at the time of his death was infected with the AIDS virus. Rubin was clearly suggesting that Greene had died of natural causes—just as the original death certificate had stated.

Why, the defense lawyer urged the jurors to ask themselves, would a highly trained doctor bother discussing poisons with a lay person? And why, if he was

guilty, hadn't Boggs run? "He never went anywhere.
He never moved. He never tried to hide. He was always there," Rubin said. "Nothing is susceptible to
one interpretation," he concluded. "Everything is
open."

Starting with the first witness, many of the jurors
and alternates began taking notes. The first to testify
were the many fire and rescue personnel, police officers, and coroner's investigators who had responded
to Boggs's call shortly after seven o'clock on the
morning of April 16, 1988. From there Jones and
MacKenzie presented the case in a straightforward but
masterful fashion, making the case easy to comprehend. There was sympathetic testimony about Ellis
Greene from his friends and relatives; about the doctor's peculiar life-style, especially from Hans Jonasson; about Boggs's attempt to murder Barry Pomeroy
from the victim himself; about the various insurance
policies; about the extensive telephone records that
linked Boggs, Hanson, and Hawkins to one another
and to Greene.

Except to the jury, much of that information was not
new. Eight months earlier, MacKenzie already had
presented the information in a truncated version to
Judge Patti Jo McKay of the Los Angeles Municipal
Court. And it was also during Boggs's preliminary
hearing that MacKenzie had offered two possible ways
that Greene had been killed—either poison or suffocation.

But now the prosecution's expert medical witnesses
were prepared to assert unequivocally that Greene had
died as a result of suffocation. In the end it would
come down to a battle of the experts, and the question
was whose experts the jury would find more believ-
able.

Dr. Michael C. Fishbein was one of the prosecution's star witnesses. Fishbein is a physician and
former Harvard Medical School professor. He was
teaching at the UCLA Medical School and practicing
medicine as a cardiac pathologist at the Cedar-Sinai
Medical Center in Los Angeles. Fishbein testified that

he had examined eighteen slides of Ellis Greene's heart tissues but found no evidence at all of myocarditis present. "There was no evidence of any heart disease at autopsy," he told the jury.

Another key prosecution witness was Dr. Michael Baden, director of forensic sciences for the New York state police. Baden, who had conducted over 20,000 autopsies in his long career, had been New York City's controversial medical examiner until he was fired after a nasty dispute with Mayor Ed Koch. At MacKenzie's request, Baden reviewed all the medical reports, photographs, examined the slides, visited Boggs's office, talked to Drs. Evancia Sy, her supervisor, Joan Shipley, and many others.

"The cause of death," Baden said flatly, "is suffocation—homicidal." Asphyxiation, he explained to the jury, can be accomplished in a variety of ways, such as by putting a pillow or a plastic bag over a victim's face, manually compressing one's neck, or even choking on a piece of food.

In addition, Baden testified, he saw no evidence that CPR had been performed, as Boggs had claimed to have done. Nor did Baden see any signs that Greene had fallen off the examination table; had Greene done so, he likely would have incurred bruises from landing on the linoleum floor. "Now, it is possible," he conceded, "that perhaps Mr. Greene stood up and then slowly collapsed or something like that. [But] I don't think he fell from the table right to the floor."

There was some evidence that an electrocardiogram had been run on Greene, Baden also conceded. But Boggs might have done so, he surmised, "to see whether he was dead or not."

Under Cooper's firm guidance, the trial sailed along at a far faster clip than anyone had dared hoped. But that was also because Jones and MacKenzie had decided in the end not to call the majority of those on their original list of potential witnesses. "We wanted to keep it simple," Jones said. "We wanted to keep the focus on Boggs." Thus the two prosecutors did not call the many witnesses from Ohio and Florida

who could have provided extensive—and damning—
testimony about Hanson and Hawkins in a variety of
ways that would have buttressed the prosecution's case.
Instead, Jones and MacKenzie chose simply to zero in
on the fact that an insurance scam had undeniably occurred—and then hope that the web of circumstantial
evidence would lead the jury to the inescapable conclusion that Greene had been murdered as a part of
that plot.

As for the defense, Rubin and Lindner knew that
their best hope of planting a seed of doubt in some
juror's mind was to offer a plausible natural cause of
death—a finding that, after all, had been reached initially by the coroner's office.

The star defense witness was Dr. Griffith D.
Thomas, a lawyer as well as a physician. A graduate
of the University of Southern California Medical
School and the UCLA law school, Thomas served as
a consulting pathologist, doing an occasional private
autopsy but otherwise practicing law. And he came
with an alternative cause of death.

Under questioning from Rubin, Thomas testified that
Ellis Greene's blood had contained 57 percent methemoglobin. Hemoglobin is a protein that carries oxygen from the lungs to the body's tissues, and carbon
dioxide from the tissues to the lungs. Methemoglobin,
Thomas explained, is a chemical change that occurs,
or is caused by, chemical agents in the hemoglobin
that changes its composition in a way that renders it
unable to carry oxygen or carbon dioxide.

"Essentially," Thomas added, "with significant
methemoglobin, you have a chemical asphyxia." The
normal levels of methemoglobin is up to two percent,
according to Thomas. Any reading above ten percent
is "clinically significant," he testified.

The next question, of course, was what might have
caused Greene's high methemoglobin reading. Again,
Thomas was prepared with a ready answer. Poppers,
or little ampules of alkyl nitrite, he said. That prescription drug is widely used by heart patients with
chest pains known as angina pectoris. The drug is a

vasodilator, or a substance that dilates the blood vessels. In recent years alkyl nitrite has become immensely popular among the gay population as a reputed aphrodisiac.

"My opinion is that he died of methemoglobenemia, acute alcohol intoxication with an already damaged liver," Thomas concluded.

And because tests also revealed that Greene had recently used cocaine, Thomas added, "It's my belief that this man at the time he died went into acute cardiovascular collapse due to the multiplicity of these substances."

In the end, Greene died as a result of an accident, Thomas said.

Jones and MacKenzie were stunned when the thrust of Thomas's testimony first became apparent, for they had been assured by Baden that there was nothing unusual about Greene's admittedly high methemoglobin reading. Taken totally off guard, the prosecutors were unable to reach Baden. Instead, after court adjourned, Jones and MacKenzie rushed to the USC medical library to read up on the subject. And what they learned proved extremely valuable back in court.

When it was finally time for MacKenzie to cross-examine Thomas, he got the witness to concede that methemoglobin naturally becomes elevated after a person dies. Moreover, Thomas had to concede as well that an extracted blood sample also can give a falsely elevated methemoglobin reading if it isn't immediately analyzed. And that was precisely what had happened with Greene's blood sample.

Jones and MacKenzie clearly had done their homework. Indeed, poring through the medical literature the previous night, they had come across the case of a man with 81 percent methemoglobin—and survived.

"So fifty-seven percent would not necessarily be fatal, would it?" MacKenzie asked Thomas.

"By itself? In a healthy individual? Most likely not," Thomas replied.

Only six weeks after the trial had begun, the time came for closing arguments.

MacKenzie called the plot "a very complicated scheme to collect money," one in which Boggs "supplied two key ingredients" for its success—his knowledge of medicine and the setting for the murder. "He violated his oath as a medical doctor not to heal but to destroy life," MacKenzie said, still speaking in his trademark monotone.

"I would suggest to you that Ellis Greene did go to the Rawhide bar. . . . And there he met Dr. Boggs," MacKenzie went on. "The reason we know that is that at 1:22 that morning a telephone call was placed from the Rawhide bar's pay telephone by Dr. Boggs, using his credit card. . . . I would suggest to you that Dr. Boggs met Mr. Greene at the Rawhide bar and brought him back to the office and murdered him as part of his scheme." The jurors listened with total concentration, several of them near the edge of their seats.

It was the prosecution's theory, MacKenzie finally said, that Boggs disabled Greene with a stun gun and then suffocated him.

"Ladies and gentlemen," he concluded, "this was an incredibly sophisticated scheme to murder an innocent man for a large sum of money. It is as cold-blooded, as premeditated, as planned, as any murder can ever be. It was almost the perfect crime."

In his closing argument, Rubin pulled another surprise. He made a whopping concession. The prosecution's evidence, he told jurors, "shows without a doubt that Dr. Boggs identified Ellis Greene as Gene Hanson, that he knew it wasn't Gene Hanson, that he did it so that Mr. Hawkins and Mr. Hanson could file false insurance claims, that he used and billed on Mr. Hanson's medical insurance for April 16th when he knew he had not treated Mr. Hanson and got payment from the insurance carrier. I'm telling you there is no reasonable doubt. It's been proved. . . . That is unquestionable. . . . It reads like a textbook." Several jurors seemed dumbstruck by the admission of guilt.

"They have proved beyond a reasonable doubt the insurance fraud. It's smooth. It follows. Each logical inference jumps from one to the other. And it makes sense,'' Rubin said. ''I cannot make one argument regarding the insurance-fraud counts. Not one. It's proved.''

Boggs had vehemently argued against conceding the fraud charges. But Rubin told him bluntly, ''What is that if not fraud? What do you want me to do—tell them you didn't do that?'' There was indeed logic in conceding the fraud counts while contesting the murder rap, Rubin finally managed to persuade Boggs. The concession gave the jury something on which to convict Boggs, and that in turn might make them less likely to find him guilty of murder. And if it worked out as well as Rubin and Lindner hoped, the doctor would already have served a good portion of any likely sentence for fraud.

Boggs went along with the strategy. Still, he was not happy about it, and as Rubin made the concession to the jury, the irate doctor surreptitiously kicked Chuck Lindner's leg under the table. Lindner felt it but it didn't hurt; the doctor had kicked him in his wooden leg.

Jones, for one, was not terribly surprised by Rubin's concession to the jury. ''I understood why he did it, and I thought it was a pretty good tactic at that point,'' he said. ''The only trouble was, it was inconsistent with Boggs's position that he was totally innocent and ignorant.''

Rubin pressed on, giving the argument all he had. ''The question is: Was there a murder?'' No, he said. A murder was not necessary to pull off the insurance fraud.

Instead, he added, ''the plan was not to murder somebody and pass that body off. The plan was to get someone recently deceased. How? Through some contacts of Dr. Boggs.''

Referring to Erik De Sando's testimony about the furniture insurance scam that Hanson and Hawkins had pulled in New York, Rubin continued, ''These were people who were scamming insurance companies all the time. They never had to kill anybody to do that.''

The prosecution had to prove that Ellis Greene had died at the hands of another, and MacKenzie and Jones had fallen well short, Rubin argued. "All of the evidence, all of these charts, all of these phone calls, are terrific circumstantial evidence that there was a conspiracy to commit insurance fraud." But there was no murder, he argued.

"If this was not a murder case, if this was straight insurance fraud, the exact same evidence would be before you. You do not have anything more to prove the murder than you have to prove the insurance fraud. That's the problem with the People's burden of proof. . . . Where's the evidence that shows that Mr. Greene was murdered?"

Rubin concluded: "Convict the doctor of insurance fraud. He's guilty of that. There's no question."

On the other hand, he said, "Have the People met their burden of proof on the homicide? Have they proved to you this theory of Dr. Boggs picking up Ellis Greene at the Rawhide and taking him back to his office and hitting him with the stun gun and suffocating him? Besides the fact that that is what Mr. MacKenzie would like to prove, where is the evidence supporting it? Where is the bartender from the Rawhide to say [Greene] was there? Where is the bartender to say he recognized Dr. Boggs? If it wasn't a big night at the Bullet, it couldn't have been a big night at the Rawhide."

By the time Rubin finished, it was late in the afternoon, and Cooper sent the jurors home. The following morning, MacKenzie delivered a brief final argument, telling the jury that the methemoglobin issue was nothing more than "a red herring." And then Cooper officially instructed the jury, as required by law. By the time she was done, it was almost lunchtime. The jurors filed back into their room and elected a foreman. After lunch they began deliberations. No one expected a verdict that day. And by four-fifteen the jurors went home for the day. They returned the next morning and resumed their deliberations immediately.

By late afternoon, they had reached their verdict. But an unexpected hitch developed. No one had expected the jury to pass judgment so quickly, and Al MacKenzie had gone to the South Bay to give a speech.

There was no way he could be reached, much less get back to the courthouse through rush-hour traffic, before the end of the day.

Rushing into the courtroom and seeing only Jones at the counsel's table, Rubin and Lindner objected to the absence of MacKenzie. But Cooper overruled them. "It's time for the jury to know Mr. Jones's true role in this case, gentlemen. It's time to take the verdicts."

"This is the ultimate reward," Jones thought to himself as he sat at the table while the jurors took their seats. Images of the past two years swirled in his head.

Behind the closed doors, there had been just one vote, and it was of course unanimous.

Boggs was guilty as charged, the jurors declared, on all nine counts of fraud, grand theft, conspiracy, assault, and first-degree murder.

In addition, the jury also ruled that Boggs had murdered Ellis Greene while lying in wait and for financial gain. These two "special circumstances" ensured still another phase to the trial. In California, the finding of just one of many possible special circumstances is sufficient to make a convicted murderer eligible for the death penalty. The law requires that the same jury return after a short break, up to a few weeks, for the "penalty phase" of the trial. Then the jury votes solely on whether to send the criminal to the gas chamber at San Quentin or to condemn him to life in prison without the possibility of parole.

As the court clerk read the verdicts, couched in stilted legal language, Boggs continued writing on his legal pad. He never looked up or displayed any emotion. His lawyers seemed more disappointed than he was.

"Boggs was a man who had a lot more in life than I did. But he just went out of control and ruined two families—his own and Ellis Greene's," said Marty Sokup, the jury foreman.

"For me it was sweet justice," said Jones. "But there was nothing to celebrate. Justice had been done and that was my reward."

Epilogue

One lovely spring morning in 1989, as jury selection
was about to get underway for Richard Boggs's murder
trial, attorney Dale Rubin walked into Judge Florence-
Marie Cooper's courtroom carrying a blue blazer and
a pair of gray slacks on a hanger. The wardrobe belonged to Boggs. Earlier, five sets of his clothes had
been misplaced by jail personnel, and so Lola Boggs
took yet another of her former husband's outfits to
Rubin's office on the edge of downtown Los Angeles.
Like all criminal defendants, Richard Boggs wanted
to look nice before a jury.

Once inside the courtroom, Rubin gave the clothes
to a bailiff to pass on to Boggs. But when the bailiff
routinely padded down the jacket and trousers, he
jabbed himself on a sharp object. Inside a pocket of
the blazer, it turned out, was an old syringe. It had
pricked the bailiff's finger. Everyone knew the doctor
was gay. And now there was reason to wonder if he
also was an intravenous drug user. The real question,
of course, was whether Boggs was infected with the
virus that causes AIDS—and if so, could the needle
have transferred the virus to the bailiff?

Terror-stricken, the bailiff quickly had himself
tested. After several agonizing days the results came
back: They were negative. At the same time Boggs
also voluntarily had himself tested, almost as a good-
will gesture. The doctor, however, got bad news: He
was infected with the AIDS virus.

The news was kept from both the public and the jury
throughout Boggs's trial. And it was kept from the jury
even after it deadlocked on the issue of whether to give

Boggs the death penalty, with ten voting for death but two holding out for life in prison without the possibility of parole.

"This never should have been a death case," said Rubin. He and Chuck Lindner had debated vigorously whether to disclose, perhaps even during the trial's penalty phase, the fact that Boggs had the AIDS virus—a death sentence in and of itself. Lindner wanted the jury to know that Boggs was certain to die anyway, in hopes that it would not vote for the gas chamber. But Rubin prevailed by arguing that the jury might be all the more inclined to vote the death penalty, lest Boggs further spread the killer virus while behind bars.

At the same time, Mike Jones and Al MacKenzie unrelentingly sought the death penalty. As Jon Perkins, the Glendale policeman, asked rhetorically, "What if they discover a cure for AIDS?"

After the first jury hopelessly deadlocked, Judge Cooper declared a mistrial. Then a whole new jury was selected and was charged solely with deciding the appropriate penalty for Boggs.

The new jury heard not only an abbreviated version of the trial testimony, so they were familiar with the case, but also from the doctor himself.

Appearing on the witness stand as a convicted first-degree murderer, Boggs nevertheless doggedly continued to maintain his innocence. He said Gene Hanson had showed up in March 1988, saying that he had embezzled a large sum of money from his business and now needed to disappear. Hanson wanted to fake his own death so that he could assume a new identity, Boggs testified.

In the predawn hours of April 16, Boggs asserted, it was Hanson who brought a stranger to his medical office. Both Hanson and his companion, who turned out to be Ellis Greene, had been drinking, according to Boggs.

The doctor said Hanson's companion was having chest pains, and so he gave the man an EKG and checked his blood pressure. It was after Boggs left the examination room that he heard "a thud," Boggs said. Rushing back into the room, he went on, he found Greene on the floor, lying on his side. Immediately he began CPR. But when he reached for the telephone to call paramedics, Hanson stopped him. "Mr. Hanson indicated that he wanted me to identify Mr. Greene as Mr. Hanson," Boggs testified. And even though the man was dead by then and Hanson offered him $25,000, the doctor said he refused. They argued for ten to fifteen minutes, according to Boggs.

Ultimately, Boggs said he reluctantly agreed, but only after Hanson threatened to expose his homosexuality. "Ninety-eight percent of my patients were unaware of it," Boggs testified. "I was afraid if he carried through on his threats, or John Hawkins did, they would totally ruin my practice. I did the stupidest thing I have ever done. I misidentified the body as Mr. Hanson."

But the doctor added, "I did not kill Mr. Greene. Nor was I any part of any plan to kill Mr. Greene."

During the trial's penalty phase, Boggs's family also took the witness stand, many tearfully pleading for his life. "I wish he wasn't in this mess," said Dana Boggs. "He's had a lot of things that have happened to him. He doesn't have any property. Everything has been taken or disappeared. His practice is gone. He has no source of money. There are still bills to pay, and yet there is no money to pay them with. I wish there was something I could do. I don't know what to do." The young man sobbed.

"He had so much going for him," added Jim Boggs, the doctor's youngest brother. "It's hard to believe it's all fallen apart."

Beulah Boggs, the doctor's elderly mother, was the most devastated of all. "How Dick got mixed up in such a mess I don't know. I can't accept it. These are things I don't understand."

Such heart-rending testimony may have touched members of the jury, but it sickened Mike Jones. "They were painting this Ozzie-and-Harriet picture of him and their family life," Jones said. "But from everything I knew, it sure wasn't *Father Knows Best* or *Ozzie and Harriet*. It was more like *Frankenstein*, or *Dr. Jekyll and Mr. Hyde*."

MacKenzie also had no sympathy for the doctor. Boggs, he told the jury, deserves "the ultimate penalty."

In the end, perhaps it was the doctor's own pitiful words that resonated with members of the jury. "I have lost everything," Boggs said. "I have nothing else—except my life."

The jury quickly voted for life in prison without the possibility of parole. Boggs would die in San Quentin. It was only going to be a matter of time.

Afterward, even Rubin was deeply saddened by such a promising life gone astray. "He could have had it all. But he wanted it quickly and without working for it. In the end he betrayed the public. He betrayed himself. He betrayed his own family. He betrayed everybody," Rubin said. "To the very end, he had this godlike attitude that you see in so many doctors. He didn't ever think he'd get caught."

By the time Boggs's fate was finally decided in February 1991, Jones was long gone from Los Angeles and the D.A.'s office. Shortly after the first jury had returned its first-degree murder conviction, Jones got a job offer from the Shasta County prosecutor's office, up in Northern California. Both he and Kim knew right away he would take the job. The pace wouldn't be the same as in L.A., but they would be closer to family. Besides, like so many people in Southern California, he and Kim were getting burned out by the congestion, the smog, the deteriorating quality of public schools, and the rising crime rate in L.A. "It was time to make the move," Jones said.

And so Al MacKenzie, the old pro at prosecuting major frauds, had to find another helper to try Gene Hanson. After much delay, Hanson's first-degree murder trial is expected to begin in late 1992. "I really don't know how he could have done the things they said he did," said Katherine Lawley, Hanson's mother. "We raise our children the best we can. But you never know what they will do." From behind bars, the defendant himself said, "I just wanted it over with. It was a relief to get caught actually."

In Columbus, Ohio, Ed Laramee and Melissa Mantz managed to keep Just Sweats afloat well into 1989, in part by closing a number of unprofitable stores. That March a buyer finally came forth. He was Dennis B. Tishkoff, chairman of Tishkoff Enterprise, Inc., a local shoe retailer with annual sales of $40 million. Tishkoff paid $145,000 for Just Sweats' assets.

"Nobody else wanted it," he said. "They were all scared off by the publicity." Proceeds from the sale went to the Fifth Third Bank, which was Just Sweats' only secured creditor. The bank was owed about $350,000. Most of Just Sweats' one hundred fifty employees stayed on after the sale, including Laramee and Mantz. But Laramee only lasted two months. He and Tishkoff quickly realized that they didn't see eye-to-eye on the company's direction. "We agreed to disagree," Tishkoff said. Mantz not only stayed on but rose to become the company's top buyer.

John Hawkins remained a fugitive, although virtually everyone connected with the case believes that he will get caught. "He'll run out of money and then he'll have to pull another scam. And that's when we'll get him," predicted Jon Perkins, who remains obsessed with nabbing Hawkins.

Until then, however, Hawkins indeed has pulled off the perfect crime.

In bucolic Northern California, Mike Jones also believes that Hawkins will be brought to justice. "They knew how to plan a perfect crime. But they couldn't quite pull it off," he said. "In the end, there really is no perfect crime. Because once it's uncovered, you'll find all kinds of mistakes."

Postscript

In August. Sardinia as usual was swarming with tourists from Italy and other countries of the Continent. Along the sun-drenched isle's picturesque, northeast coast, the countless marinas were teeming with pleasure boats of every color and size.

It was hardly the ideal time or place to be searching for an international fugitive said to be sailing a red catamaran. But John Hogan was determined. As the special agent in Sardinia for the U.S. Naval Investigative Service, a little known worldwide civilian government agency, Hogan was hot on the trail of John Hawkins.

For more than three years, Hawkins had eluded an international manhunt, brazenly traveling incognito throughout the United States, Britain, Greece, Spain, the Netherlands, France, Canada, Mexico, Australia, and the Caribbean, often sailing from port to port. Occasionally police in Glendale, California, would receive reports of sightings of Hawkins, and sometimes these reports were even accompanied by photographs of the fugitive in some exotic locale, looking every bit the high roller having the time of his life. Invariably the tips were spawned by the many true-crime shows on U.S. television, most notably *America's Most Wanted,* that often featured the murder of Ellis Greene and the continuing search of Hawkins. But always such information arrived in California too late. Every time the authorities closed in, Hawkins was long gone.

But by late July, the tips were coming in almost daily, and Hogan knew that he was very close indeed to capturing the elusive murder suspect, who was quietly being considered by the FBI for its Most Wanted list. All Hogan had to do was find the red catamaran.

Two weeks earlier, the *Oprah Winfrey* show had done a feature segment on *America's Most Wanted,* the phenomenally successful Fox Network program that regularly led to the apprehension of fugitives from the law. And that July 14 segment included a riveting account of the Just Sweats murder-for-insurance plot, including a live interview with Jon Perkins, the pugnacious Glendale homicide detective, who had come prepared with numerous photographs of Hawkins on the lam, many of them sent in by tipsters from around the world.

In Amsterdam, a willowy twenty-four-old woman saw the show and nearly retched in horror. The dashing young man she had known and loved as Bradley Bryant had turned out to be a two-timing, bisexual scammer who, police said, was really John Hawkins and had been involved in an innocent man's murder.

Livid, she picked up the telephone and called the Winfrey show. From there, she was referred to *America's Most Wanted,* whose producers had long grown accustomed to handling such calls. They in turn called Perkins in Glendale, and he quickly got in touch with her.

Still infuriated, the woman told Perkins she had met "Bradley Bryant" a year earlier while sailing near Ibiza, Spain, and later he had visited her several times in Amsterdam.

Working with Perkins, Jerry Treadway, the fraud investigator at the California Department of Insurance, called Rod Miller, the special agent in charge of the Southern California office of the Naval Investigative Service. Treadway was well familiar with the crack agency. At the time, in fact, he had an agent working out of Miller's office on an unrelated insurance fraud case, and he hoped that Miller's agency, given its maritime expertise, could help out, and quickly.

As Treadway began describing the case, Miller quickly recognized it; he remembered reading about the trial and conviction of Dr. Richard Boggs. Miller immediately received approval from his Washington headquarters to join the chase.

Initially, Navy investigators concentrated in Spain, particularly on the island of Ibiza, based on the woman's information. But two days later, Perkins called Miller with urgent new details. A second Dutch tipster, the father of a man who had been traveling with Hawkins, advised authorities to look instead in the south of Sardinia. Thus Miller called on Hogan, who knew the mountainous island well, for he was stationed at the U.S. Navy submarine base on La Maddalena, a tiny island just off Sardinia's northeast coast.

Miller, in the meantime, again called Washington, asking the Justice Department's office of international affairs to quickly prepare an international arrest warrant for Hawkins and send it to Rome over the Interpol wires. Miller was adept at cutting through bureaucratic red tape. When the Pentagon's Operation Ill Wind had still been unfolding three years earlier, it was Miller who had been summoned to Washington to help coordinate the covert investigation of high-level corruption in military procurement contracts.

From a hotel room in San Diego, where he was vacationing with his family, Perkins stayed in close contact with Miller—as well as with the second tipster. The man seemed to have fresh information on Hawkins's movements almost on a daily basis. Look in the north of Sardinia, the tipster now advised.

Hogan thus doggedly worked his way back up the coast, stopping even in the drydocks. It was frustrating work, in just one thirty-mile stretch of the shoreline, there were at least thirty marinas. But Hogan persisted. About two-thirty on the afternoon of August 1, as he gazed out across the shimmering harbor of Cannigione, a bright Mediterranean sun behind him, Hogan at last spotted a red catamaran. It was tied up at the pier. Its name was *Carpe Diem,* Latin for "Seize the day."

And from afar, he thought he spotted Hawkins. The fugitive had left the $113,000 boat that he purchased with cash in France seven months earlier and was now walking along the marina. Hawkins was deeply tanned and fit. He had done nothing to alter his appearance.

On foreign soil, Hogan had no authority to arrest Hawkins. So he quickly summoned local Italian authorities. They already knew that Hogan was in pursuit of a fugitive wanted on murder charges in the United States, but they did not think Hogan would catch his prey. And they had even laughed—thinking Hogan was joking—when the special agent told them that among Hawkins's identifying marks was a splotch of discolored skin in his groin area.

But now, when Hogan telephoned them from a harborside restaurant, the Italian cops quickly responded, sending three armed officers to the dock to rendezvous with Hogan. They waited patiently. Hours went by. At five-thirty the unsuspecting Hawkins returned, his newly streaked blond curls bobbing in the gentle breeze off the Tyrrhenian Sea.

"That's him," Hogan said with a timbre that defied skepticism.

The burly Italian officer swooped in and arrested a stunned Hawkins after a brief scuffle, causing a commotion that stopped gaggles or tourists strolling along the harbor. Loudly insisting that the cops had made a terrible mistake, Hawkins presented them with a British passport bearing his photograph but the name of Gregory Donald Henson. It was one of many passports bearing Hawkins's photograph—but a different name— in his possession.

The officers took Hawkins to the village police station and during a routine strip search saw for themselves that Hogan had not been kidding about Hawkins's skin discoloration. They later confirmed his identity through more conventional means, relying on photographs and fingerprints.

From behind bars in a dank jail ceil in Cagliari, Sardinia's capital, Hawkins unwaveringly proclaimed his innocence. "I don't have anything to do with any murder. The doctor's responsible. I didn't kill anyone. He's the architect of the whole thing," Hawkins told

La Republica, an Italian daily newspaper. "I had to flee because they suspected I was involved. It would be a crime if you sent me back."

But it also would only be a matter of time before Hawkins was extradited to California, where he, like Melvin Eugene Hanson, faces first-degree murder charges.

ABOUT THE AUTHOR

Edwin Chen is a Washington-based correspondent for the *Los Angeles Times*. During the Persian Gulf war in 1991, he served as bureau chief in Dhahran, Saudi Arabia.

He also has written for the *Washington Star*, the *Detroit News*, the *Washington Post*, the *Atlantic Monthly*, the *New York Times Magazine*, the *Nation*, the *Progressive*, and *People* magazine.

Chen, forty-three, is the author of *PBB: An American Tragedy* and a contributing author to *Science of the* New York Times: *A Survey*.

He won the American Bar Association's Silver Gavel Award in 1985 and twice was awarded the Gold Medallion for Public Service by the State Bar of California, in 1984 and 1985.

Born in Nanking, China, Chen is a 1970 journalism graduate of the University of South Carolina and studied as a Nieman Fellow in 1984 and 1985 at Harvard University.

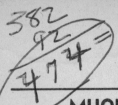

MURDEROUS MINDS

☐ **THE SLEEPING LADY:** *The Trailside Murders Above the Golden Gate* by **Robert Graysmith.** The law finally caught David Carpenter, whose thick glasses and shy stammer concealed an insatiable sexual appetite and a murderous anger. This is the detailed story of the hideous crimes, the gripping manhunt, the sensational series of trials, and the secret self of the killer who *almost* got away with it. (402553—$5.99)

☐ **DEATH SENTENCE:** *The Murderous Odyssey of John List* by Joe Sharkey. The riveting story of mass-murderer John List, who savagely killed his mother, his wife and three children—then "got away with it" for eighteen years! One of the most chilling true crimes of the century. (169476—$4.95)

☐ **THE SEARCH FOR THE GREEN RIVER KILLER** by **Carlton Smith** and **Tomas Guillen.** In this book you will meet the young women who died hideously. You will meet the men hunting for their killer. But there is one person you will not meet. The Green River Killer himself. Like London's Jack the Ripper, this one is an unsolved serial murder case. (402391—$4.99)

☐ **FATAL VISION** by **Joe McGinniss.** The nationwide bestseller that tells the electrifying story of Dr. Jeffrey McDonald, the Princeton-educated Green Beret convicted of slaying his wife and children "A haunting story told in compelling detail."—*Newsweek* (165667—$5.95)

Buy them at your local bookstore or use this convenient coupon for ordering.

NEW AMERICAN LIBRARY
P.O. Box 999, Bergenfield, New Jersey 07621

Please send me the books I have checked above.
I am enclosing $_____ (please add $2.00 to cover postage and handling).
Send check or money order (no cash or C.O.D.'s) or charge by Mastercard or
VISA (with a $15.00 minimum). Prices and numbers are subject to change without
notice.

Card #_____ Exp. Date _____
Signature_____
Name_____
Address_____
City _____ State _____ Zip Code _____

For faster service when ordering by credit card call **1-800-253-6476**

Allow a minimum of 4-6 weeks for delivery. This offer is subject to change without notice.